D1192038

Sartorial Strategies

Sartorial Strategies

OUTFITTING ARISTOCRATS AND FASHIONING

CONDUCT IN LATE MEDIEVAL LITERATURE

Nicole D. Smith

UNIVERSITY OF NOTRE DAME PRESS

NOTRE DAME, INDIANA

Library of Congress-in-Publication Data

Smith, Nicole D.

   Sartorial strategies : outfitting aristocrats and fashioning conduct in late medieval literature / Nicole D. Smith.

        p.   cm.

     Includes bibliographical references and index.

     ISBN-13: 978-0-268-04137-3 (pbk. : alk. paper)

     ISBN-10: 0-268-04137-7 (pbk. : alk. paper)

   1. English literature—Middle English, 1100–1500—History and criticism. 2. Social history—Medieval, 500–1500.   3. Clothing and dress in literature.   4. French literature—To 1500—History and criticism.   5. Literature, Medieval—History and criticism. I. Title.

  PR275.S63S65   2012

  820.9'001—dc23

                                    2012005301

For my parents

and my husband

Contents

Illustrations

Acknowledgments

My greatest debt is to the teachers whose commitment to students and incisive scholarship encouraged me to pursue medieval studies. I owe thanks to David Aers for introducing me to medieval literature. He then led me to Susan Crane, who directed this project when it began as a dissertation. This book owes more than I can express to Susan for her dedication to academic rigor, her delight in things medieval, and her enduring support. Her model for research, teaching, and service continues to inspire me, and I am honored to have this opportunity to share how much she has meant to me as a mentor and friend. I also thank Larry Scanlon and Stacey Klein for their invigorating graduate seminars at Rutgers University, during which the seeds for this book were planted. The intellectual generosity and continued guidance I receive from all of my mentors have benefitted my work in countless ways.

Friends and colleagues at the University of North Texas have made suggestions to improve this study. Robert Upchurch graciously read and commented on the entire manuscript more than once. My appreciation for his critical acumen is deep, and my debt to him is great. I thank, too, Jacqueline Vanhoutte, whose valuable feedback and rhetorical expertise encouraged me to rewrite the details of my argument. I also benefitted from conversations with Christophe Chaguinian, Jacqueline Foertsch, Stephanie Hawkins, David Holdeman,

Jack Peters, and Alexander Pettit at various stages of this project. My graduate research assistant, Jodi Grimes, was meticulous, reliable, and resourceful at every turn. Diana Holt and Andrew Tolle provided administrative support and savvy.

A National Endowment of the Humanities Summer Seminar in 2006 facilitated research for chapters 3 and 4. I thank Richard Newhauser for his tutelage, Rebecca DeYoung for her philosophical perspective, and Michelle Duran for her photographic expertise during our time at Cambridge University. I am particularly appreciative of the grants from the University of North Texas that supported the research and writing of this study. Because some of the questions I raised in this study led me down unfamiliar roads, I have benefitted from the kindness of scholars, archivists, and librarians in the United States and overseas, especially Catherine Batt, E. Jane Burns, Leo Carruthers, Frank Grady, Laura Hodges, Richard Hoggett, Kathy King, Anne Marshall, and Robin Netherton. I thank Harvard University Archives for access to Charles Lionel Regan's doctoral dissertation.

It is a stroke of good fortune that *Sartorial Strategies* found a home at the University of Notre Dame Press. I am grateful to Stephen Little and Rebecca DeBoer for their support of this project and generous advice. Ann Aydelotte and the Press's anonymous readers provided thorough and thoughtful responses that have helped me improve this study.

I give heartfelt thanks to Jo-Anne Christoffel, Gwyeth T. Smith, Jr., Dan Christoffel, and Kathi Reilly, my four parents, who have expressed unflagging interest in and enthusiasm for my work, as only parents can. They, along with Jean and Josiane Rigaud, provided countless hours of child care and support, without which this book would not have been completed. My children, Vincent James Llewellyn and Elodie Simone Josephine, were no help at all but brought immeasurable joy to my life during this project. Finally, I am especially grateful to my husband, Philippe Rigaud, an astute listener whose optimism, conviction, and love has sustained me throughout.

Earlier versions of chapters 1 and 4 appeared as "Estreitement bendé: Marie de France and the Erotics of Tight Dress," *Medium Ævum* 77, no. 1 (2008): 96–117, © 2008 Society for the Study of Medieval Languages and Literature; and "The Parson's Predilection for Pleasure," *Studies in the Age of Chaucer* 28 (2006): 117–40. I acknowledge permission to use material from these essays here.

Introduction
"Out of Old Clothes, Something New"

In order, then, that your theme may assume a rich costume, if the expression is

old, be a physician and make the old veteran a new man. . . . [W]hen I see

what its proper apparel is in a similar situation, I change the covering and

transform for myself, out of old clothes, something new.

—Geoffrey of Vinsauf, *Poetria nova*

The epigraph to this introduction reveals an idea about clothing and literature that is central to this book: clothing, as represented in written texts, has transformative properties.[1] In the above instance, the medieval scholar of literary arts, Geoffrey of Vinsauf, writing ca. 1208–13, conceives of dress as a metaphor that renders old, familiar expressions new and refreshing. Figurative changes of clothing thus invite literal changes in meaning. But what happens when literal garments change? Or the dress stays the same, but the circumstances in which the clothing is worn shift anew? If these alterations of costume and context can modify themes of literary texts, then what indeed is at stake for authors who embrace more literally Geoffrey's notion of the transformative potential of representations of dress? By attending to figurations of actual attire, their metaphorical impact, and the cultural fields within which dress operates, this study seeks to answer these questions.

Abbess Heloise's (ca. 1090–1163/64) well-known change from quotidian to religious clothing and her subsequent transformation of mind indicate an overlap of the literal modes of vestimentary representations and their potential figurative meanings.[2] More commonly in the texts examined here, however, the shift of literal and figurative costume and contexts is not so stark. This study targets literature in which aristocratic attire prominently and persistently becomes a sign of moral behavior that, in turn, can vary considerably depending on context. The presence and possibility of multiple meanings attached to aristocratic attire alerts readers immediately to the contested nature of such literary renditions. As new fashions emerged in England and France through which the nobility expressed wealth, power, and largess, romance writers celebrated luxurious outfits as indicative of the responsibilities of and commitments to a courtly ethos, while churchmen denounced those garments as invitations to and manifestations of sin. Dress and its accessories consequently negotiate particular social agendas while they materialize in medieval texts as articles crucial to understanding the appearance, social behaviors, and moral values of both finely dressed protagonists and the nobility whose tastes writers have sought to accommodate or curtail.

Cutting across the bias of texts produced by medieval churchmen and courtly writers alike, *Sartorial Strategies* argues that four vernacular poets deeply interested in clothing situate expensive attire as an index of morally upright conduct in light of revolutionary changes in medieval fashions and pastoral care. My examples are drawn primarily from English and French texts generated between the mid-twelfth and late fourteenth centuries, when a confluence of material and moral forces shaped literary and artistic figurations of aristocratic bodies as the church increased its attention to promoting virtuous behavior. During this time, two significant changes in dress styles altered the way that people thought about dress in social, political, economic, and literary contexts.[3] In the twelfth century, loose, expansive garments became drawn tightly to the body with laces, belts, and knots, while in the fourteenth, the technology of plate armor prompted the construction of garments tailored to fit the contours of the body through the use of darts, curved seams, and rounded armholes.[4] These new fashions were both excessive and expensive because of their extravagant use of material: they either required inordinate lengths of fabric that were manipulated to render the body exaggerated in appearance in the 1100s or relied on wasteful cutting to achieve a form-fitting silhouette in the 1300s. Medieval writers acknowledge the interchangeability between terms of fashion, excess, and expense, yet they interpret these qualities of clothing primarily in two very different ways according to genre. On the one hand, romances used descriptions of fashionable clothing to express aristocratic beauty, wealth, and social standing. On the other, clerical chronicles and spiritual guides highlighted a growing trepidation that these provocative garments could express prideful excess or incite lascivious passions. These documents specifically condemn women wearing a laced or belted tunic, known as the *bliaut*, and men clad in short, tight jackets and fitted hose, which showcase, as Geoffrey Chaucer memorably describes in his *Parson's Tale*, "shameful privee membres" and "buttokes" (X.424–25).[5]

The innovative changes in garment construction of the twelfth and fourteenth centuries might contribute to pinpointing the "birth of fashion," but my interest rests with the medieval notion of "facioun" as both a "style" and "a mode of behavior," the latter of which could, I argue, be informed by the dress one wears.[6] As a system of meaning and a historical phenomenon, fashion delineates a particularly social occurrence that describes the smaller, ever-changing details of garments and the larger silhouettes of style modified over time. Yet "fashion" did not always mean sartorial changes at historical moments. Rather, medieval writers use the term more generally to refer to one's appearance, stature, or conduct.[7] "Fashion," as I employ it in this study, pursues such a dual trajectory. As I draw upon the modern sense of the word in order to refer to representations of dress born from one of two watershed moments in clothing history, my readings of these fashionable aristocrats in literature, in turn, extend to the medieval sense of "fashion" as a synonym for how dress in the four following chapters communicates meaning about modes of behavior. To describe these behaviors, I rely primarily on two words: "conduct" and "comportment." Although the English term "conduct" does not mean "moral soundness" until the fifteenth century, "comportment" shares its linguistic history with "port," the term Chaucer uses to describe the demeanor of pilgrims in his *General Prologue* to the *Canterbury Tales*.[8] Because "conduct" and "comportment" denote modern and medieval senses of appropriate ways of being, I use them interchangeably throughout this study to indicate behavior that is, in my view, virtuous and consonant with Christian teaching in the later Middle Ages.

Fashion changes coupled with innovations in pastoral care ultimately influenced clerical and poetic understandings of aristocratic attire. Pope Innocent III's Fourth Lateran Council in 1215 was the best-attended general council of the Middle Ages and arguably the most interested in its attention to the care of souls.[9] In its goal "to eradicate vices and plant virtues, to correct faults and reform morals, [and] to remove heresies and strengthen faith," as Innocent writes in his convocation, the council produced seventy constitutions and a decree for crusading in the Holy Land that outlined general reforms for the church.[10] Sartorial regulations that specify styles and colors of clothing appear for the first time in the history of the ecumenical decrees: canon 16 prohibits clerics from both participating in secular entertainments, games, and festivities at taverns and wearing garments usually associated with the nobility. As if to curb ecclesiastical pride and excess, the directive encourages moderation in attire: outer garments should be "neither too short nor too long," and clerics should avoid "superfluous ornamentation" in embroidered sleeves, shoes with pointed toes, dress of red and green, and buckles and belts adorned with gold or silver.[11] In short, clergy must distinguish themselves from laity in appearance and behavior by observing, among other things, strict discipline in attire.

Where canon 16 shapes identity and behavior through sartorial reform, canon 21 cultivates both public and private identities of clergy and laity through penitential reform.[12] Mandatory confession at least once in a lifetime had long been a part of church practice, but canon 21, known famously by its opening phrase *omnis utriusque sexus*, stipulated that all the faithful of either sex, after having reached "the age of discernment, should individually confess all their sins in a faithful manner to their own priest at least once a year."[13] This directive gave renewed emphasis to the long-standing requirement that parish priests attend to the penitent's inner disposition, provide guidance for appropriate conduct, and administer penance as punishment for sin. As a result of such personal assistance in self-reflection, sinners would ideally reform their desires and thereby gain contrite hearts.[14] Canon 21 thus prompted individuals who confessed annually to admit responsibility for sin through heightened self-awareness, and it required that priests administering the sacrament have a broad understanding of the nuances of vice and virtue so as to counsel their flock. In the face of the directive, this ongoing interchange, simultaneously reflexive and intrapersonal, found greater prominence in the pastoral landscape.

The added emphasis on penance—and the educational requirements for clergy and laity to realize Innocent III's directives—changed social and literary landscapes in ways that affected representations of aristocratic attire in religious didactic texts. Faced with the challenge of educating clergy, students, and laity in the arts of penance, churchmen produced a plethora of instructive literature, predominantly in Latin in the thirteenth century and in the vernacular in the fourteenth, that demarcated vice and virtue.[15] Confessional manuals taught the tripartite structure of penance (contrition of heart; confession to a priest; and satisfaction of sin, the penalty performed to reconcile the sinner to God and to the Christian community) and the nuances of the seven deadly sins. Most often, sartorial sinfulness would appear in relation to either the most deadly sin of pride or lust, with clergy condemning expensive attire either as a superfluous ornamentation that flaunts personal wealth or as a means of inciting onlookers to lust.

With the increase in output of penitential guides that demanded newfound consideration of sin, churchmen amplified a well-established discourse connecting immoral conduct with respect to attire that had existed long before 1215. In an often-cited example from the early third century, Tertullian denounces women's excessive sartorial decoration as deceiving or encouraging lustful actions in his memorable *De cultu feminarum* ("Concerning the Apparel of Women").[16] Nearly a millennium later, French theologian Peter the Chanter reviles fashion's vivid colors and novel long trains as unnatural additions that display human vanity in "Against the Superfluity and Expense of Clothing" and "Against the Form of Clothes," part of his *Verbum abbreviatum* (1191–92), a well-known late twelfth-century manual of moral theology for preachers.[17] So, too, do Latin clerical chronicles and histories of England, from Orderic Vitalis's *Ecclesiastical History* in the late eleventh century to the anonymous *Eulogium* in the fourteenth, condemn fashion for its detrimental effects on the English population, therefore supplementing denunciations popular in vernacular *pastoralia*.[18]

Once again cutting across this bias, *Sartorial Strategies* draws from four writers who both frame their texts with references to vice and virtue and present literary depictions of courtly attire in order to interrupt the strong current of negative moral commentary on medieval dress promulgated by clerics. I assert that stylish aristocrats serve as exemplary figures in pedagogical programs that present even the finest dress as an opportunity for educating clergy and laity in moral conduct. In particular, I argue that Marie de France, the preeminent female poet of the twelfth century, Heldris de Cornuälle, the otherwise unknown thirteenth-century French composer of *Silence*, the anonymous fourteenth-century poet of *Sir Gawain and the Green Knight*, and his contemporary Geoffrey Chaucer all reject the perception that fashionable attire expresses immorality in favor of one that identifies aristocratic garments as signs of virtuous behavior.

I seek to take an innovative approach to understanding depictions of medieval dress, royal culture, and social identity in the vernacular literature of the Middle Ages by systematically attending to the moral value of aristocratic attire in romances and spiritually informed texts in light of cultural changes in fashion and pastoral care. From artifacts that survive as remnants of history to poetic renditions that cover textual bodies, dress and its many representations produce, influence, or transform courtly identities. Long studied by social historians and scholars of art, costume, and culture, dress has been the focus of anthropological and economic inquiries, and it has gained increasing popularity with literary critics who examine textual illustrations of clothing as signs that communicate meaning.[19] Frequently, medieval literary critics have construed clothes as indices of wealth and status, and thus personal identity. Dress demarcates gender. It signals membership in church, military, or chivalric communities.[20] Yet clothing also kindles desire, as is the case for many a knight who falls love-sick at the sight of his magnificently clad beloved.[21] It provokes anxiety, as many medieval moral treatises and sumptuary statutes reveal in their attempts to regulate sartorial appearance.[22] When conceived of as fashion, a term that refers to manipulating textiles so as to produce innovative dress styles, clothing becomes a conceptual system that attends to performance, artifice, pleasure, and discipline.[23] This study builds upon the foundational work of social and costume historians, while contributing to the advances made by literary scholars interested in medieval dress, by focusing on romance's representation of aristocratic clothing as a tool for shaping moral comportment in courtly contexts.

While romances are intended for a different social situation of reading than clerical reading, they nonetheless provide fertile ground for an investigation of clothing and conduct. As the leading secular literary genre of the Middle Ages, romance documents and perpetuates cultural ideals that both reflect and influence aristocratic social values.[24] The genre informs the behaviors and aspirations of its noble and upwardly mobile readership largely by deploying stock motifs— the arming of the hero before leaving for battle, the demarcation of feminine beauty through a catalogue of a lady's physical and sartorial splendor, or the moral and martial challenges presented to and overcome by a knight in exile soon to return home—that reappear "faithfully and abundantly," much like a genetic "meme," as Helen Cooper explains, while adapting to cultural and social change over time.[25] Despite the genre's tendency toward superlative, medieval romances can, writes Neil Cartlidge, "depict topographies through which the contours of the real can sometimes be perceived."[26] Here, I take the "contours" of which Cartlidge speaks in quite a literal way. Specifically, romance outlines the contours of its protagonists' bodies through its descriptions of fashionable attire and thereby demonstrates a real interest in contemporary sartorial practice.

Although the extensive descriptions of lavish dress and accessories, known as the rhetorical trope *effictio*, can register exaggerated luxury or unrealistic expense, Cooper reminds us that "romance as we know it is the product of identifiable and specific changes in social practices, and therefore [is] much more closely modeled on the immediate conditions of contemporary life." Citing the rise of chivalric accoutrements (the stirrup, in particular), Cooper argues that this new technology provided narrative content for the romancier; within fifty years after the stirrup's arrival, the fictional knight appeared in courtly literature mounted in stirrups, with a lance under his arm and ready to joust.[27] Similarly, with the change in fashion for the courtly elite in the twelfth and fourteenth centuries, heroes and heroines appear in medieval literature outfitted *en vogue:* women consistently wear the tightly fitted long dress, known as a *bliaut,* in romances of the high Middle Ages, while fashion-savvy noblemen appear in constricting short coats and clinging hose in later medieval texts. In these ways, the meme of fine dress as a requirement of courtly appearance occurs time and again while registering changes in fashion as they existed in the later Middle Ages.

Sartorial Strategies understands representations of contemporary dress in certain romances as an important component of each poem's pedagogical enterprise, suggesting that aristocratic attire can reveal ideals of virtue and discipline to both laity, who understand expensive trappings as integral to their elite lives, and clergy, who often read these garments as signs of sin in their excess. The examples that I cite all purposefully position fashionable attire as a staple of court life that invariably influences moral comportment. In this way, the romances offer didactic lessons for their audiences.[28] That the genre promotes moral instruction has been well argued by C. Stephen Jaeger, who sees romances written by clergy in the twelfth century as creating chivalric values—rather than reflecting extant ones—so as to correct and instruct aristocratic behaviors: "courtliness as a sublime ethical code" either begins with or entirely comprises "a process of education."[29] In a like manner, the romances I read here negotiate correspondences between expensive garments and issues of moral teaching central to the genre. For instance, Marie de France's stunning *pucèle* [maiden], clad in a revealing costume in *Lanval*, appears as a testifying figure who successfully persuades Arthur's tribune to acquit her lover from crimes that he never committed. Alternatively, the description of luxurious garments and textiles given to Gawain upon his arrival at Hautdesert reinforces a chivalric code of hospitality blatantly absent when the Green Knight first entered Camelot at the beginning of *Sir Gawain and the Green Knight.* Whether worn on the body or exchanged between fellow noblemen, dress promotes an imagined, ideal courtly appearance as well as exemplary comportment. In this way, the genre of romance finds affinities with medieval drama, a form that relies on fashionable costume as an index for understanding its *dramatis personae.* But whereas plays in the Middle Ages offer didactic lessons that often correlate extravagant fashion with worldliness and sin, particularly in the figure of the gallant who flaunts his short gown, tight hose, and slashed jacket, the texts that I read illustrate stylish garments as signs of virtue.[30] Consequently, the garments that I examine in romances and religious texts teach not only laity to embody the ideals of chivalric behavior envisaged by clerical instructors, as Jaeger would have it, but also clergy to reevaluate their condemnations of attire in chronicles, sermons, and spiritual guidebooks.

Romance's presentation of aristocratic attire as an index of virtue sheds light on a conversation between romances and texts of clerical didacticism often marked by the latter's critique of the former. Latin and vernacular ecclesiastical works directed toward pastoral care often register discontent with romance and, in so doing, foster an unfavorable link between the form and function of both genres. In rousing his inattentive audience by invoking King Arthur and then chastising his listeners for their apparent indifference to stories of God, one cleric articulates an anxiety common among clergy who fear that literary fictions distract laity from more religious exempla.[31] So, too, would Abbot Gevard likely be empathetic to the cleric bemoaning his parishioner who listens inattentively to the narrative of Christ's Passion but is moved to tears at the romance of *Guy of Warwick*.[32] These two clergymen understand romance as a genre that conveys such

pathos that lay audiences experience intense, lasting emotional re-
actions to fiction rather than to the didactic stories delivered in church
to inform and bolster their faith.

The bifurcated responses to matters of romance and religion are
further explored beyond the pulpit by clerical authors who suggest
that biblical stories and hagiography warrant consideration as enter-
taining literature despite subject matter that is clearly distinct from
romance. The often-cited *Cursor Mundi,* an early fourteenth-century
account of the history of the world from the Creation to the Last
Judgment, illustrates the seductiveness of romance's content while
inviting readers to consider stories of Jesus and Mary as equally en-
joyable.[33] The 30,000-line poem begins by addressing the literary desires of its readership: "Man yhernes rimes for to here, / And romans
red on maneres sere" [Man yearns to hear rhymes and read romances
on different manners] (lines 1–2). It then outlines several important
romances of the period, including stories of Alexander, King Arthur,
Isumbras, Roland, and Tristram, and concludes that those readers so
taken by such rhymes and romances no longer like any other entertainments.[34] Similarly, the twelfth-century court poet turned monk
and contemporary of Marie de France, Denis Piramus, claims in the
beginning of his *Vie seint Edmund le rey* that his saint's life provides more
moral edification than the folly illustrated in romance.[35] These writers
believe that different values inform romance and religious literature,
and they aspire to draw an equally enthusiastic audience to their ecclesiastical works.

Penitential manuals, too, register similar despair with the content of romance and often appropriate imagery of the stylish subject
into expositions of undisciplined and therefore sinful behaviors. Similar to the complaints advanced by the sermonists, *Speculum Vitae* (ca.
1350–75), an important medieval instructional treatise that invokes
the Lord's Prayer to combat the seven deadly sins and to cultivate the
seven virtues, finds itself in competition for the same audience as such
romances of *Octavian, Isumbras, Bevis of Hampton,* and *Guy of Warwick.*[36]
Promising "na vayne carpynge / of dedes of armes ne of amours"
[no worthless chatter of military feats or love] (lines 36–37), the

Speculum writer instead offers "[t]o carp of mast nedefull thynge / Þat sykirest es for saul and lyf" [to speak of the most needful thing that is most spiritually safe for one's soul and life] (lines 50–51), namely, how to rule one's being and govern well one's senses so as to find the way to heaven.[37] By preceding the promise to speak of the most "needful" topics with a list of romances about which the writer's "carpynge sal nogt be" [speaking shall not be] (line 47), *Speculum Vitae* depicts the content of romance as a luxurious excess that counters the very notions of self-governance integral to the narrative's project as articulated in the introductory lines.

Such ideas of personal discipline both resonate thematically with other penitentials, which disapprove of readers who enjoy romance, and throw into relief the striking choice of authors who use their romances as venues to present a more disciplined sense of self-regulation in aristocratic attire. For instance, as early as the twelfth century, Peter of Blois, an important ecclesiastic who figured prominently at Henry II's court, indirectly seconds the critiques advanced by writers of religious texts and sermons in his *Liber de confessione,* complaining that "the laity wept copiously over the tragedies of Arthur, Gauvain, and Tristan but were indifferent to the stories of God's love and shed no tears of repentance."[38] The lay audience's affective response to the trials of romance's heroes not only opposes its indifference to Christian exempla but also forestalls any self-awareness that would evoke penitent behavior in worldly men or women. The fourteenth-century vernacular penitential, *The Clensyng of Mannes Sowle,* might be read as a response to Peter of Blois's grievance.[39] By providing a model of confession to those sinners who wish to repent for misdeeds in thought, speech, and deed, including the reading of romances, the *Clensyng* encourages the kind of self-reflection that would redress sin. For the individual suffering from sloth, the *Clensyng* proposes the following formula:

> Also in such tymes & festes I haue left holy redynge & syngyne, & willfully I haue rad on romaunces, fables, & songes and carolles of dishoneste & synne & nycetees. Also in such tymes & daies, when I might & schulde haue praied, or taught, or lerned, or spoke good, þan I haue

spoken harm of oþer, or of tidynges, lesynges, or of fleschly synnes &
mayne idell wordes to hyndrynge of my soule.

—

[Also during such times and feasts, I have left holy reading and singing,
and willfully I have read romances, fables, songs and carols of dishonesty and sin and foolishness. Also at such times and days, when I might
and should have prayed or taught or learned or spoken well, I have spoken ill of another or of rumors, lies, or of fleshly sins and many idle
words to the detriment of my soul.][40]

The *Clensyng* finds the secular adventures of knights and their ladies
incongruent with matters of virtue and atonement. Romance belongs
in the same abysmal category as "those tales, songs, and carols of dishonesty, sin, and foolishness," in entertainments that apparently do
not convey anything approaching the good derived from "holy reading
and singing." It promotes condemnable behaviors commensurate with
the ill effects of speaking rumors, lies, or of fleshly sins.[41] All of these
religious texts, from sermons to penitentials, decry romances as works
devoid of any virtue, which seduce laity away from the morally edifying readings found in *pastoralia*.

That these aforementioned examples of pastoral care repeatedly
denounce romance bespeaks an engagement between the two genres
concerning form and function that is taken up in this book with respect to aristocratic clothing. In the most drastic sense, writers of
penitentials and other spiritual guides do not believe that the form of
romance can address any of the functional characteristics inherent in
guides of pastoral care. Yet, as Richard Newhauser has remarked, "no
form can be limited to one function alone in a literary system and no
function can be fulfilled exclusively by one type of literature."[42] In
other words, romance, though emphasizing different means, can arrive
at an end similar to that of the penitential manual: it can offer access
to those upright codes of behavior demanded by treatises on sin in its
depiction of knights and ladies whose sense of moral conduct derives
from ethical conduct based on Christian teaching.

It might be argued that I have highlighted a favorable divide between clerical and poetic analyses of sartorial display by drawing on

moral complaints about fashion in treatments of vice: clergymen condemn expensive, novel attire as sinful, while romanciers celebrate material luxuries as courtly necessities. To be sure, there are models of costly clothing as measures of moral comportment in descriptions of virtue that persist in religious texts from the biblical Parable of the Wedding Feast (Matthew 22:11–14) to commentaries by William of Malmesbury in the twelfth century and Thomas Aquinas in the thirteenth.[43] Absent, however, from these representative examples are specific styles that name either the long, tightly laced *bliaut*, belts cinched around the body, or fitted hose and constricting jackets. Instead, the passages that promote virtue through dress rely on generalized descriptions of sartorial splendor that do not engage historical changes.

In terms of this study, I examine romances and religious guides that negotiate a space for virtuous aristocratic behavior through connections to stylish dress conventionally condemned by clerics in their considerations of sin. Aristocratic garments, often understood to demonstrate excessive consumption or to excite lust in men and women, inspired many clerics to insist on sartorial reform as a part of moral reform. But *Guigemar, Silence, Sir Gawain and the Green Knight,* and the *Parson's Tale* all recognize such attire as a means to fruitful and meritorious ends.

Though not a romance, Geoffrey Chaucer's *Parson's Tale* merits inclusion with such literary company because it shares a similar strategy with the romances in figuring attire ultimately as virtuous. Penitential manuals consistently position aristocratic dress as symptomatic of sin, and the *Parson's Tale* initially follows suit. However, Chaucer returns to dress imagery to convey spiritually sound behavior, effectively appropriating the fashionable aristocrat from romance in order to propose a new understanding of pleasure in attire absent from the other twelve vernacular penitentials examined in chapter 4. This interest in creating a nexus between court practice and moral comportment may be explained in part by Chaucer's deep commitment to fictions that address aristocratic life, values, and fashions (in both the medieval and modern sense of the word): nearly all of his poetry before the *Canterbury* project, from the *Book of the Duchess* with its reliance on courtly love motifs to his translation of the *Roman de la rose* to his composition of the historical epic romance, *Troilus and Criseyde*, could be considered courtly.[44] Even if the poems were not intended specifically for the court, they nevertheless engaged ideas and discourses concerning material wealth and goods familiar to the nobility in ways informed by his work for the monarchy. From the time that Chaucer was a member of the Royal Household in 1367 through the last years of his life when he was affiliated with the future Lancastrian king Henry IV, Chaucer regularly received gifts of clothing.[45] As controller of customs between 1374 and 1386, he computed and collected taxes levied on exported wool and cloth.[46] He was thus exposed to or engaged with the very textiles upon which the nobility relied as part of their lifestyle for the fifteen years prior to his composing the *Canterbury Tales,* a fact that may explain the precise sartorial details that he channels into each pilgrim's portrait in the *General Prologue.*

Despite his interests in courtly clothing and the wealth of the wool industry, Chaucer chooses not to include sartorial splendor in his longest romance in the *Canterbury* collection, the *Knight's Tale.* More peculiar is that the only extensive consideration of male aristocratic attire occurs in his moral treatise, the *Parson's Tale,* which is far removed from his romance both in content and placement. Where the *Knight's Tale* appears first, features a narrator who is the highest-ranking secular pilgrim in the group, and takes as its subject questions of love, chivalry, and aristocratic romance in poetry, the *Parson's Tale* appears last, features a tale-teller of the lowest-ranking member of the clergy among the religious pilgrims, and takes as its subject a prose treatise concerning the sacrament of penance and the seven deadly sins. In featuring the very image of aristocratic fashion that pervades contemporary medieval romances, Chaucer crystallizes the literary concerns of romance as ethical concerns much in the same way as do Marie de France, Heldris de Cornuälle, and the *Gawain*-poet.

While *Guigemar, Silence, Sir Gawain and the Green Knight,* and the *Parson's Tale* are perhaps surprising for their collective differences—two appear in French (one in Anglo-Norman, the other in a Picard dialect of thirteenth-century Continental French), two are Middle English, and, moreover, the *Parson's Tale* is not a romance at all but a prose text on penance—as four texts in dialogue they represent three distinct threads of a complex conversation informed by historical changes in fashion and in ecclesiastical reform. First, each relies on dress as a central plot motif. Second, they all engage with England to some degree. And third, all bear witness to a developing interest in virtue and vice evident in their textual or codicological frames.

Clothing and its accessories become crucial for narrative development in each of the literary works examined in the following pages. Marie de France's *Guigemar* draws upon the innovation of using belts, laces, and knots to fit garments closely to the body by featuring a knot and a belt as integral to advancing the plot: the hunting wound that Guigemar suffers in his thigh, which he then binds tightly with his shirt in a sort of knot to staunch the bleeding, precipitates his journey to find his beloved. The two lovers eventually swear fidelity in love by exchanging sartorial tokens—a belt for her and a knotted shirt for him—that ultimately serve as recognition devices at the end of the short romance. Where the twelfth century marks the beginning stages of carefully defining the aristocratic silhouette in fashion history, the thirteenth presents a heightened interest in controlling virtuous behavior through dress appropriate to one's station. By choosing transvestism as a strategy that not only governs the narrative trajectory of over half the poem but also explores moral virtue and filial loyalty at a time when vice-ridden courts came under fire in literature, Heldris de Cornuälle invites a reassessment of Lateran IV's sartorial directives in canons 16 and 68. The church may wish to correlate dress with social station by preventing religious from wearing the colorful, fashionable garb designed for the nobility so as to avoid the sin of superfluity in canon 16, and it may seek to reveal human essence by requiring Jews to mark themselves in dress so they do not marry Christians in canon 68, but Heldris interrupts such direct correspondence between clothing, essence, and virtue by presenting a woman who is meritorious in behavior even as she transgresses social codes and gender boundaries through cross-dressing.

Like the aforementioned French romances, the Middle English texts position dress and its accessories as central concerns. *Sir Gawain and the Green Knight* first registers the great fourteenth-century fashion change of fitting garments closely to the body through novel tailoring techniques in its rendition of the Green Knight entering Camelot in a short, tight jacket with hose clinging to his legs. Yet the *Gawain*-poet ultimately figures one piece of the fashionable aristocrat's ensemble as essential to the poem's narrative climax, *dénouement*, and conclusion. In the case of the *Parson's Tale*, aristocratic attire allows Chaucer to stage a paradigmatic shift in the way readers should understand delight in dress. These romances, and the one vernacular penitential written by the same layman who also authored various poems committed to exploring the generic conventions of romance, thus respond directly to the accusations of religious narratives that condemn the genre specifically for its inclusion of dishonesty, sin, and niceties—including luxurious, fashionable garments—that hinder the soul.

In addition to featuring dress as a central concern, each text engages with English political systems in direct or indirect ways. Marie de France dedicates her *lais* to a noble king who was most likely Henry II Plantagenet, ruler of England, and she writes in Anglo-Norman, known increasingly as the "French of England" for its use from the time of the Conquest in 1066 through the middle of the fifteenth century.[47] Both *Silence* and *Sir Gawain and the Green Knight* weave English politics into their narratives through examinations of loyalty at court, and Geoffrey Chaucer, an employee of the crown, produces the first penitential manual written in Middle English by a layman.[48] Whether literal or linguistic, the four texts insert ideas of England into narratives that represent the effect of aristocratic attire on social conduct and moral behavior.

While I correlate romances and spiritual guides because of their shared interests in representing the clothed body in the literature of or pertaining to England, one of the most compelling reasons to read these particular texts together is for their explicit connections to virtue and/or vice in their manuscript contexts. Marie de France and Heldris de Cornuälle make this connection in the prologues to their poems: Marie argues that readers should use literature as a means to guard themselves from vice in general (*Prologue*, lines 23–25), while Heldris digresses at length to condemn avarice in particular (lines 23–106). Though not in the prologue proper, *Sir Gawain and the Green Knight* pursues an examination of "sourquydrye" [presumption]—defined as the third branch of pride in medieval taxonomies of sin—that the Green Knight first mentions when challenging Arthur's courtiers to a holiday game (line 311) and that Bertilak later references in his revelatory discussion with Gawain (line 2457).[49] As a penitential manual, the *Parson's Tale* outlines and examines each of the seven deadly sins and, like the romances, uses dress to manifest both vicious and virtuous behaviors.

The manuscript context in which these works circulated attests to a real interest in combining moral instruction with courtly fiction, as if to teach in a single codex how a reader might acquire both social grace and grace from God. Marie's *Guigemar* and Chaucer's *Parson's Tale* appear in multiple codices but, even when texts such as *Silence* and *Sir Gawain and the Green Knight* survive in solitary exemplars, there is still evidence of an intertextual thematic arc that spans courtly and moral teachings. For instance, of the eleven *fabliaux* that appear alongside *Silence* and five other verse romances in Nottingham, University Library, MS Mi.LM.6, four feature religious protagonists or themes.[50] In the case of London, British Library, MS Cotton Nero A.x, Art. 3, all four poems of the *Gawain*-poet are deeply enmeshed in the trappings of courtly life while ever cognizant of spiritual practices.

The best examples of romances existing alongside works of clerical didacticism for the purpose of this study appear in London, British Library, MS Harley 978, and Cambridge, Magdalene College, MS Pepys 2006. In the case of the former, Marie de France's entire twelve *lais* appear in their sole complete form alongside no fewer than fifteen separate works on moral teaching, four of which address confession or fashion changes and worldly vanities.[51] In the case of the latter manuscript, Pepys 2006 is the only known codex to excerpt the two prose *Canterbury* tales (*Melibee* and *Parson*) and to include them with a collection of courtly poetry largely by John Lydgate and Geoffrey Chaucer. It has been suggested that Pepys 2006 "consists of elements from (probably) two originally distinct manuscripts," but an examination of the two hands responsible for the Chaucerian prose and following lyrics reveals an interest in bridging religious and secular concerns of the nobility.[52] Since one hand writes *Melibee* and part of the *Parson's Tale*, and the second hand continues the *Parson's Tale* and the subsequent courtly poetry, it is impossible to separate the moral and courtly interests along scribal lines. As Mary Erler argues of Pepys 2006, "whether one person selected the material is impossible to tell, but because the writing of the collection's disparate items took place at about the same time, it seems likely that the personal taste of a single figure is reflected."[53] Pepys 2006 thus testifies to the same medieval interest of reading courtly narratives alongside Christian ones that extended well into the seventeenth century, when the unique copy of the *Gawain*-poet's courtly and Christian works were bookended with a prayer and a small penitential manual.[54]

Scholars of medieval textual criticism argue that meaning derived from texts cannot be divorced from their codicological contexts: individual works become informed by intertextual thematic arcs that span an entire codex, thus revealing personal tastes and reading habits that combine romances with moral treatises, as found in inventories of medieval personal libraries.[55] A record of the library of King Edward III's son, Thomas Woodstock (1355–97), duke of Gloucester, notes more than eighty books, including romances, histories, and theological tracts. Thomas's eleven romances, likely the primary source of his leisure reading, were complemented by texts such as Gregory's *Cura pastoralis* and a book of vices and virtues.[56] Smaller libraries of aristocrats reveal similar holdings of romances and treatises of sins and their remedies: in the last decade of the fourteenth century, Margaret Courtenay (née de Bohun, 1311–91), second countess of Devon, bequeaths several books including one of vices and virtues along with three romances. Following suit, Isabella of Castile (c. 1355–92), duchess of York, gives a book of vices and virtues to Sir Lewis Clifford and a Lancelot romance to her son, Edward of Norwich. Like the previous women's bequests, the rather large manuscript collection amassed by Eleanor de Bohun (1366–99), duchess of Gloucester, includes a book of vices and virtues, Gregory's *Cura pastoralis,* and a single verse romance known as the *Histoire de Chivaler a Cigne.*[57] Based on these inventories, essential reading appears to be romances complemented by late medieval teachings on penitential practices and behaviors.

In considering the connections between literary renditions of sartorial delights and clerical regulation of contemporary aristocratic

dress, each chapter of this book highlights a particular sartorial strategy that challenges the widespread assumption that stylish individuals were in need of spiritual rehabilitation. First, the French texts of
Marie de France and Heldris de Cornüalle employ dress to articulate
productive and virtuous behaviors. Second, the Middle English works
of the *Gawain*-poet and Chaucer use fourteenth-century fashion as
outward signs of pleasure that paradoxically encourage penance. The
two texts in French and two in English represent the cross-pollination
of literary ideas and sartorial fashions first registered by French
and English chroniclers in their descriptions of political alliances,
conflicts, and disseminations of "foreign" dress practices in England.
The twelfth-century cleric and historian of England and Normandy,
Orderic Vitalis, born in England and educated at a monastery in
St. Evroult, France, collapses distinctions between the French and
English in his *Ecclesiastical History* when he describes clothing worn at
the English court of King Rufus (William Rufus, otherwise known
as William II), grandson of Robert II of France. When Orderic notes
that "our ancestors used to wear decent clothes" [Illi enim modestis
uestiebantur] and "now almost all our fellow countrymen are crazy"
[nunc uero pene uniuersi populares cerriti sunt] with their "frivo-
lous fashion" [friuolam adinuentionem], it is unclear whether he
means English or French predecessors and contemporaries.[58] However, fourteenth-century chroniclers are more explicit in naming the
French as responsible for propagating problematic dress styles: Guillaume de Nangis reports that the English witness new short fashions
during Edward III's victory at Sluys in 1340, while John of Reading
laments the English adoption of French fashion after Philippa of
Hainault (granddaughter of Philippe III of France) arrives in England soon after Edward III's coronation.[59] These historians point to
a cultural exchange across the Channel that I pursue in this study with
respect to morality and attire.

    Chapter 1 argues that Marie de France sidelines the notions of
immorality inherent in depictions of fitted garments as they appear
in clerical histories and other contemporary romances, such as the
Roman d'Enéas, in favor of a poetics that teaches restrained behavior
through constrictive clothing. As an illustration of the claim in her

Prologue that readers must protect themselves from vice, Marie's sartorial strategy in *Guigemar* takes fitted belts and knotted shirts as indicators of virtuous love. She appropriates the twelfth-century fashion change of drawing garments close to the body with belts, laces, and knots to morally edifying ends. In responding primarily to contemporary clerical chronicles, which decry the practice of tight lacing in the same scathing rhetoric that later pervades the moral treatises of the thirteenth and fourteenth centuries, Marie de France situates herself as a vigorous participant in an active debate concerning the broader issue of literature's moral value.

For Heldris de Cornuälle, clothing functions in different but equally compelling ways. Chapter 2 asserts that garments do not matter for Heldris's cross-dresser, a young woman who passes as a knight and minstrel at the king's court, in the same way as they do for either medieval clerics who find transvestism to be a sign of individual immorality or for modern literary critics who see it as an invitation to consider the text's gender politics. To mark ideal moral conduct at two salient moments, Heldris deploys *effictio,* a rhetorical device conventionally used to delineate the appearance of the fashionable body in romance, to signal what Marjorie Garber calls a "category crisis" that emphasizes moral dissonances in the poem.[60] *Silence* reinvents the transvestite as a figure who highlights, somewhat surprisingly, the moral crisis of her fellow knights instead of the protagonist's errant soul, as traditional clerical condemnations would have it. Although thirteenth-century church reforms encouraged the sort of individual spiritual reflection that would likely occasion the transvestite's self-evaluation, *Silence* refuses such an approach. Rather, Heldris uses the transvestite to measure the ethical conduct of others who engage directly with her. In reconceptualizing transvestism as a kind of moral barometer, the chapter seeks to provide a new interpretive key to understanding the poem's engagement with the sins that plague aristocratic courts.

Drawing from a range of contemporary texts that feature aristocratic belts in both spiritually sound and unsound contexts—from chivalric works, such as the "Complainte de la bataille de Poitiers" and Geoffroi de Charny's *Livre de l'ordre de chevalerie,* to religious guides written by clergy as well as by the lay knight Henry of Lancaster—chapter 3 maintains that the *Gawain*-poet refashions unease associated with the ornamented silk garments of the aristocratic court to educate his audience in the arts of penance. Gawain's famous girdle, which he accepts from Bertilak's wife as a love-token with magical life-saving properties, prompts the Green Knight to punish his opponent for betraying their agreement. The belt then leads Gawain to confess and subsequently reevaluate his behavior. By figuring the belt as a penitential garment worn to satisfy sin and thus to reconcile the penitent to God and to his immediate Christian community, the *Gawain*-poet transforms our understanding of a garment originally infused with sexual and immoral connotations. His sartorial strategy takes the expensive, ornamented belt, which churchmen would condemn for prideful excess, as a catalyst for religious conversion.

The final chapter turns not to romance but to Geoffrey Chaucer's vernacular penitential manual, the *Parson's Tale*, which both serves as a key witness to the religious sentiment of its time and includes the most vivid rendition in Chaucer's entire canon of a fashion-savvy aristocrat. While romances in the *Canterbury Tales* avoid standard sartorial tropes to indicate social standing, wealth, or beauty, the *Parson's Tale* appropriates the fashionable aristocrat from romance in order to stage a paradigmatic shift in the way that readers should understand delight in dress. Like the *Gawain*-poet, Chaucer uses expensive attire to prompt penitential behavior. However, Chaucer's rhetoric of dress, which is original narrative in a tale that is primarily a translation of two source texts, creates systems of pleasure-in-attire that appear in his exposition of the three components of penance: contrition, confession, and satisfaction of sin. Beginning as signs of displeasure for the unremorseful whose clothing will not protect them from the fires of hell and seen subsequently as illicit pleasures associated with the deadly sin of pride, figurations of attire ultimately return as the means to the spiritual bliss that the Parson finds necessary to reconciliation with God. Chaucer's initial two treatments of dress in the *Tale* make explicit an implicit concern about fashion and moral conduct: new styles of clothing exemplify prideful excess because they reveal the body and demand excessive amounts of labor and fabric. But in the typical Chaucerian manner, the poet overturns such an assumption, and in this case it is to serve positive ends: his redirection of dress as expiatory becomes a tangible means to shepherding penitents to celestial bliss—arguably, a central concern of a majority of writers in the Middle Ages. That Chaucer mobilizes contemporary understandings of dress in vivid, original narrative that derives from no source found to date furthermore addresses the broader issue of the *Tale's* literariness that Chaucerians have often found missing.

These sartorial strategies demonstrate the value, productivity, and cultural significance of the fashions that so troubled and inspired medieval writers. Ranging from renditions of the fashionable body as expressions of cultural values to reconfigurations of courtly attire as incentives for inner spiritual transformation, the image of the stylish aristocrat in romance shifts the contemporary conversations about dress away from a discourse of sin to one of virtue. Court culture, with its celebration of aristocratic attire, must serve the larger literary frames of virtuous conduct, and for this reason each writer of romance complicates the traditional opposition between sacred and secular polemics on dress: Marie de France, Heldris de Cornuälle, and the *Gawain*-poet refuse clerical critiques of fashion because the larger frames of their poems (vice for Marie, avarice for Heldris, and a codicological context for the *Gawain*-poet whose romance sits alongside the spiritual texts, *Cleanness, Patience,* and *Pearl* in the only extant manuscript) demand that sartorial tropes work in edifying ways. The consequences of such sartorial strategies reshape clerical material for aristocratic use in the vein of vernacular theology, which in turn makes clerical culture all the more relevant to medieval aristocrats, as the *Parson's Tale* illustrates when it engages with social questions that pertain especially to the aristocracy and rising bourgeoisie. While religious and political documents decried the immorality inherent in sumptuous clothing and attempted to restrain the behavior of individuals wearing stylish garments, the works featured in the chapters that follow re-imagine fashion-savvy aristocrats as models of morally sound behavior in a pedagogical program advanced not by preachers but by poets.

Marie de France

Guigemar and the Erotics of Tight Dress

Clothes need to be more disciplinary.

—Pearl (tight-lacing enthusiast)

In the twelfth century, a startling change in dress styles occurred. Garments that were once expansive and flowing became tightly fitted across the body with belts, knots, and laces. Short hemlines— characteristic of Anglo-Saxon tunics, dresses, and jackets—lengthened, and fitted sleeves and bodices revealed the body's contours and exaggerated the dimensions of the arms and torso in the early 1100s.[1] Belts and laces tightened loose fabrics closely around the upper body, and dressmakers achieved a fuller skirt by first cutting vertically from the lower hem to halfway below the waist and then placing a triangular gore into each of the slits.[2] The resulting silhouette featured a marked contrast between a fitted bodice and a full skirt, the train of which was often knotted, perhaps to avoid dragging costly fabric on the ground. According to fashion historians, this moment in the high Middle Ages marks "the early, modest beginnings of tight-lacing."[3]

Literary and artistic representations of the tightly bound body appear in a variety of genres, from medieval romances to illuminated manuscripts, and generate vastly different responses depending on context. While this novel dress emblematized fashion *savoir faire* in romances and select manuscript images, it prompted various complaints in religious histories and moral treatises: either tightly clad women seduced men to sin or noblemen placed national security at risk because they were distracted by their own fitted fashions.[4] From these strikingly different understandings of attire emerges a solitary voice in twelfth-century romance that purposefully recasts clerical critiques of fashion toward positive ends. In particular, the poet known as Marie de France situates tight dress as a sign of virtuous behavior, thereby providing a moral justification for aristocratic trappings.

As a writer of short romances, beast fables, and spiritual adventures in the form of a knight's quest to purgatory (*Espurgatoire Seint Patriz*) and hagiography (*La vie seinte Audree*, attributed), Marie de France demonstrates a real interest throughout her work in exploring intersections between a courtly ethos and Christian conduct, which is in turn amplified by codicological contexts.[5] Of the five extant manuscripts in which at least one of Marie's *lais* survive, all present a "web of interlocution" between courtly necessities and moral refinement that Marie already figures at the sartorial level in her *lais*.[6] The only extant manuscript to include all of Marie's *lais* along with her *Prologue*, London, British Library, MS Harley 978, bespeaks such an interest by situating the short romances alongside no fewer than fifteen works of moral edification.[7] Each of the remaining four extant manuscripts includes at least one of Marie's *lais* coupled with a saint's life, secular hagiography, or *pastoralia*, as if to offer a similar interlocutory promise: the teachings of romance complement those of clerical didacticism (and vice versa), suggesting that one genre can both inform and influence the other.[8] This chapter pursues the codicological concern of interweaving courtly and Christian practices more locally in Marie's *Guigemar*, which presents tight dress as a sign of honorable comportment. Such a sartorial strategy allows Marie to acknowledge the arrival of new fashions by creating a new art of courtly love through restraint in attire that both responds to and redirects clerical anxieties. In so doing, Marie's romance both engages with and contributes to a collection of penitential and religious writings that aimed to teach its audience about virtue, vice, and moral conduct in the last quarter of the twelfth century.

Tight dress, knots, and belts often appear as signs of aristocratic beauty, sexual continence, and military prowess in medieval literature, but they acquire particular historical import when read in light of evolving social attitudes toward fashion during the reign of Henry II (1154–89) and Eleanor of Aquitaine. Gervase of Tilbury, a devout and learned layman, attests to "the changes in fashion brought by time" when writing of his close relationship with Henry II and his aristocratic circle: "men and women alike . . . wear very tight clothes . . . so that one gets the impression that their bodies have not just been dressed (*induta*) in their clothes, but have actually been sewn (*insuta*) into them."[9] Gervase's observation suggests that the Angevin court witnessed the transformation of fashionable dress among its elite. Given the monarchy's support of arts and letters, it is also possible that Henry II and Eleanor indirectly encouraged the dissemination of textual representations of sartorial changes through literary patronage.[10] Not surprisingly, contemporary works offer various interpretations of what the new fitted attire means: romances tend to use tight dress as a mark of noble birth or beauty, while histories and sermons authored by various clerics often figure the fashion as a sign of pride or sexual licentiousness because it communicates the individual's investment in worldly goods.

The *lais* of Marie de France, a compilation of twelve short Breton romances written in the 1160s for a "nobles reis" [noble king] (*Prologue,* line 43), who may have been Henry II, registers the fashion change that Gervase describes in order to communicate wealth, beauty, and martial prowess.[11] The *lai de Guigemar,* however, is particularly noteworthy because it reconciles literal and metaphoric understandings of tight dress in an innovative way that accords with aristocratic value while appealing to the moral concerns in clerical sermons and histories. As the first in the series as it appears in London, British Library, Harley 978, *Guigemar* establishes fitted attire as an expression not only of noble beauty but also of an original pedagogical enterprise that seeks to demonstrate tight dress as virtuous for laity and clergy. Rather than espouse the clerics' view, which perceives tight lacing as sexually licentious, Marie responds to them by redirecting the inherited convention in romance.

To be sure, Marie's use of common romance motifs accords with those of the genre: the eponymous protagonist falls in love with a seemingly unattainable woman (she is married to a jealous husband who keeps her under lock and key); the two experience love in the typical Ovidian sense (as a constraining malady that affects body and mind); elements of magic infuse the narrative (from a talking hind who curses Guigemar to a magical ship that transports lovers to foreign lands); lovers exchange gifts that affirm their commitment (a knot in Guigemar's shirt and a belt for the lady), and these gifts serve as a recognition motif should the lovers become separated and then reunited. *Guigemar*, though, departs from convention with respect to Marie's use of aristocratic costume because she conceives dress through a poetics of restraint that signifies broadly across discourses of fashion, courtly love, and morality. Instead of adopting the Ovidian notion that love, which constricts the body, must be abandoned, Marie advocates becoming *estreitement bendé* [tightly bound] (lines 58, 139–40, 373) in attire. In this way, the *lai*'s protagonists model an innovative, virtuous *art d'aimer* rather than the morally dangerous behaviors that trouble so many churchmen.

Guigemar's relative popularity in extant manuscripts (it survives in three of five) attests to the potential of teaching a wide audience of laity and clergy two important lessons: first, that tight dress signals discipline, moderation, and self-control; and second, that the moral "sen" [sense] (*Prologue*, line 16) that they may gloss from descriptions of dress in *Guigemar* includes fitted attire as an illustration of positive, faithful sexuality.[12] Marie's portrayal of lay nobility in turn teaches both laity and clergy a socially responsible version of the sartorial discipline advocated by the modern corset designer, known simply as Pearl, in the epigraph to this chapter.[13]

Pedagogy and the *Prologue*

Marie's *lais* register an awareness of two incongruous interpretations of aristocratic attire—that of beauty and wealth advanced by demands of the genre, and that of anxiety registered by clerics—and respond with a new art of loving that embraces virtue and orthodoxy. On the one hand, various *lais* consistently feature lavish costume as a sign of wealth in an ideal aristocratic world that was, in fact, marked by an increase in trade, conspicuous consumption by nobles and non-nobles alike, and, as a result, a decrease in what has been described as the "material stability" in the world of the twelfth-century aristocracy.[14] On the other, the collection's much-commented-upon *Prologue* proposes a curriculum for understanding literary representations in an orthodox manner that would, in turn, help readers guard themselves from sin, a position consonant with the project of the few penitential manuals that emerged in the twelfth century before the great proliferation of such spiritual handbooks in the following two hundred years. Marie's audience should thus "gloser la lettre" [gloss the letter] (line 15) and supply "sen" [sense] (line 16) to the text so that they "se savreient garder / De ceo k'i ert a trespasser" [would know how to keep themselves from whatever was to be avoided] (lines 21–22).[15] In drawing upon an exegetical tradition that prompts readers to find ethical significance through proper interpretation of text, Marie suggests both that her own work merits similar attention[16] and that the amorous adventures of her protagonists include lessons to edify the moral fiber of her clerical and lay readership.

The *Prologue* thus announces that the *lais* that follow will provide an example of a didactic initiative. To become courtly in Marie's world means to abide by what C. Stephen Jaeger calls "a sublime ethical code" that underpins romance's tacit "program of education."[17] Susan Crane describes the pedagogical phenomenon as such: "Openly and joyfully [romances] adopt from religious writing the doctrine, the models of conduct, and the narrative patterns that can deepen their ultimately secular endeavor."[18] Indeed, Marie's *Prologue* names "vice" as the central danger against which her reader must protect himself. He should therefore "study" [estudïer], "listen" [entendre] (line 24), and "begin [the] weighty work" [A grevose ovre comencier] (line 25) of reading the *lais* in order to "keep vice at a distance and free himself from great sorrow" [Par ceo s'en puet plus esloignier / E de grant dolur delivrer] (lines 25–26). However, descriptions of passionate love, expensive costume, and lavish tournaments pose a noteworthy challenge for Marie's educational program because such courtly practices draw vastly different responses from clergy and aristocratic laity. While the nobility might understand love, costumes, and tournaments literally as chivalric ideals, moralists would likely read them figuratively as sinful excess.

Denis Piramus, a twelfth-century cleric contemporary with Marie de France, exemplifies this latter concern by criticizing romance as a genre that promotes more folly than faith. After identifying Marie as a particularly popular court poet in the beginning of his *Vie seint Edmund*, Denis asserts that the content of his hagiography rather than her short romances "can cure souls and protect bodies from shame":

> Jeo vus dirray par dreit fei
> Un deduit qui mielz valut asez
> Ke ces autres ke tant amez,
> E plus delitable a oÿr;
> Si purrez les almes garir
> E les cors garaunter de hunte.
> Mult deit homme bien oyr tel cunte:
> Homme deit mult mielz a sen entendre
> Ke en folie le tens despendre.
>
> (lines 60–68)
>
> —
>
> [I will tell you truly a pleasant tale that is worth much more than those others you love so much and is more delightful to hear. And it can cure souls and protect bodies from shame. One should surely listen well to such a story. Better that one should pay attention to sense than waste time on folly.][19]

Denis's assertion that the lives of saints rehabilitate souls and protect bodies from shame unlike "those other" tales accords with ecclesiastical condemnations that find romance at odds with religious teachings.[20] Despite the clerical commonplace that romance does not necessarily offer spiritual edification to its readership, Marie conceives of the genre as one that possesses restorative properties. The *Prologue* to the *lais* engages in what may be considered a secular version of pastoral care by affirming that reading romance helps "guard oneself from vice" [Ki de vice se voelt defendre] (line 23) so that one may lead a spiritually sound life.

That Marie encourages such moral conduct through dress is noteworthy, given clerics' anxieties over fashion in combination with their view of romance as devoid of moral teaching. In *Guigemar*, the first *lai* that follows the *Prologue*, Marie responds to these concerns by deftly demonstrating tight dress as an expression of virtuous love, which in turn announces her mission to use poetic images to productive ends. Rather than compose a text wherein "the description of lay nobility becomes a pedagogic instrument in the hands of the clergy for the correction and instruction of the laity,"[21] Marie depicts aristocratic fashion in romance so as to revise notions of clerical didacticism. That she does so at a crucial time in church history, when books and aids to pastoral care were hardly in existence, affords us one explanation of why she treats fashion so virtuously.

Of course, works by Augustine and Gregory, along with Celtic and Anglo-Saxon penitential manuals, serve as witnesses to a tradition of the *cura animarum* (the care of souls) in Marie's distant past.[22] However, as Joseph Goering and Leonard E. Boyle have respectively argued, the manuals attending to sin and sacraments that first emerged in the second and third quarters of the twelfth century (such as Bishop Bartholomew of Exeter's *Penitentiale*), and that in turn encouraged the production of at least ten to twelve more manuals between the Third and Fourth Lateran Councils (1179–1215), provided a foundation upon which practical literature on virtue and vice would flourish.[23] These guides "blaze a trail" in their "very deliberate attempts to communicate to the pastoral clergy at large the current teaching, whether theological or legal, on the pastoral care in relation to the needs of the times, and on the sacraments, particularly penance, matrimony and the eucharist, in respect to the latest in learning."[24] Marie's *Guigemar*, and arguably her entire collection of *lais* with their interest in virtue, marriage, and (in the case of *Yonec*) the Eucharist, may be understood as blazing its own trail, treating fashion as virtuous in order to reflect to the nobility lessons analogous to those articulated in the pastoral tradition.

"Mariees au deable": Tightly Laced Women in Clerical Commentaries

In response to clerical condemnations in histories and sermons of tight dress as signifying an unbridled body, Marie de France draws upon contemporary innovative styles to present a new art of courtly love in *Guigemar* that reshapes clerical material for aristocratic use. As clothing emphasized a more slender figure in the twelfth century through the use of belts, laces, and knots, new questions arose concerning the meaning of fashion. Medieval clerics, following the positions of early church fathers, construe tight dress as arousing lust in men and conveying the wantonness of fashionable women.[25] In general, they perceive fashionable garments as both concealing a woman's sinful nature and broadcasting its immoral tendencies.

Twelfth-century clerics expand their warnings to both women and men who wear tight or laced attire. Orderic Vitalis's *Ecclesiastical History*, notable for its rendition of the Anglo-Norman events between 1050 and 1141 and its understanding of lay aristocracy, condemns the effeminate nature of courtly men who wear "long, over-tight shirts and tunics" [strictis camisiis . . . tunicisque].[26] William of Newburgh (ca. 1136–98), an Augustinian canon and historian, echoes Orderic's concerns about the sinfulness of fitted vestments. Remarkable for its window on the early years of Henry II's reign, which are not usually chronicled, William's *Historia rerum Anglicarum* describes clothing restrictions for male pilgrims searching for the Cross: "no man [may] have clothes that are slashed or laced" [quod nullus habeat pannos decisos vel laceatos], presumably because the laced garments cling to the body in a way that is inappropriate for such a sacred endeavor.[27] In a move that combines Orderic's ethical condemnation of tight dress with William's suggestion that laced individuals have no business engaging in religious pursuits, Bishop of Paris Maurice de Sully (ca.

1120–96) extends his sartorial diatribe to women whom he considers diabolical and lascivious for their choices in fashion:

> Celes qui leur cols et leur cheveuls descuevrent et oignent leur sorcilz et vernicent lor faces come ymage et lacent leur braz et leur costez et vont comme grue a petit pas, chiere levee que l'en les voie, cestes sont fornaises ardanz de luxure et sont mariees au deable et enfers est leur doaires, et si font meint ardoir entor euls par le jeu de luxure.

> ——

> [Those women who bare their necks and heads and grease their eyebrows and paint their faces like images, lace up their arms and bodices and walk with mincing steps like a crane, face uplifted so as to be seen, these women are burning fires of licentiousness married to the devil, with hell as their dowry. They make many around them burn through their lustful tricks.][28]

Recent scholarship has highlighted Maurice's mention of cosmetics in this passage as an example of clerical antifeminism and anxieties over secular wealth, but equally important is his denunciation of tight lacing.[29] In addition to deriding women with greased eyebrows and painted faces, Maurice implicates the fashionably fitted woman in a conventionally misogynistic paradigm of sin: her tight garments represent "burning fires of licentiousness" that make her a worthy spouse for the devil.

Such figuration of fashionable women as brides of Satan is unique to neither Maurice nor the high Middle Ages. Indeed, Maurice and other clerics perceive constraining clothing as a symbol for an unbridled body that is, or will become, uncontrollably sinful. For example, sermonist Gilles d'Orléans articulates nearly a century after Maurice the diabolical nature of a belted woman:

> En apercevant une de ces femmes, ne la prendrait-on pas pour un chevalier se rendant a la Table-Ronde? Elle est si bien équipée, de la tête aux pieds, qu'elle respire tout entière le feu du démon. Regardez ses pieds: sa chaussure est si étroite, qu'elle en est ridicule. Regardez sa taille: c'est pis encore. Elle serre ses entrailles avec une ceinture de soie, d'or,

d'argent, telle que Jésus-Christ ni sa bienheureuse mère, qui étaient pourtant de sang royal, n'en ont jamais porté.

—

[In viewing one of these women, would we not take her for a knight going to the Round Table? She is so well equipped from head to toe that she breathes entirely the fire of the devil. Look at her feet: her shoe is so narrow that she is ridiculous in it. Look at her waist: it is worse yet. She tightens her entrails with a belt of silk, gold, silver—that which neither Jesus Christ, nor his blessed mother, who were nevertheless of royal blood, ever wore].[30]

Just as Maurice notes that tight lacing signals devilish behaviors, so does Gilles emphasize that belted garments may jeopardize the spiritual well-being of those who are tightly bound. The concern over belts would continue into the fourteenth century in *Sir Gawain and the Green Knight* and in a contemporary religious treatise that similarly describes women who wear "rydelid [gathered] gownes and . . . lacis" in dialogue with the devil over their worldly pride and inclination toward fornication.[31] For these clerics, belts and laces announce depravity on par with the devil's and, when worn by women, accentuate the body's contours to such an extent that those who witness such attire will fall into sin.

"Estroit vestue": Redirecting Romance's Trope of Fitted Fashion

In responding to the clerical position that fitted attire signals an unbridled body, Marie recasts a conventional trope used in romance to moral ends. Romances contemporary with Marie's *lais* tend not to emphasize representations of tightness as sins, but rather as popular indicators of beauty, high social standing, and sexual titillation. The *romans antiques*, which include the anonymous *Roman d'Enéas*, *Roman de Thèbes*, and Benoît de Sainte-Maure's *Roman de Troie*, use extensive descriptions of fitted garments to characterize attractive female protagonists of noble descent. Written in the twelfth century, likely under the patronage of Henry II and Eleanor of Aquitaine, these adaptations of Latin texts infuse sartorial elements of courtly love into vernacular historical narratives that Marie arguably knew.[32] The *Roman d'Enéas* depicts Dido, queen of Carthage, "in a precious red garment, banded very beautifully with gold around the body until the hips as well as along the sleeves" [La raïne se fu vestue / d'une chiere porpre vermoille, / bandee d'or a grant mervoille / trestot lo cors desi as hanches / et ansement totes les manches] (lines 1466–70);[33] regal Antigone appears in a belted *bliaut* with incisions that show her naked flesh in the *Roman de Thèbes*;[34] and Benoît de Sainte-Maure describes the *bliaut* that Calchas's daughter, Briséida, wears as a garment that could enhance the beauty of any woman in the *Roman de Troie*.[35] As a representative example of attire in Continental romances, Jean Renart's early thirteenth-century *Roman de la rose ou Guillaume de Dole* adopts the trope of tight dress as an indicator of nobility when describing courtly ladies at a garden party.[36] Whether in England or in France, writers of romance consistently use a noble woman's tight dress as a metonym for wealth and beauty.

Like Marie's *lais*, medieval romances produced in France and England during the high Middle Ages extend this familiar trope: in addition to objectifying social status and physical appearance, the lens of clothing also focuses on sexuality. In covering naked flesh, Mireille Madou asserts, dress "reveals the norm of decency and modesty," and fitted attire consequently introduces the body into a "field of eroticism" by emphasizing contours: "cinching the waist, for example, attracts attention to that very place, which is not without consequences in the relation between a man and a woman."[37] Dido's garment, which she dons just before seducing Enéas in the *Roman d'Enéas*, reveals her sensual body and arouses sexual attraction, as does Antigone's laced *bliaut*, which incites Parthenopex's desire in *Roman de Thèbes*.[38]

The same is true for the courtly women in a range of other romances. As a more "realistic" romance that sidelines marvelous adventures in favor of titillating accounts of affairs between handsome knights and clever women, *Guillaume de Dole* exploits the power of women's fitted attire to seduce.[39] Jean Renart depicts aristocratic ladies who "enter the rush-strewn tents where the knights were waiting to stretch out their arms and draw them under the covers" [Erent mout bien enharneschiées / Tot chantant es tentes jonchiées / Vont as chevaliers quis atendent, / Qui les braz et les mains lor tendent; / Ses traient sor les covertors] (lines 209–13). Just as their dress excites prospective suitors, so does it spur desire in Thomas of Kent's Anglo-Norman *Roman d'Alexandre ou le roman de toute chevalerie* (ca. 1175–85), a text noteworthy for its inclusion of chivalric behavior and moral teachings. More *chanson de geste* than romance because of its insistence on militaristic activity and its inconsistent treatment of the love affair between Alexander and Queen Candace, the *Roman d'Alexandre* nevertheless presents its queen in a tightly laced tunic immediately before an intimate conversation of "amur fine" [courtly love] (line 7755), a euphemism for the lovers' consummation of desire.[40] While the aforementioned examples depict the ways in which women's clothing incites male desire, another *chanson de geste*, the continental *Prise d'Orange* (ca. 1160–65), illustrates in a parody that dress can affect the physical state of a lover: Queen Orable's *bliaut*, which is "tightened with laces over her torso" [estroit a laz par le cors] (line 686), makes her lover's "whole body tremble" [tot le cors li fremist] (line 687).[41] The fitted bodice has become a sartorial sign of a body in love.

Of the works that may have constituted Marie's audience's "horizon of expectation,"[42] the *Roman d'Enéas* stands out as particularly notable because it not only echoes the religious concern that tight dress reveals unrestrained female sexuality, but it also imagines a narrative lesson that corresponds to contemporary clerical views for those who clothe themselves in aristocratic fashions. Wearing fitted attire titillates observers and marks excessive behavior that the *Enéas*-poet penalizes. These revelations operate in conjunction with two of the major revisions made by the *Enéas*-poet to his source text, Virgil's *Aeneid:* while Virgil sympathetically depicts Dido as a tragic queen and dismisses Camille, queen of the Vulcans, as a minor character, the French text sees Dido as an amoral adulteress and features Camille as a woman warrior who finds tremendous pleasure and reward on the battlefield.[43] Dido and Camille, in constricting attire, appear as women with excessive liberty who are subsequently punished. The queen of Carthage ends her extreme and ultimately unrequited love for Enéas by her own suicide and thus suffers perpetual torment as a result of her adultery. She had promised to stay faithful to her deceased husband, Sychaeus, but her affair with Enéas betrays that pledge. Consequently, Dido remains a dishonored outcast in the afterlife, avoiding all contact with her husband.[44] Her destiny, which here is a revision of Virgil's commentary that Dido is lovingly, but sorrowfully, faithful to Sychaeus in death, corresponds to medieval clerical views on punishment for lascivious behavior associated with wearing tight dress. So, too, does the *Enéas*-poet portray Queen Camille in lavish garments, the concern for which ultimately marks her downfall. Camille's appearance—"estroit vestue" [tightly dressed] in black with a tightened belt—not only expresses what her Trojan opponent, Tarquin, understands as unbridled sexuality, but it also prompts him to offer her money for pleasure.[45] Camille defends her honor by killing Tarquin in combat, yet the poet resists figuring Camille as completely virtuous. She becomes distracted on the field when first perceiving and then coveting a fallen knight's magnificent battle gear. She is therefore unprepared to defend herself against the enemy's attack and, as a result, is killed. In thus depicting both Camille's and Dido's ruin, the *Enéas*-poet envisions drastic ends for the aristocratic woman who clothes herself in fitted finery.

Women's Dress in the *Lais* of Marie de France

Like the *Enéas*-poet and other writers of romance who first emphasize clothing as a sign of social status, Marie's *lais* imagine fitted attire as part of a larger sartorial hermeneutic that features luxurious, aristocratic dress more generally as evidence of beauty, noble lineage, and chivalric prowess.[46] Most often, Marie uses dress to suggest nobility: the embroidered silk robe in *Fresne* (lines 208–10) and the fur-trimmed coverlet of *Milun* (lines 103–4) both convey an infant's aristocratic lineage. However, other, equally compelling representations persist as signs to be interpreted throughout the collection. *Eliduc* expands an understanding of noble costume to include beauty, when the protagonist falls in love with the king's daughter, who is "Vestue fu d'un drap de seie / Menuëment a or brosdé, / E un curt mantel afublé" [dressed in a silk gown, finely embroidered with gold, and wrapped in a short cloak] (lines 796–98). In other *lais,* members of the nobility rely on garments to indicate social standing: *Yonec* features a family "richement s'aparaillast" [all richly attired] (line 476) when going to a festival, just as the son of a count takes with him "riches dras" [rich clothes] (line 133) when he leaves for Salerno in *Les Deus Amanz.* While these instances reinforce the notion that self-presentation is important to nobility in romance, other examples include commentary on chivalric manners and customs. Clothing serves as a method of civilizing in *Bisclavret,* a *lai* in which the eponymous hero changes from a werewolf to a nobleman by dressing himself (lines 72–75). Alternatively, garments emphasize valor when knights are richly attired either on their deathbed—the case in *Chaitivel* (lines 167–68)—or upon leaving home in search of fame in tournaments or war—as happens in *Eliduc* (line 76).

Marie deploys fitted garments, in particular, as an expression of aristocratic splendor that arouses observers in *Lanval* and *Guigemar,* the only two *lais* that feature body-hugging clothing. She confirms the popular clerical view, articulated above by Maurice de Sully, that tightly clad women stimulate perilous desires in men. Ultimately, however, Marie redirects such an idea through a sartorial strategy that depicts women in tight dress as figures of virtue. To be sure, the fitted *bliaut* accentuates feminine beauty in *Lanval:* the *pucèle's* maidens, "Vestues furent richement, / Laciees mut estreitement / En deus bliauz de purpre bis" [were richly dressed, tightly laced, in tunics of dark purple] (lines 57–59), pique Lanval's curiosity and prompt him to seek his future benefactress, who in turn exemplifies how an image of a tightly laced woman can shift common clerical expectations. It is not surprising that Lanval's lover, who wears a form-fitting shift "Que tuit li costé li pareient, / Ki de deus parz lacié esteient" [that revealed both her sides since the lacing was along the side] (lines 561–62), titillates those at Arthur's court: the judges who saw her "A grant merveille le teneient" [marvelled at the sight] (line 582) and were subsequently "eschaufast" [warmed with joy] (line 584). The novelty of Marie's strategy appears in *Lanval* when tight dress subsequently communi-

cates an ethical code lacking in Arthur's court: Lanval's lover, in revealing and erotic clothing, emerges as a testifying figure who clearly
speaks truth and supports virtue. Her appearance prompts Arthur's
attendants to acquit Lanval of his crime so as to please the well-
dressed lady.

   Guigemar presents a more complex engagement with Marie's
sartorial strategy that has largely gone unnoticed by scholars, despite
the recent critical emphasis on costume as a crucial point of entry to
literary representations of medieval court culture.[47] Those who address Guigemar's knotted shirt and his lady's belt tend not to read
them in light of the twelfth-century fashion that drew garments close
to the body with laces, belts, and knots,[48] while other critics comment
on Marie's use of dress as a visual expression of female identity in
lais other than *Guigemar*.[49] These latter interpretations demonstrate a
specific engagement with dress as it pertains to aristocratic women's
subjectivity, but they nonetheless overlook Marie's use of costume in
relation to the historic onset of tight lacing and knotted attire. *Guigemar* features contemporary fashion in conventional tropes that describe
aristocratic men and women, while offering a revision to the ways in
which belts and knots have previously been understood as either common folklore motifs or familiar Christian religious symbols—two
considerations that have prevented modern readers from understanding more local and cultural significances of belts and knots for a
twelfth-century medieval audience.

   In terms of women's dress, *Guigemar* depicts the paradox that belts
and laces can serve as important signifiers of excessive, passionate love
that is nevertheless honorable and restrained. For men, the *lai*'s sartorial strategy reveals that male desire demands control. Like the judges
who preside over Lanval's trial, *Guigemar*'s Lord Meriaduc behaves as if
he were warmed with joy when he observes Guigemar's lady, whose
laced *bliaut* accentuates her figure. After she faints, Meriaduc proceeds
to cut the laces of her dress, finds the belt that Guigemar gave to her,
and tries to unfasten it because "Kar de bon quor la peot amer" [he
wanted to love her with all his heart] (line 720). His behavior may be
perceived as an example of precisely what clerics fear—tightly bound

women prompt men to succumb to uncontrollable sexual desire—and thus warrants correction. Where *Lanval* depicts women in fitted attire stimulating men, *Guigemar* shows that women's apparel prompts potential suitors to take drastic measures in order to satisfy their illicit desire.

While Guigemar's lady's laced *bliaut* first arouses Meriaduc's passion, her belt underscores not lascivious sexuality, as might be construed if in fact the belt were a kind of chastity device, but rather fidelity to her beloved:[50]

> Il veit sovent a li parler,
> Kar de bon quor la peot amer;
> Il la requiert, el n'en ad cure,
> Ainz li mustre de la ceinture:
> Jamés humme nen amera
> Si celui nun ki l'uverra
> Sanz depescier.
> (lines 719–25)

> ——

> [Meriaduc often came to speak with her, since he wanted to love her with all his heart. He pleaded for her love; she paid no attention to him, instead she showed her belt: she would never love any man except the one who could open the belt.]

Unlike the belt that churchman Gilles d'Orléans recognizes above as a sign of decadence, this one serves as a materialization of the virtuous love that thwarts Meriaduc's desire. Meriaduc finds no success in wooing Guigemar's lady with language of *fin amour*; despite his efforts to "speak" to her because he "loved her"; "she paid no attention" to him because of her "belt," a point reinforced by the couplet, "cure" and "ceinture." By positioning the belt as an impenetrable accessory that frustrates Meriaduc's advances, Marie demonstrates the lady's loyalty and continence for the man who can "open" it in addition to emphasizing that male desire is in need of restraint.

Refiguring Ovid's Acts of Love

Marie views tight attire not so much as an indicator of excessive sexual behavior, as churchmen do, but as a sign of restraint that can be used as an example for arts of courtly love. Meriaduc's failure at opening the lady's belt, despite his initial success in cutting the laces of the *bliaut*, can be considered as an object lesson in Ovidian arts of love.[51] According to Tracy Adams, Ovid's position on desire features a tormented lover who must "learn to love wisely and safely" by "enact[ing] his love artfully according to the wishes of the lady." Adams further observes that "during the course of the *lai*, Marie illustrates this process of refinement from the abrupt onset of love up to the moment it is definitively mastered."[52] To map the lover's development, Marie includes dress and its accessories as part of the refinement process, presenting fitted garments as the artifice—the Ovidian *ars*—that aids the lover in first controlling love and then in learning the finer points of erotic play. In the case of Meriaduc, Marie stipulates that the belt must be "despleiat" [untied] (line 810), which is quite a different skill from Meriaduc's attempt to "trenche" [cut] (line 738) or "ovrir" [to open] (line 739) the lady's *bliaut*. This small detail is analogous to learning how to love. One cannot love recklessly; one must be educated. One cannot cut the belt; one must know how to untie it. The belt defeats Meriaduc because it highlights his ignorance when it comes to arts of courtly love.

Guigemar thus addresses how one can love ardently, yet appropriately; how one can engage with courtly motifs of secret, erotic passion, yet demonstrate control in devotion. Marie creates a poetics of restraint in order to extend the Ovidian convention of love's vise-like hold on the body to include pedagogical signs of fidelity that are ultimately registered in tight dress. In order to assuage physical pain, Ovid teaches men how to "control ruinous passions" and free themselves from the restraints of love by rejecting it altogether.[53] In a prelude to persuade the lover to abandon the pains caused by love, the *Remedia amoris* repeatedly draws attention to metaphors of burdening—whether by yoke [laesuro] (line 90) or chains [vinclis] (line 213)—and to the reprieve upon freeing oneself from love's excruciating hold on the body. Ovid highlights the lover's pleasure in escaping these metaphorical chains: "he best wins the freedom for himself who has burst the bonds that hurt his breast, and once for all o'ercome the smart" [optimus ille sui vindex, laedentia pectus / vincula qui rupit, dedoluitque semel] (lines 293–94). Ovid's lover, bridled with emotional discomfort, learns first to loathe what he initially desired and then to seek liberation from his bonds. In this case, the Classical poet espouses language of restraint, which invites infidelity in love.

Marie, too, expresses lovesickness in a similar way, but she understands the by-products of restraint differently. Instead of rejecting feelings of self-discipline and doing away with love, Guigemar and his lady adopt the constraints of tight dress as signs of their mutual commitment. Like Ovid, Marie draws upon language that describes the psychological pains of love that act upon the body in visible ways: Guigemar's countenance betrays internal suffering when his lovesickness registers externally as "la dolur / dunt il ot pale la colur" [pain that drained color from his face] (lines 423–24). So, too, does his courtly lady suffer: "ele senteit / . . . cum Amur la destreineit" [she was feeling . . . how love constricted her] (lines 419–20), a point first made clear by the couplet, "senteit" [felt] and "destreineit" [constricted], and then reiterated when Marie explains that the lady "Veillé aveit, de ceo se pleint; / Ceo fet Amur, ki la destreint" [had been awake all night; that was her complaint. It was the fault of love, pressing her hard] (lines 429–30). The lady's anguished demeanor— "Amur la destreineit" [love oppressed the lady] (line 420) —reveals her passion for Guigemar as a constrictive force, which encourages the commonplace reading that links interior love wounds to physical oppression.

Marie adopts and adapts Ovid's binding metaphors to her own purposes, thereby modifying convention in order to propose that lovers should incorporate control into courtship. She asserts a relationship between teaching and tightness in a scene that depicts Guigemar's lady held prisoner by her husband. In an attempt to thwart sinful desires, the lady's husband has locked her in a room with painted murals that encourage virtuous love.[54] While this much-quoted passage does not consider tight dress specifically, it does illustrate Marie's interest in expressing the positive effects of tightness in a way that contrasts with Ovid's use of images that restrain, constrain, or burden the body:

> La chaumbre ert peinte tut entur;
> Venus, la deuesse d'amur,
> Fu tres bien mise en la peinture;
> Les traiz mustrout e la nature
> Cument hom deit amur tenir
> E lealment e bien servir.
> Le livre Ovide, ou il enseine
> Comment chascuns s'amur estreine,
> En un fu ardant le gettout,
> E tuz iceus escumengout
> Ki jamais cel livre lirreient
> Ne sun enseignement fereient.
>   (lines 233–44)

———

[The room was painted with images all around; Venus the goddess of love was skillfully depicted in the painting, her nature and her traits were illustrated, whereby a man might learn how to behave in love, and to serve love loyally. Ovid's book, the one in which he instructs lovers how to control their love, was being thrown by Venus into a fire, and she was excommunicating all those who ever perused this book or followed its teachings.]

Critics are largely in agreement that Venus burns the *Remedia amoris*,[55] the text that promotes love as a restraining force that encumbers the lover. Marie suggests that erotic love can exist for a couple if the individuals remain *estreitement bendé* [tightly bound] (line 373) in dress, unlike Ovid, who wishes to manage love by eradicating it entirely. The burning of the book is not to be read as casting off restraint but as an affirmation of love, which need not be suppressed as Ovid would do, but rather restrained, directed, or constrained so as to manifest itself virtuously. Marie affirms her kind of love, which is controlled and restricted but still erotic, in the rhyming couplet above of "tenir" and "servir," which describes Venus teaching a man how he should "hold" love and "serve" it well and loyally (lines 237–38). Her immediate turn to Ovid's book, in which he teaches how lovers should control their love (lines 239–40), which illustrates a lesson seemingly consonant with her own, ultimately results in her rejection of the text because Ovid promotes freeing the body from restraints in love, not succumbing to them. In place of promoting painful bonds that convince lovers to abandon love altogether, Marie develops a relationship between education and restraint through the line-ending rhymes "enseine" [teach] and "estreine" [tighten] above. She advocates restraint that leads to virtuous ardor in place of the Ovidian notion of restraint that results in love's demise. Consequently, having found Ovid's position on "teaching" and "tightness" unacceptable—Venus, after all, throws Ovid's text into the flames—Marie proposes an alternative one in the belt and knot that the lovers eventually exchange. Her didactic strategy transforms common ideas of restriction and accessibility into an original expansion of convention: a woman's faithful and erotic love can be read in the garments she wears.

Marie's deployment of dress thus responds to dominant clerical positions in the twelfth century, which tend to condemn women's fitted attire and the passions it evokes. Furthermore, religious discourse on fashion rarely acknowledges a woman's ability to love virtuously. Ovid's *Remedia amoris* both affirms this stance by stating that women's faithful love is impossible and by declaring erotic love to be a constraining burden on men. Marie, however, takes issue with these two positions, particularly in *Guigemar*, and transforms the idea of a woman's virtuous, erotic love into a new *art d'aimer* based on a poetics of restraint. By literalizing love motifs made popular by Ovid through representations of dress, Marie responds rhetorically to clerical anxieties about fitted attire and unrestrained sexual behavior. Her novel understanding of fitted costume as an *art d'aimer* contributes to a larger pedagogical project of educating clergy and nobility in the finer points of courtly love, one of which includes the merits of contemporary fashion.

Just as Marie incorporates women's tight dress into the *lai*'s pedagogical project, so does she deploy a similar tactic in terms of men's. Tightness teaches Guigemar a particular skill of courtly love that draws upon the Ovidian notion that "arte regendus amor" [love must be guided by skill] (*Ars amatoria*, line 4).[56] Marie's *art d'aimer* specifies that one can wear tight clothing and behave virtuously, a point that clerics might consider a paradox. Such an *art* resembles what courtier Andreas Capellanus describes in his late twelfth-century treatise, *De amore:* the courtly lover will shine with *virtu*, a virility that encompasses moral behavior, military prowess, and the arts of making love.[57] Guigemar should present himself as a strong, courageous knight who demonstrates sound ethical values through his faithful love for one woman. Yet Marie separates such components of courtly love for her protagonist. Although the valiant Guigemar emerges victorious in battles in Flanders and France, he is inept when it comes to techniques of lovemaking because "De tant i out mespris Nature / Ke unc de nule amur n'out cure" [in forming him Nature had so badly erred that he never gave any thought to love] (lines 57–58). In order to educate Guigemar in the finer points—specifically, to rectify Nature's error and to encourage Guigemar to "think of love"—Marie extends the relationship between "teaching" and "tightness," which she first articulates with respect to Ovid, to include dress and its accessories.

Whereas Ovid (in *Remedia amoris*) and select clerics encourage either abandoning love for its constrictive hold or identifying tight dress as a sign of illicit pleasures (in Maurice de Sully), Marie adopts the knotted shirt for her courtly protagonist as a visible manifestation of virtuous, albeit sometimes painful, love. *Guigemar* therefore presents its sophisticated lesson in male socialization by having fitted garments precipitate Guigemar's tutelage in virtuous arts of love. His re-education begins after he fatally wounds a marvelous hind, takes an arrow in his own leg, and is cursed by the dying animal: unless Guigemar finds a woman who will love him as much as he loves her, his leg will not heal.[58] The knight responds by making a tourniquet with his shirt—"De sa chemise estreitement / Sa plaie bende fermement" [with his shirt he bound his wound tightly] (lines 139–40)—so that he then can mount his horse, board a magical ship, and find a lover.

Upon meeting the lady who has been locked away by her jealous husband, Guigemar's physical injury is transformed into a psychological love-wound, which Marie attends to through motifs of aristocratic clothing. In so doing, Marie departs from stock conventional tropes in romance by suggesting fitted attire as a remedy for lovesickness. Only through a mutual expression of love and a subsequent exchange of tightened garments do Guigemar and his lady find relief from love's pains.

Folklore, Ecclesiastical Textiles, and Clerical Condemnation

Marie expands the popular motifs in romance of recognition and gift-giving, which tend to indicate loyalty in either familial or erotic love, in order to show that constricting garments may contain the body in positive ways.[59] While Guigemar's initial inability to make love was first evident in the form of a "plaie" [wound] (line 140) in his thigh, his lovesickness has since transformed into a "plait" [knot] (line 559) that his beloved makes in his shirt. Noting the homonymic play between *plaie* and *plait*, Sun Hee Kim Gertz sees Guigemar's wound, the knot, and the belt that he gives his lady as tokens "of recognition that should remind [Guigemar] (and Marie's readers) of the wounded hind and its prophecy, of how they met, and of how they are 'bound' to one another in love."[60] The knotted garment and belt thus appear in the generically conventional practice of gift-giving as a means to affirm identity.

In addition to engaging the strategy of knotting as a recognition motif, Marie exploits the popular medieval belief that associates belts and knots with the supernatural so as to propose a novel understanding of sartorial ties.[61] The tradition of knots in folklore and magic from which Marie draws is at least as old as Virgil's *Eclogues* and is evident in later medieval texts, such as Albert the Great's thirteenth-century *De animalibus* (ca. 1250) and the *Pearl*-poet's fourteenth-century *Sir Gawain and the Green Knight*.[62] Just as Virgil and Albert write of a magical knot that can promote either success or impotence in love, so does Marie's *Guigemar* demonstrate that those who exchange knots and belts remain loyal and continent.[63] *Sir Gawain and the Green Knight* features "knots" in the form of a pentangle and a girdle—the former called an "endeles knot" (line 630) and the latter "loken vnder [Gawain's] lyfte arme . . . with a knot" (line 2487)—as restraints for both the soul and body that affect Gawain's martial and spiritual behaviors, as the third chapter in this study argues.[64] The pentangle decorates the exterior of Gawain's shield as a reminder of the knight's Christian attributes, while the knotted belt, according to Bertilak's lady, has magical properties that will save him from harm. So, too, do Guigemar's knots (the tourniquet and his shirt) impact his chivalric exploits. The former allows the knight to staunch his hunting wound so he can eventually meet the woman who will capture his heart, while the latter protects him from the enthusiastic Breton ladies who seek to undo his shirttail in order to seduce him.

Although the later-medieval examples of *De animalibus* and *Sir Gawain and the Green Knight* rely on the supernatural elements of knots in order to ensure continence, the instances in *Guigemar* do not. As Helen Cooper argues, romances characteristically lean on magic, but magical powers often do not determine events in the narrative. Rather, the protagonists' own initiatives or emotions do.[65] Such is the case in *Guigemar.* As if to exemplify Cooper's argument, Marie offers an interesting revision to the conventional use of supernatural knots in romance by employing magic "non-magically," so that her hero "bring[s] out something in himself."[66] Guigemar's and his lady's knots demonstrate their mastery of self-control. Their discipline is morally sound, despite their appearance as tightly clad individuals who, according to the clerics, would probably behave sinfully. In this *lai*, knotted attire therefore acts as a metonym for fidelity, not as a magical talisman that either ensures or wards off love. That Guigemar's tied shirt serves as a materialization of his everlasting presence when he can no longer be by his lover's side might be understood as Marie's sartorial rendition of lovers who are tied together in devotion. In this way, Marie anticipates what Andreas Capellanus's courtier proposes to his beloved in *De amore:* "I may seem to depart from you in body, but in my heart I shall always be bound to you" [et ego, quamvis corpore videar discedere, corde tamen vobis colligatus exsisto].[67] Guigemar may leave his lady after their affair is discovered, but their knots emphasize a faithful connection, much like the one experienced by Andreas's lover when he ties himself figuratively to his beloved—a tie that endures through mutual agreement rather than through magic.

By associating the manipulation of garments with virtuous behavior, Marie once again engages with the clerical understanding of dress that presents expensive clothing as a measure of moral conduct in the political histories and penitential guides that emerge on the literary scene toward the end of the twelfth century. Clerics would recognize the handling or knotting of fabric in one of two apparently incompatible ways: either as a metaphor to illustrate chaste behavior, or as a sign of diabolical sexual excess in accordance with dominant views of garments tightened by laces and belts. For the former, William of Malmesbury describes "elegance in countenance and in raiment" when "courtesy" of language accords with "brilliance" of apparel, and John of Salisbury recognizes that one wears a belt when performing "merit of virtues excelling others."[68] Henry II's clerk, Gerald of Wales (ca. 1145–1223), in the most striking literary context with respect to *Guigemar*, features language of restraint in conjunction with descriptions of textiles and physical desire. As both a critic and beneficiary of the Angevin court, Gerald was a prolific writer of poetry, letters, polemics, and moral treatises. Indeed, morality appears as a driving force in his *Gemma Ecclesiastica*, a favorite guide of Pope Innocent III on the sacraments that instructs its readers in virtuous living, which includes a rhetoric of restraint associated with cloth.[69] Gerald describes cotton textiles, which he sees as analogous to carnal and mental desires that must be drawn back tightly: "Bissus retorquetur in cortinis tabernaculi, quia lumbi carnis et mentis restringendi sunt, ut lascivis caro motibus et cor refrænetur cogitationibus" [cotton is pulled and twisted into curtains for the tabernacle because the loins of our body and mind have to be pulled back tight in order that the flesh may restrain its wanton desire and the heart its lustful thoughts].[70] The differences between the *Gemma* and Marie's *lais* are many: cases have been made for the *Gemma*'s audience as either religious or scholarly, not necessarily courtly as Marie's is thought to be; the textile described is not a garment for the body, but for the church;

and these curtains for the tabernacle are not knotted but rather pulled and twisted.[71] Despite the obvious discrepancies, the analogy between the appearance of textiles and corporeal sensuality still resonates with the sartorial strategy that Marie proposes, and the sense of pulling and tightening associated with the verb "restringere" furthermore echoes practices of knotting and tying in *Guigemar*. In this way, Marie's stance resembles Gerald's, whose record of his impressions of Henry II's reign relates textiles to sought-after moral behavior and whose *Gemma* foreshadows some of Innocent's concerns in the Fourth Lateran Council.[72]

Just as fitted attire prompted competing understandings of the people who wore such garments, so do knots encourage bifurcated readings. In contrast to Gerald of Wales's positive analysis of tightly pulled textiles, English author John of Salisbury notes that knots in men's fashion betray a foolish attention to dress "that verges upon indecency" in his *Policraticus* (ca. 1159).[73] Written in the early years of Henry II's reign, the *Policraticus* critiques immorality at court by situating knots as signifying an individual's prideful investment in self-presentation, the very sartorial behavior that an anonymous sermon condemns: "se devraient chatier cil et celes qui ainment les orguilleuses vesteures, les miparties, les entaillies, les haligotées, les grans trains" [Those men and women who like prideful costume—two-tone gowns, robes with frontal slits and shoulder knots and long trains—should castigate themselves].[74] These literary renditions, which depict knots as sinful, are complemented by manuscript illuminations that figure fitted attire as diabolical. The Winchester Psalter, likely commissioned sometime between 1145 and the 1160s by the cathedral's bishop, Henry of Blois, caricatures the devil dressed in an amalgamation of what Margaret Scott sees as "the most extreme elements of male and female fashion of the period": a tightly laced gown with knotted sleeves (likely derived from women's dress) and a knotted side-split overskirt (coming from men's attire) (see fig. 1, lower left).[75] While churchmen would understand knotted clothing as signs of pride and lascivious excess, Marie instead aligns her use of knots with a positive penitential tradition that accords more closely with Gerald's notion of pulling textiles together as a sign of continence.

Figure 1 "Temptations of Christ," Winchester Psalter, ca. 1145–55. London, British Library, MS Cotton Nero C. IV f. 18. © The British Library Board.

In *Guigemar*, Marie transforms the image of tied garments from signs of indecency and overindulgence to indicators of masculine fidelity and controlled eroticism when Guigemar's lady knots his shirt. During the time that the lovers spend apart, Guigemar's knotted shirt gestures toward erotic restraint. However, in their reunion, Marie reveals that Guigemar no longer wears his knotted shirt, unlike his lover who remains belted. Critics have understood this peculiar incongruity in the lovers' pledge of fidelity as Marie's way of emphasizing Guigemar's imperviousness to love's temptations. Suzanne Klerks, for instance, reads Guigemar's refusal to wear the shirt as a thematic device that highlights his invulnerability to the women who come to court in an effort to unknot his shirt.[76] Unlike Guigemar's lady's body, which Meriaduc exposes and threatens to violate as he attempts to open her belt, Guigemar's remains safely out of reach while courtly ladies try to untie his shirttail. Thomas Reed offers a slightly different reading that builds upon clerical antifeminist sentiment when he argues for "a double standard in a relatively ideal relationship." Guigemar does not wear his shirt because he does not have to. After all, "women are more physically vulnerable in matters of physical love than men."[77] Both critics understand that Guigemar's body cannot be contained by his knotted shirt—even though his lover's stays belted—because men's physical integrity is not compromised so easily as women's.

Reading the knot and the belt alongside clerical commentaries describing the effects of tight dress on martial behaviors, however, suggests another explanation. Clerics would understand men wearing fashionable knotted garments as more interested in sartorial luxuries than in military discipline. We know that Orderic Vitalis laments the "undisciplined" nature of men who "loved to deck themselves in long, over-tight shirts and tunics" [summopere comebant, prolixisque nimiumque strictis camisiis indui tunicisque gaudebant].[78] Moreover, the writer of the *Itinerarium peregrinorum et gesta Regis Ricardi* complains that in the year 1192, French crusaders "had left the military life and indulged in the amatory life" [relictis castris militaribus, jam amatoriis indulgebant], a change reflected by their fitted garments:

Their luxurious dress was further evidence of the effeminate life they were leading: the seams of their sleeves were held closed with intricate lacing; their wanton flanks were bound by intricate belts; and to reveal the fitting of their pleated garment more clearly to onlookers, they wore their cloaks back-to-front, twisted round to the front of their body and compressed between their arms.

——

[. . . luxus quoque vestium otium loquebatur effœminatorum: manicarum nimirum hiatus multiplici laqueo claudebantur; operosis constricta cingulis latera lasciviunt, et ut rugosæ vestis conclusio manifestius intuentibus pateret, chlamydes in anteriora contortas ordine præpostero comprimebant inter brachia.]⁷⁹

Here, laced sleeves and belted flanks do not indicate restrained passion, as they do in *Guigemar.* Instead, the clothing that exposes the contours of the male body denotes decadent and hypersexual behavior: these same tightly clad men "passed sleepless nights in drinking parties, and then, inflamed by wine with desire for girls, they used to frequent the brothels" [noctes in compotationibus deducuntur insomnes, iamque mero æstuantes puellarum solebant frequentare prostibula]. Furthermore, if other men had been "admitted on the same business" and the crusaders found themselves locked out, they would "tear down the doors."⁸⁰ So, too, does John of Salisbury worry that knights find themselves corrupted by extravagance in dress. He asserts that "military discipline is necessary" for those who wrongly conceive of "military glory . . . in so squeezing and twisting their linen or silken garments as to make them cleave as close to the body as a second skin. [Such knights are] more proficient in the arts of pleasure than notable for valor."⁸¹ He concludes that "there is nought which less befits a soldier than too delicate attire and the exquisiteness of too luxurious clothing, unless perchance, spurning Mars, he has like Traso dedicated his service to Venus for the capture of the stronghold of [the famous Greek courtesan] Thaïs" [Nichil est quod minus deceat militem quam cultus mollior, et deliciae uestium exquisitae, nisi forte cum Trasone ad munitionem Taidis expugnandam Veneri deuouerit militiam suam Marte contempo].⁸² Ever mindful that outward appearance expresses inward desires, John suggests that those knights preoccupied with fitted attire fight with an eye toward decadent rewards rather than toward the defense of the realm of England.

Marie's Redirection of Religious Positions in *Guigemar*

Guigemar acknowledges that "twisted" garments that "cleave close to the body" may affect a knight's performance in war. As if to respond to John of Salisbury's position that "luxury always conquers," the courtly hero keeps the shirt in his possession, but not on his body. By refusing to don his knotted shirt, Guigemar conveys disciplined passion, which appears secondary to his desire to do his duty. He sidelines a popular fashion in favor of developing his martial strength. In so doing, Guigemar demonstrates what clerics deem appropriate behavior—he jettisons knotted clothing, registers the "discipline" for which John advocates, and remains valorous in matters of both love and war.[83] As a lover, he stays devoted to his lady; and, as a knight, he succeeds so well that he acquires a retinue of over one hundred knights, who accompany him to Meriaduc's home when he is called to unbuckle his lover's belt (lines 753–54). When his lady unknots the shirt, Guigemar's education in moral behavior, military prowess, and courtly love all come together. No longer "tied" in love, Guigemar converts the energy that restrains love into that which fights for it. He besieges Meriaduc's castle, kills the lord, and frees his lady (lines 879–80). Neither his *virtu*—the ability to show his military prowess while attending to the arts of courtly love—nor his "knightly discipline"— which John of Salisbury or another contemporary, William of Malmesbury, might have found "relaxed"—is questioned.[84] Rather, Guigemar's experience demonstrates that "use of arms" and pursuing "pleasures of women," two endeavors that Geoffrey of Monmouth finds incompatible in his *History of the Kings of Britain*, are not mutually exclusive after all.[85]

By keeping Guigemar's lady "tightly bound" and therefore maintaining one element of sartorial control between the lovers, Marie suggests that, even in their reunion, fitted garments convey restrained, yet productive passion. This productivity can be considered in the same clerical register that addresses clothing and martial behaviors. Whereas John of Salisbury, in particular, tends to highlight excessively tight dress as compromising men's militarism and morality, he positions belts in an opposite way. As the means by which knights hold swords close to their bodies, so indeed do belts express "merit of virtues excelling others" [eos prae ceteris uirtutum merita insignirent] because the soldier "shall always be girded up for the service of the commonwealth" [Et recte cingulo decoratur ad militiam quisquis accedit, quia eum expeditum esse ad munia rei publicae officii sui necessitas exigit]. "The belt," as John construes it, "is therefore a symbol of labor, and the labor deserves honor" [Cingulum ergo indicium est laboris, labor honoris meritum].[86] Marie understands similar virtue in belting Guigemar's lady. Of course, Guigemar's lover neither wears the belt on top of her clothing, nor does she possess a sword. But Marie is not beyond figuring steadfast women with swords: *Yonec* demonstrates one such heroine, who carries her lover's sword after his death. Yonec's lady finds "comfort" [cunforte] (line 442) in her knight's sword, which she will give to their unborn son when he comes of age so that he can avenge his parents. In *Guigemar*, Marie girds Guigemar's lady for the benefit of the heart. In this way, the lady emblematizes the type of woman who fights for and enables love throughout the collection—from Fresne, who remains faithful to Gurun despite his brief marriage to her twin (*Fresne*, lines 349–54), to the heroine in *Les Deus Amanz*, who instructs her lover in how he might overcome the arduous challenge proposed by her father for any man who wishes to marry his daughter (lines 93–126).

Reading Guigemar's lady as a woman who assumes an active role in promoting love, like other female protagonists in Marie's *lais*, suggests in turn a reconsideration of Guigemar's girded lady as reflecting the predominant medieval conception that women's behavior needed to be controlled by men. Although Marie repeatedly figures Guigemar's lover in areas or garments that enclose—her jealous husband imprisons her in a tower, Meriaduc keeps her in custody at his castle, Guigemar belts her—she endows Guigemar's lady with important responsibilities epitomized by the belt. Guigemar's lady appears as a faithful servant to both love and her lord when she liberates Guigemar from his knotted shirt and consequently prompts his re-education in popular aristocratic notions of courtly love.

Preempting the *Roman de la rose*

Marie's strategy of figuring women's competency in service, chivalry, and faithful love, as evident in the laced *bliaut* or belt, appears as an important precursor to the sartorial strategy of Guillaume de Lorris, who would highlight men's fitted attire, rather than women's, as a requisite for pursuits of love in his *Roman de la rose*. In his commentary on the role of elegance in attire, Guillaume's personification of Love instructs:

> Moine toi bel, selonc ta rente
> Et de robe et de chaucemente.
> Bel robe et bel garnement
> Amandent home durement,
> Et si doiz ta robe baillier
> A tel qui la sache taillier,
> Qui face bien seanz les pointes
> Et les manches vestanz et cointes.
> . . . .
> De ganz, d'aumoniere de soie
> Et de ceinture te cointoie,
> Et se tu n'ies de la richece,
> Que faire nel puisses, si t'estrece,
> Mes au plus te doiz deduire
> Que tu porras sanz toi destruire.
>   (lines 2139–46, 2153–58)

———

[Outfit yourself beautifully, according to your income, in both dress and footwear. Beautiful garments and adornments improve a man a great deal. Therefore you should give your clothes to someone who knows how to do good tailoring, who will set the seams well and make the sleeves fit properly. . . . Deck yourself out with gloves, a belt, and a silk purse; if you are not rich enough to do so, then restrain yourself. You should, however, maintain yourself as beautifully as you can without ruining yourself.][87]

"Beautiful garments and adornments improve a man a great deal": Marie, too, in the preceding century, arrives at the same conclusion for her courtly lovers. Both women and men benefit from their fitted attire in that they learn to love virtuously and passionately. So, too, does Love's lesson in the *Rose* address the potential for vice in clothing, thereby openly confronting clerical anxieties, while Marie engages indirectly with religious histories and sermons that deride physical adornments as invitations to sin. As if to acknowledge the clerical concern advanced by Maurice de Sully that attention to cosmetics may encourage sin, Love notes that the courtier should not "rouge or paint [his] face, for such a custom belongs only to ladies or to men of bad repute" [Mes ne te farde ne ne guingne: / Ce n'apartient s'au dames non / Ou a ceaus de malves renon] (lines 2168–70). Instead, Love permits the courtier to "sew [his] sleeves and comb [his] hair" [Queus tes manches et ton chief pigne] (line 2167). Guillaume thus presents the elegance of tight dress not as an indicator of sin— "Cointerie n'est pas orguiaus" [Elegance is not pride] (line 2135)— but as an enabler of serving a woman, for "he who is tainted with pride cannot bend his heart to serve nor to make an entreaty" [Et qui d'orgueil est entechiez / Il ne puet son cuer emploier / A servir ne a souploier] (lines 2126–28). In so doing, the *Roman de la Rose* suggests that laced and belted dress is fundamental for men who serve love.

Marie de France, in preempting this position, situates those garments on her female protagonist so as to advocate women's important role in the services of love. She gives a literary example of what Stephen Jaeger describes as the rise of women as teachers of moral discipline in the realm of courtly love,[88] and does so through representations of luxury garments. Fitted attire, whether worn by Guigemar's lady in Marie's twelfth-century romance or by the courtier in the thirteenth-century *Roman de la rose*, operates as a crucial component in educating courtly lovers.

Although clerical histories prominent in literary critical landscapes demonstrate the idea that tight dress evokes transgressive sexuality, *Guigemar* shows otherwise, instead aligning itself with at least one penitential guide that contributes to the proliferation of manuals attending to pastoral care in the thirteenth and fourteenth centuries. Garments and their accessories signal neither the uncontrollable sexual desires often articulated by churchmen, nor the restraining sentiments of love that Ovid expressly rejects. Rather, fitted attire broadcasts meritorious behavior. It transforms the uncouth and immodest into the disciplined, modest, humane, and elegant. By recasting tight dress as a sign of positive corporeal restriction in *Guigemar*, Marie deploys a pedagogical strategy that radically repositions the signification of twelfth-century fashion and the conventional rhetorical tropes that employ costume to convey virtuous meaning. As such, her nuanced understanding of fashion in *Guigemar* contributes twofold to a broader perception of courtly dress as a didactic tool: she anticipates meritorious depictions of fashion in subsequent romances and demonstrates that the goals of romance are not unlike those of the literature on political histories, sermons, and penance, in that these genres encourage readers to shun vice in favor of virtue. In Marie's world, becoming *estreitement bendé* means to be well versed in a new *art d'aimer* that edifies both heart and soul.

CHAPTER TWO

Heldris de Cornuälle

Telegraphing Morality through Transvestism

Trangression is not immoral.

—Jean Beaudrillard, *The Ecstasy of Communication*

Whereas the last chapter situated Marie de France's sartorial strategy as a response to disapproving judgments on tight attire by contemporary chroniclers and, by extension, as a contribution to religious writings on moral edification in the twelfth century, this chapter turns to the complex intersection between Heldris de Cornuälle's *Roman de Silence*, the rhetorical trope known as *effictio*, the sin of avarice, the subject of cross-dressing, and one of the thirteenth century's major social changes, which depended on an alteration not in garment styles but in religious practices promoted in the reforms advanced by the Fourth Lateran Council. In crafting a sartorial strategy that uses transvestism to address moral perfection, despite the vehement clerical condemnation of cross-dressing as sinful, Heldris de Cornuälle demonstrates, as Jean Beaudrillard would write nearly a millennium later, that transgression need not be immoral.[1]

The year is 1215. Innocent III, the most powerful and ambitious pope of the Middle Ages, calls religious officials to Rome to the

Fourth Lateran Council "to eradicate vices and plant virtues, to correct faults and reform morals, [and] to remove heresies and strengthen faith" of clergy and laity alike.[2] The directives issued from the Council had special significance for the people of England, who, from 1208 to 1213, had lived under an interdict from Innocent that suspended Christian services and the administration of some sacraments in response to King John's refusal to accept the pope's appointment of Stephen Langton as Archbishop of Canterbury. For six years the country lacked religious direction and continuous pastoral care. After Innocent lifted the interdict in 1213, the legislation enacted at Lateran IV two years later provided English bishops with a syllabus to rekindle religious sentiment among the population while drawing back into the fold the errant priests who, during their forced sabbatical, had taken wives and mistresses and moved their daily activities from church to tavern.[3] During the same period of England's interdiction, Latin grammarian and poet Geoffrey of Vinsauf dedicates his highly influential poem on rhetorical theory, *Poetria nova*, to the engineer of the Great Council, Innocent III. Citing the pope's unequalled virtue, gentle heart, and munificent gift giving, Geoffrey offers a "little book" [opus exiguum] that is "full of worth" [viribus amplum] (line 42) in its exposition of rhetorical devices that amplify narrative beauty. Among the many literary tropes that Geoffrey names is *descriptio*, which expands poetry's content to the pleasure of a reader's eyes and ears by including an *effictio*, the head-to-toe description of a person's anatomy or attire that becomes a standard convention in romance to indicate a woman's beauty and wealth or a man's social standing and military prowess. Both texts, the canons of Lateran IV and *Poetria nova*, propose methodologies to instill a sense of honor in their audience—a newfound respect for the Christian faith in the case of Innocent's canons and for the poetics that figuratively dress narrative content in appealing ways in Geoffrey of Vinsauf's rhetorical guide.[4]

I cite this pope and poet, these canons for moral teaching, and this rhetorical theory concerning attire because they weave substantial threads into a "web of interlocution" that includes sin, cross-dressing, and a thirteenth-century Northern French romance about the kingdom of England extant in one manuscript, the *Roman de Silence*.[5] In positioning *Silence* at the center of this web, I aim to show that its poet, Heldris de Cornuälle, speaks to issues of vice and virtue central to the pedagogy of Lateran IV through the use of *effictio*, a trope which, consonant with Geoffrey's rhetorical treatise, conveys notions of discipline. As if drawing from the values of kindheartedness and largess articulated in the dedication of Geoffrey's "little book" to Innocent, Heldris incorporates complaints against avarice into a narrative that pins upright moral behavior and integrity of heart to its female protagonist, a transvestite knight who finds success and valor at the king of England's court, despite her cross-dressing, a practice that contemporary clerics heartily denounce. Heldris's commitment to exploring the intersection between sin, dress, and morality in *Silence* furthermore extends to the poem's codex (Nottingham, University Library, Mi.LM.6), a series of texts that contribute to a narrative trajectory addressing morality across the manuscript.[6] Heldris's romance encapsulates a central ethical concern, often overlooked by critics, apparent in the codicological context, that contributes more broadly to ecclesiastical reforms aimed at personal reflection and clothing's ability to reveal proper behavior.

Long condemned in religious teachings as a sin against nature, transvestism, in the sense of adopting, counter to one's sex, masculine or feminine identity through dress, invites medieval and modern interpretations founded upon questions of sexuality. Consonant with such a position, critics of *Silence* understand the romance's deployment of transvestism in terms of sex and gender in myriad and often contradictory ways. These critics frequently conclude that cross-dressing somehow necessitates a consideration of a woman's sexual nature or gender identity with respect to her status at court.[7] While gender and sexual politics associated with transvestism register as crucial issues in the text, equally important and often overlooked is the connection that the poem fosters between clothing and moral virtue as it derives from thirteenth-century church reforms, which, for the first time, feature sartorial markers as signs that indicate appropriate moral conduct or human essence. To consider the transvestite in this way means to understand cross-dressing as a practice that can, as Marjorie Garber has argued, signal meaning in categories other than gender, a point to which I will return later in the chapter.[8]

Given the poet's attention to the capital sin of avarice in the prologue and his use of *effictio* on two occasions, I argue that Heldris de Cornuälle employs transvestism as a sartorial strategy to investigate moral conduct. In particular, dress and the literary devices used to demarcate it allow for an examination of upright behavior in two separate spheres: that of the cross-dresser who, according to medieval theologians, goes against nature and consequently would invite vice; and that of the kings and courtiers who interact with the cross-dresser. Heldris reinvents the transvestite as a figure whose beauty mirrors an ethically sound demeanor, evident in the first *effictio* describing Silence as a woman. In the second *effictio*, Heldris redirects the condemnation traditionally reserved for the cross-dresser to those who behave poorly in chivalric endeavors. As a result, the transvestite both conveys and prompts moral perfection.

While social and religious discourses particular to thirteenth-century church doctrine encourage individual spiritual reflection and would thus likely occasion the transvestite's self-evaluation, *Silence* refuses such a strategy. Despite the poem's insistence on localizing moral virtue at the heart and thereby encouraging personal reflection at key moments, Heldris employs the transvestite to stimulate others to assess their own ethical comportment. No longer the object of clerics' disapproval, the eponymous heroine serves as an index for the appropriate moral countenance evident in her perfection of heart.

The Frame of Avarice

Like Marie de France's *lais*, *Silence* draws upon conventions central to the mode of romance and its generic demands: it illustrates a love story, flight from court, the protagonist's return, and the text's resolution of conflict.[9] Heldris de Cornuälle begins *Silence* with a discourse on avarice, claiming that stingy folk have robbed the courts of pleasure by hoarding their wealth and refusing to support entertainments, including story-telling, tournaments, and making love. The prologue concludes with an admonition for honor and generosity. In the next 1,700 lines or so, Heldris recounts the love story of Cador, count of Cornwall, and his wife, Eufemie. It terminates with the birth of their daughter, Silence, whom Cador disguises and raises as a boy because Ebain, the king of England, has forbidden women to inherit. When Silence comes of age, the allegorical figures of Nature and Nurture (understood as the cultural forces that influence one's behavior and/or appearance) debate on two separate occasions as to which of the two will prevail in the transvestite's life. Will Silence successfully suppress her nature as a woman and continue to live as a knight in Ebain's realm, as Nurture hopes? Or will Nature convince Silence to abandon men's dress and chivalric pursuits for the domestic practices associated with women at court?

After several adventures—which include Silence's escape from her guardian, further disguise and then success as a *jongleur* in foreign lands, attempted seduction by Ebain's licentious queen, Eufeme (whose name is nearly identical to Silence's mother's), and resulting exile in France—Silence returns to England to fight on Ebain's behalf against four rebel counts. Following Silence's valiant victory, Eufeme renews her amorous designs on Silence, who rebukes her a second time. Eufeme then plots Silence's death by having Ebain send the cross-dressed knight on what seems to be an impossible mission: he commands Silence to capture Merlin and bring him to court. Should Silence fail, she would no longer be welcome in Ebain's realm. Since Eufeme is well aware that Merlin will be captured only by a woman's trick, she believes that Silence will be exiled from Ebain's court forever. To her surprise, Silence returns with Merlin, who later reveals how dress has duped the king. True to the prophecy, Merlin is captured by a woman, Silence, who has lived her entire life in man's dress out of respect for her father's wish that she be eligible to inherit his wealth. As if to respond to the frame of the poem, which names avarice as a sin that destroys honor, Ebain munificently restores to women the right to inherit. No longer bound by her filial promise to pass as a man, Silence presents herself at court to be clothed as a woman. In the end, the king executes his adulterous queen, whose male lover cross-dressed as an attendant nun. Nature removes all signs of masculinity from Silence, and Ebain takes the newly feminized Silence as his wife.

The shift from twelfth to thirteenth centuries, and from the literature of Marie de France to that of Heldris de Cornuälle, reveals a diachronic change in the representation of vice and its relation to the didactic concern of romance to address righteous behavior. Where Marie de France defends the composition of her poems as a means to guard oneself from vice in general, Heldris frames his with a concern for avarice in particular, which will reappear later in the poem in regard to Silence's transvestism. Noting in no uncertain terms his ideal audience of those who know good storytelling and who "proisent mains honor d'argent" [value honor more than money] (line 10), Heldris develops a pressing concern with avarice that engages contemporary religious reforms, political events, and literary responses to them.[10] In the romance's first 106 lines, Heldris bemoans the plight of those minstrels or *jongleurs* who have difficulty earning a living at court because "stingy people" [gent avere] (line 23) "have so robbed it of all pleasure" [vos le paravés desjué] (line 33). Promoting a position paralleled in a variety of French and Latin texts, from John of Salisbury's poem *Entheticus* (a didactic satire composed on or after 1155 for the Angevin court) to the short poems of Raoul de Houdenc (writing in the late twelfth or early thirteenth century in France), Heldris articulates the common complaint of minstrels who bemoan "avere gent, honi et las" [greedy, nasty, petty people] (line 31) "que si n'ont soing c'om puist joïr / De gueredon qu'il voellent rendre" [who do not care to make a man happy with some reward they might wish to give] (lines 12–13).[11]

These complaints, evident in the "money-satires" that proliferated after 1100 and enjoyed great popularity until 1300, have been linked to the introduction of coinage in the European economy at the turn of the millennium.[12] As Lester Little notes, since capital exchange in the form of cash was slowly replacing gift exchange in the eleventh and twelfth centuries, personal ties between lords and vassals and the aristocracy and peasantry weakened.[13] These social disturbances furthermore registered along an ethical spectrum by moralists who were convinced that the influx of coinage yielded "an emphatic focus on avarice as the source of deviant ethical behavior."[14] Like the moralists, Heldris de Cornuälle acknowledges a collapse in relations between the nobility and travelling performers that he attributes to greed: courtly folk have become so "intoxicated with avarice" [enbevré en Avarisse] (line 39) that they have given up chivalric pastimes in favor of hoarding wealth.

While *Silence* aims at stingy aristocrats who deprive the court of a minstrel's songs, it arguably targets more specifically the church and court politics of the thirteenth century that sought to promote interest in Christian piety. The canons of Lateran IV provide two points of contact with Heldris's romance: equally significant are an anxiety for avarice and a desire to restrict participation in courtly amusements. Acknowledging the clerical tendency toward reaping pecuniary benefits in ecclesiastical practices, the canons name *cupiditas* and *avaritia* in various instances that outnumber any mention of other cardinal sins. Canons 29, 49, 56, and 66, in particular, seek to curb greed in practices of multiple benefices (canon 29), excommunication (canon 49), contracts (canon 56), and simony (canon 66). A concern for upright clerical behavior can also be seen in canon 16: "clerics shall not hold secular offices or engage in secular and, above all, dishonest pursuits. They shall not attend the performances of mimics and buffoons, or theatrical representations." It seems that secular entertainment also compromises ecclesiastical dignity.[15] As part of the seventy constitutions and the Holy Land Decree written at Lateran IV under Innocent III's leadership, these particular directives aid in reforming then-prevalent abuses by controlling spiritual and temporal matters.

Heldris de Cornuälle translates Lateran IV's concern for avarice and its move to suppress clerical attendance at courtly performances to his romance by launching a critique of avaricious kings that, in turn, engages with contemporary French politics and literature. In 1261, King Louis IX of France issued an ordinance that banned *jongleurs* from the royal palace; he was likely economizing in preparation for the Eighth Crusade, in which he would die in 1270.[16] The French poet Rutebeuf, writing in the second half of the thirteenth century, takes a particularly strong stance compared to other poetic works against Louis IX's measures to protect his realm from threats from the East that purportedly menaced Christianity.[17] As Edmond Faral and Julia Bastin describe it, the king imposed a series of practices designed to evoke penitential behaviors: "prayers, processions, fasts, sanctions against blasphemy and sin, suppression of excess at meal times and in clothing, and an indefinite interruption of tournaments and gaming."[18] Yet, despite this royal asceticism that would foster piety, poets understood these new behaviors as a cover for the state's greed. For instance, Rutebeuf's *Complainte de Constantinople* (lines 102–3) decries the prohibition of minstrels caroling in banquet halls, as if they were undermining the integrity of the kingdom; and his *Renart le Bestourné* criticizes the avarice of the nobility by alluding to the 1261 ordinance in its political satire.[19] Less a political satire than Rutebeuf's aforementioned works, and concerned predominantly with the royal court in England rather than in France (although Silence finds refuge with the French king for a period of time), the *Roman de Silence* nevertheless engages similar dissatisfactions with avaricious nobility who do not remunerate clever, well-received minstrels ["Bons menestreus bien recheüs"] (line 26).

In pointing to the political context of Louis IX's ordinance while gesturing to a disposition of heart-felt kindness that may be connected to the canons of Lateran IV, the conclusion of *Silence*'s prologue concretizes the moral context of largess and virtue as desirable characteristics alongside which Heldris positions his transvestite knight. By stating that "honest poverty" [povertés honeste] (line 97) is more valuable than wealth without joy and that "it is better to be gracious and frank than to be stingy and King of France" ["Et volentés gentils et france / Qu'avers a iestre et rois de France"] (lines 99–100), Heldris emphasizes generous behavior at court that depends upon wholesomeness of heart and honest conduct. His use of the adjective, "france," which denotes not only "noble status by birth" but also the sense that the will is "free," "unburdened," or "unencumbered," suggests a liberality that Heldris will later connect to the heart of his protagonist, Silence, when he describes her as having a "cuers . . . francise" [noble . . . heart] (line 3197) while she lives and works as a cross-dressed minstrel alongside villainous colleagues who plot her demise.[20]

This move to the heart illustrates Heldris de Cornuälle's commitment to exploring the kind of personal introspection with respect to honorable behavior promoted in Lateran IV's church reforms.

Canon 21, also known as *omnis utriusque sexus*, offers the most explicit invitation for Christians to examine their consciences in its stipulation for the annual auricular confession of sins:

> All the faithful of either sex, after they have reached the age of discernment, should individually confess all their sins in a faithful manner to their own priest at least once a year, and let them take care to do what they can to perform the penance imposed on them. Let them reverently receive the sacrament of the Eucharist at least at Easter unless they think, for a good reason and on the advice of their own priest, that they should abstain from receiving it for a time. Otherwise they shall be barred from entering a church during their lifetime and they shall be denied a Christian burial at death.
>
> ——
>
> [Omnis utriusque sexus fidelis, postquam ad annos discretionis pervenerit, omnia sua solus peccata confiteatur fideliter, saltem semel in anno proprio sacerdoti, et iniunctam sibi poenitentiam studeat pro viribus adimplere, suscipiens reverenter ad minus in pascha eucharistiae sacramentum, nisi forte de consilio proprii sacerdotis ob aliquam rationabilem causam ad tempus ab eius perceptione duxerit abstinendum; alioquin et vivens ab ingressu ecclesiae arceatur et moriens christiana careat sepultura.][21]

Often seen as an important point in the history of penance, *omnis utriusque sexus* places an increased demand on the individual to question and evaluate his or her conscience because it invites individuals to confess alone [*solus*]. About to become obsolete were the days when the church asked parishioners to confess either together a common list of sins that may or may not have been committed or else alone only once in a lifetime.[22] Because of the greater frequency of confession, canon 21 prompted a flourishing of practical spiritual guidebooks based on those produced in the twelfth century to teach clergy, scholars, and laity the concepts and categories of vice, virtue, and redemption so as to acquire a better understanding of what and how to confess.[23] Because these manuals were designed to educate confessors in current teachings of canon law, popular theology, and recent church reforms that focused on penance, they often included itemized discussions of the seven deadly sins. As if aware of Lateran IV's focus on the avarice of clergy, Heldris presents his own condemnation of the sin with respect to courtly conduct.

In condemning avarice at court and applauding aristocratic kindness in heart and wealth in the poem's frame, Heldris uses romance as a secular counterpart to the kind of reflective piety promoted by Lateran IV, which finds roots in the twelfth-century theology of Anselm of Canterbury (d. 1109) and Bernard of Clairvaux (1090–1153). Building upon the Rule of Saint Benedict, which aims to control the will and body through communal discipline, Anselm encourages knowledge of God by stimulating the mind. To this end, Anselm revises Benedict's Rule so that its twelve steps "touch the individual alone in the intimacy of his own mind and will."[24] Following Anselm, Saint Bernard ultimately promotes self-knowledge as the means to find union with God. These interior spiritual movements arguably become the foundation for personal inward turns evident in late twelfth- and thirteenth-century romances, which situate at court heroes and heroines who suffer peril alone until their wounded hearts unite with the desired object.[25] In Heldris's romance, the interior struggle located at the heart concerns Silence's exterior appearance as a transvestite knight.

In depicting Silence as a cross-dressed figure, Heldris further correlates his romance with Lateran IV's reformations of sartorial matters in the only two directives that mention clothing. Much more so than at earlier councils, the legislation of Lateran IV regulates dress in detail in order either to promote a sense of disciplined morality, as in canon 16, or to convey human essence, as in canon 68. Where canon 16 prohibits clergy from wearing garments often associated with the nobility, including articles that are too long, too short, or overly ornamented, canon 68 requires Jews to distinguish themselves through dress so they do not marry Christians. Together these two directives may be understood as Lateran IV's sartorial program to use dress as an effective means to convey both ethically sound comportment and an individual's natural essence. *Silence* reflects a similar idea with important modifications: Silence's physical beauty and knightly garb raise issues of individual and public morality, but her garments do not disclose her female self until the end of the romance, when she dons women's attire for the first time in her life.

Geoffrey of Vinsauf's *Poetria nova* and Silence's First *Effictio*

This section turns to the advancements in rhetorical theory made by Geoffrey of Vinsauf at nearly the same time of Lateran IV in his *Poetria nova*, which, as a strand in the web of interlocution informing *Silence*, connects themes of discipline and moral conduct located at the heart through its exposition of *effictio*. While traditionally associated with representations of attire in narrative, the first *effictio* in *Silence* addresses the protagonist's unclothed physical perfection as a sign of honorable behavior.

Commonly understood as an elaborate description of the body's physical characteristics, the *effictio* appears as a rhetorical device in *Silence* at two salient moments profoundly interested in moral comportment. The first describes the protagonist's feminine features as the allegorical figure of Nature creates the perfect daughter for Cador and Eufemie. Like other poets, Heldris is part of a long tradition that understands *effictios* of women as emphasizing primarily magnificence, aristocratic wealth, and high social standing. Homer, for instance, reveals Hera's beauty from head to toe as she adorns herself before seducing Zeus in the *Iliad*, while Marie de France announces the regal nature of the female protagonist in *Lanval*. In the fourteenth century, Chaucer's *Miller's Tale* presents Alison's penchant for an expensive wardrobe as if clothing could assist her aspirations for social mo-bility.[26] Common among these various literary examples is the centrality of dress in rendering women highly desirable.

In the thirteenth century, *effictio* garners renewed attention from medieval grammarians, Matthew of Vendôme and Geoffrey of Vinsauf, who extend the Classical notion of the trope as a device that conveys character, appearance, lineage, and talent to include a literary exercise through which descriptions of clothing, jewelry, armor, and weaponry transform both figurative language and the figure portrayed into more beautiful entities.[27] Geoffrey of Vinsauf's *Poetria nova*, a 2,000-line Latin poem, was the most renowned of the several guides that taught poetic style and structure, as it influenced poets in England and on the Continent from its inception ca. 1210 through the fifteenth century.[28] While it has been noted that Geoffrey proposes few significant innovations in rhetorical arts, instead relying on reiterating Classical lessons,[29] he alone among his contemporary Latinists emphasizes the value of dress for rendering a woman's body attractive.[30] Furthermore, Geoffrey notes that readers can understand the rhetorical technique of *descriptio* best through an example that includes an *effictio* of clothing. Equating the "rich expression" with luxurious dress, which in turn dignifies "rich content," Geoffrey instructs fellow writers: "Do not let a wealthy matron blush in a pauper's gown." Indeed, the quality of women's attire reflects her true physical nature.[31] He likens the artifice of fine language with clothing that showcases a woman's beauty:

> If to beauty so portrayed you wish to add clothing: let her hair, dressed down her back in braids, be entwined with gold. Let a band of gold give radiance to the brightness of her brow; let her face be bare, clothed only in its own color; let a starry necklace circle her milk-white neck; let her hem be white with linen, her mantle burn with gold; let a girdle everywhere bright with jewels cover her waist; let her arms be rich in bracelets; let gold circle her fine fingers, and a jewel prouder than gold pour forth its beams; let art contend with fabric in her bright attire. Let neither hand nor imagination be able to add anything to such array.[32]

In using *effictio* to exemplify *descriptio*, Geoffrey literalizes this poetic maneuver by dressing the body in garments that accentuate her beauty to such an extent that no literal or imaginative addition could make the female body more magnificent.

Absent from Geoffrey's *effictio* is any mention of the influence that garments have on the behavior of the woman who wears them. Unlike

Marie de France, who positions belts and fitted attire as central to controlling love and demonstrating virtuous passion, Geoffrey does not find discipline apparent in attire. Rather, the *effictio* demonstrates order associated with the unclothed body. As he traces a woman's attributes from her forehead down to a foot of "excellent smallness," Geoffrey asserts the primacy of Nature's artful discipline in creating a naked form:

> Let Nature's compass describe first a circle for her head. Let the color of gold be gilt in her hair; let lilies spring in the eminence of her forehead; let the appearance of her eyebrow be like dark blueberries; let a milk-white path divide those twin arches. Let strict rule govern the shape of the nose, and neither stop on this side of, nor transgress, what is fitting. Let the lookouts of her brow, her eyes, shine, both of them, either with gems' light or with light like that of a star. Let her face rival the dawn, neither red nor bright, but at once both and neither color. Let her mouth gleam in a form of brief extent and, as it were, a semicircle; let her lips, as if pregnant, rise in a swell, and let them be moderately red: warm, but with a gentle heat. Let order compose her snowy teeth, all of one proportion; let the fragrance of her mouth and that of incense be of a like scent. And let Nature, more potent than art, polish her chin more highly than polished marble. Let a milk-white column be with its precious color a handmaiden to the head, a column which bears up the mirror of the face on high. From her crystal throat let a kind of radiance go forth which can strike the eyes of a beholder and madden his heart. Let her shoulders adjust together with a certain discipline, and neither fall away as if sloping downward, nor stand, as it were, upraised, but rather rest in place correctly; and let her arms be pleasing, as slender in their form as delightful in their length. Let substance soft and lean join together in her slender fingers, and appearance, smooth and milk white, lines long and straight: the beauty of the hands lies in these qualities. Let her breast, a picture of snow, bring forth either bosom as if they were, in effect, uncut jewels side by side. Let the circumference of her waist be narrowly confined, circumscribable by the small reach of a hand. I am silent about the parts just below: more fittingly does the imagination speak of these than the tongue. But let her leg, for its part,

realize its length in slenderness; let a foot of excellent smallness sport in its own daintiness.[33]

Explicit within Geoffrey's description is a concern for order, regulation, and control as Nature constructs the female body: she shapes the nose according to a "strict rule," which is careful not to "transgress what is fitting"; "order" creates teeth; shoulders move together "with a certain discipline" and "rest in place correctly." Whereas Geoffrey utilizes dress in narrative to underscore a woman's natural beauty in an earlier *effictio*, this description of a body unencumbered by dress articulates notions of order and regulation. The *effictio* thus functions twofold: when it attends to the exterior garments, the device highlights feminine splendor; when it focuses on the naked body, it emphasizes that body's discipline.

Heldris de Cornuälle endorses distinctions similar to Geoffrey's, but with modifications. Whereas Geoffrey predicates order as part of the process that creates naked bodies, Heldris views such discipline in connection with morality. Like Geoffrey, Heldris depicts Nature crafting the perfect woman from head to toe in the first *effictio* in *Silence*. Working from "biele et pure" [beautiful and pure] (line 1865) material, Nature "Metrai plus de bialté ensanble / Que n'aient ore .m. de celes / Qui en cest monde sont plus beles" [assemble(s) more beauty than a thousand of the most beautiful girls in the whole world] (lines 1882–84). Heldris's recurring enunciation of Silence's beauty (lines 1907, 1920, 1923, 1926, 1929, and 1934) may be understood as an amplification of the cataloguing technique that Derek Pearsall sees as a defining characteristic of the trope: conventional medieval description "depends upon the accumulation of all available detail. The ideal is richness, ornament, elaboration."[34] However, Silence's magnificence in this case does not depend on any accessory that Nature adds to her body. Heldris instead lists Silence's superior physical qualities, from "mains petites, lons les dois" [small hands, long fingers] (line 1938), to "cuisses moles et faitices" [thighs soft and shapely] (line 1942), to "piés, et ortals a mesure" [feet and toes in proportion] (line 1944).

While Pearsall reads the cataloguing techniques of *effictio* that medieval writers employ as a mere literary exercise, Heldris uses them as a means to address beyond the literary text the contemporary social issues of spiritual conduct at play. To be sure, the very superficial nature of the medieval *effictio* lends itself to transcribing aspects of life informed by contemporary fashion—Marie de France's attention to the fitted *bliaut* in *Lanval* highlights twelfth-century aristocratic splendor, while Geoffrey Chaucer represents fourteenth-century tailoring practices of inserting triangular pieces into the bottom of a skirt to make it fuller, as with Alison's gored skirt in Chaucer's *Miller's Tale.*[35] Heldris de Cornuälle, however, crafts his initial *effictio* so that it addresses one of the thirteenth-century's major social changes, which depended not on an alteration in garment styles but on an alteration in religious practice that emphasized moral discipline and integrity of heart, namely, in annual confession, which prompted self-reflection and control.

Heldris invokes such moral comportment at the conclusion of the romance's first *effictio* during an extended affirmation of Silence's perfection that nevertheless subtly directs attention to her inner beauty, found "en la puciele" [in the maiden] (line 1952):

Ainc belizors voir ne vesqui
De li el monde, ne nasqui,
Al plus droit que jo puis esmer.
En li n'a nïent a blasmer
Fors solement qu'ele est trop biele,
Que tant en a en la puciele
Qu'a .m. peüst assés savoir,
Se tant en peüscent avoir
Et de bialté et de faiture.
Ainc n'ovra mais si bien Nature
A rien ki morir doive vivre.
                (lines 1947–57)

——

[But never in truth lived a more beautiful creature in this world, nor was anything more lovely ever born. As near as I can estimate, there is absolutely nothing wrong with this girl—except that she's too beautiful. For there is so much beauty in the maiden that it would be plenty for a thousand, if they could share such beauty and workmanship. Never again did Nature work so effectively to give life to a mortal creature.][36]

Despite the extended consideration of Silence's physical appearance that precedes this intrusion, by Heldris, he concludes that Silence's loveliness appears internally, rather than externally in the line-ending rhyme of "trop biele" [too beautiful] (line 1951) and "en la puciele" [in the maiden] (line 1952). Heldris furthermore shifts attention away from the contours of Silence's body to an interior essence that drives her behavior as she lives in the world by completing the *effictio* with "vivre," a move quite typical of this rhetorical technique to address inner virtue through exterior appearance.

No longer merely an allegorical architect that constructs physical frames, Nature is a force that works within by generating the spirit and values of the heart that will motivate the body's movements and behaviors. While remaining committed to infusing Silence with beauty both inside and out, Nature gathers the material that will render her masterpiece "un vallant home" [a noble human being] (line 1826), since the refined clay that she works always yields "les buens" [good folk] (line 1834) "sans falle" [without fault] (line 1833). If, however, Nature works carelessly and mixes coarse clay into the refined, then the integrity of the heart is threatened: "Cil gros se trait al cuer en oire" [this coarse matter attacks the heart right away] (lines 1835–39). In asserting that the faults made by coarse clay threaten the constitution of the heart, Heldris examines the precarious status of the heart, which could easily dictate vile behavior:

> Et se ses vils cuers li fait faire
> Qu'il ne s'en puissce pas retraire,
> Dont est il sers et ses cuers sire,
> Espi! quant tels cuers le maistyre.
> (lines 2429–32)

———

[But if his vile heart forces him to do (wrong), so that he cannot stop doing it, he is the servant and his heart the lord. See what happens when such a heart is master!]

According to Heldris, the more vile the heart, the more it threatens to lead the body to vice.

By localizing such energy specifically at the heart, *Silence* licenses *effictio* to communicate ideas of internal reflection that underpin both the larger project of Geoffrey of Vinsauf's *Poetria nova* and Augustine's *Confessions*. The first lines of Geoffrey's treatise liken the creation of poetry to the construction of a house, both of which require personal examination. The place where this internal reflection occurs is not immediately at the mind, but in the heart so that the heart provides a solid frame within which the body can move: "the work is first measured out with [man's] heart's inward plumb line . . . ; his heart's hand shapes the whole before his body's hand does so" [intrinseca linea cordis / Praemetitur opus, . . . totamque figurat / Ante manus cordis quam corporis].[37] Such primacy of the heart as a moral index furthermore finds its roots in Augustine's *Confessions,* in which the bishop consistently figures the heart as a moral barometer that not only registers vice and virtue but also prompts the body to behave in vicious and virtuous ways: the heart differentiates between "love's serenity and lust's darkness" (II.ii.2); if a man is "dull of heart," then he loves vice (IX.iv.9), whereas "total concentration of the heart" allows for wisdom (IX.x.24).[38]

Charles Taylor notes that Augustine's language of inwardness "represents a radically new doctrine of moral resources" for his time, but by the high Middle Ages his theological understanding of self-reflexion does not appear as a radical departure from Christian belief.[39] Rather, it emerges as an issue that helps churchmen establish the role of the individual in his path to salvation, as seen in the enthusiastic debates between Anselm of Canterbury, Abelard, and Peter Lombard, all of whom question Augustine's notion of the individual's will and its relationship to sin.[40] In terms of positioning the heart as important to ethical conduct, the thirteenth-century theologian contemporary with Heldris, Thomas Aquinas, shares a particular affinity with Augustine in that both understand the Christian ideal of "purity of heart" as a crucial element in Christian happiness.[41]

If Aquinas's interest in situating morality in the heart, as Augustine did, is indicative of a particular trend in ways of thinking about

Christian ethics in the thirteenth century, then it is not surprising that those spiritual sensitivities also resonate in the work of Heldris de Cornuälle, who, in *Silence*, positions the heart as central to chivalric behavior and, by extension, to morality. For bodies that fall victim to vice, Heldris responds with a sartorial strategy that at once echoes and revises popular usage of *effictio* in literary texts: moral integrity is mani - fested best in a metaphor of dress. Take, for example, Geoffrey of Vinsauf's use of garments in *effictio*. While Geoffrey sees magnificent attire as a sign of female elegance, Heldris inverts this view to show that unrefined clothing reflects poor behavior. *Silence* addresses the relationship between attire and morality by likening the body of an individual with a vile heart [vil cuer] (line 1843) to coarse, simplistic fabric [sarpelliere] (line 1844) in the preamble to the *effictio* describing Silence's perfect beauty:

> Ne poés vos sovent trover
> Vil cuer et povre, et riche cors
> Kist sarpelliere par defors?
> Li cors n'est mais fors sarpelliere,
> Encor soit de la terre chiere;
> Mais li cuers ne valt une alie
> K'est fais de grosse et de delie.
> (lines 1842–48)
> —
> [Don't you often find a poor, vile heart with a rich body, which is nothing but sackcloth on the outside? The body is mere sackcloth, even if it is made from the finest clay, and the heart made of coarse mixed with fine isn't worth a crab-apple.]

Heldris's consideration of clothing finds similarities to Geoffrey's in that both see a relationship between physical beauty and the value of dress. Geoffrey may focus on the merits of exterior appearance in order to emphasize what lies underneath clothing, but Heldris highlights the opposite. He sees tattered and besmirched clothing as evidence of man's transgressions: "li cuers de la grosse terre" [the heart of coarse clay] (line 2322) symbolizes "nature vils" [vile nature] (line

2321), which "solle la parmenterie" [soils fine apparel] (line 2324). In moving from interior fault of character to exterior pollution of clothing, Heldris establishes the negative standard against which he will define Silence. Vile nature may foul adornments, but the narrative does not realize such a threat to Silence because she is a paragon of virtue.

In this way, filthy or simplistic garments operate differently in Heldris's romance than they do in other medieval texts. For instance, Alain de Lille, William Langland, and the *Gawain*-poet all situate foul clothing on morally injured bodies: Alain's twelfth-century *De Planctu Naturae* features a down-trodden Nature wearing a tunic that man has torn with his own injuries and insults; Langland's fourteenth-century *Piers Plowman* depicts the personification of *Activa vita*, called Haukyn, wearing a coat stained with his own offenses; and the *Gawain*-poet's contemporary exemplum, *Cleanness*, conceives of man's persistent sin in dirty garments that offend aristocratic courtiers.[42] These texts all portray soiled clothing as signs of the protagonists' transgressions. Conversely, the *Roman de Silence* cannot associate foul dress with its heroine because she is the epitome of moral perfection. Instead, the romance here dresses a generalized aristocratic population in sackcloth because "many nobles are sullied, dragged down by the vileness of their hearts" [maint noble sont sollié, / De lor vils cuers entoëllié] (lines 1855–56). For the morally perfect protagonist, Heldris chooses garments for a transvestite—a surprising choice, because cross-dressing traditionally invites scathing clerical commentary. Yet Heldris refuses to condemn Silence for a sartorial decision imposed by her father. Rather, as the second *effictio* will show in the next section, the poet displaces moral correction from Silence to her fellow knights because they are likely to fall short of the high moral standard that the heroine exhibits despite her own sinful sartorial practice.

Transvestite Romances and Silence's Second *Effictio*

As a thirteenth-century romance, *Silence* is particularly noteworthy for its interest in transvestism. Perhaps most familiar as a central motif to ensure chastity in the lives of female saints, transvestism emerges in romance as a means by which noble women benefit from masculine privilege. Beginning with the woman-warrior Camille in the twelfth-century epic *Roman d'Enéas* and extending to the female protagonists in the so-called transvestite romances of the thirteenth and fourteenth centuries, *Aucassin et Nicolette, Yde et Olive, Tristan de Nanteuil,* and *Silence,* women disguised as men demonstrate ingenuity and success in chivalric endeavors of love and war.[43] Of the transvestite romances, all but *Silence* and one of its primary source texts, *Lestoire Merlin,* position love as a motivator for women to pass as men. For instance, both Yde and Blanchadine remain cross-dressed so as to continue as lovers of women, and their sex is miraculously changed when their transgressions are about to be revealed in *Yde et Olive* and *Tristan de Nanteuil.* In *Aucassin et Nicolette,* the heroine briefly dons men's dress in order to travel safely in search of her beloved Aucassin.[44] *Silence* stands as a notable exception among these texts because it engages transvestism initially with respect to inheritance instead of to the pursuit of a love relationship. To be sure, the poem employs Silence's cross-dressing in ways that address sexual behaviors associated with cultural constructions of gender, practices of courtly love, and laudable martial talents, as many critics have shown, but the dominant trends in *Silence* scholarship overlook a crucial issue that transvestism engages: ethical behavior at a time when the poet finds moral conduct lacking at court.

While gender and sexual politics associated with transvestism license readings that engage those very terms, Marjorie Garber has persuasively shown that the figure of the transvestite can signal a crisis in categories other than gender, "calling attention to cultural, social, or aesthetic dissonances."[45] Despite serving as an external indicator of self-presentation, transvestism, according to Garber, operates in myriad texts as a subversive practice that "indicates a category crisis elsewhere, an irresolvable conflict or epistemological crux that destabilizes comfortable binarity and displaces the resulting discomfort onto a figure that already inhabits, indeed, incarnates the margin."[46] Consequently, the cross-dresser highlights potential problems in other social discourses, such as those of race and class.[47] In the case of *Si-*

lence, the cultural discourse in which the transvestite registers disso-
nance is that of morality.

Silence conveys dissatisfaction with immoral noblemen through its
descriptions of cross-dressing. Concordant with the laudatory remark
in the prologue directed to honorable individuals who shun avarice,
the second *effictio,* which describes Silence outfitted as a knight about
to embark on a military campaign in defense of King Ebain, articulates similar praise for those who practice largess and ultimately diverts
attention from the sartorial subject to munificent individuals. The description attends closely to Silence's exterior appearance by noting his
fine vestments, including the "ganbizon de soie" [padded silken tunic]
(line 5336), "obierc malié" [finely meshed hauberk] (line 5337), "cal-
ces" [leggings] (line 5342), "esporon" [spurs] (line 5344), "sa bone
espee" [his good sword] (line 5349), "ventalle" [hood] (line 5352),
and "elme" [helmet] (line 5353).[48] But just as the first *effictio* subverts
certain conventions of the trope by ignoring dress as a traditional indicator of physical beauty, so does the second *effictio* revise common
understandings of how the trope communicates meaning. Unlike
other literary portrayals of magnificent attire in romances that broad-
cast chivalric virtue, that of Silence's does not indicate his martial
prowess and virtuous character. As a result, the poet's figuration of Silence's battledress neither correlates with Chrétien de Troyes's description of the beauty, nobility, and valor epitomized by Erec's exemplary
attire in *Erec et Enide,* nor articulates the knight's multifaceted goodness
and bravery, which is the case in *Sir Gawain and the Green Knight,* as the
following chapter will show.[49]

The twelfth-century *Roman d'Enéas* presents a case more closely re-
lated to the martial *effictio* in *Silence* in that it describes the appearance
of a transvestite knight, Camille. However, where Heldris refuses a
catalogue of Silence's moral or knightly attributes, the *Enéas*-poet's *effictio* attends to Camille's chivalric talents much like the *effictios* of Erec
and Gawain. Despite Lorraine Stock's assertion that Camille's *effictio*
should not be considered as a typical description of the arming of a
hero since there is no mention of weaponry, it is a valuable example to
read alongside *Silence* because the *Enéas*-poet perpetuates the standard

use of dress in *effictio* to reveal behavior.[50] The text presents Camille as a warrior who "a mervoille par estoit bele / et molt estoit de grant poeir" [was marvelously beautiful and of very great strength] (lines 3962–63). She "molt ama chevalerie / et maintint la tote sa vie" [loved chivalry greatly and upheld it her whole life] (lines 3969–70), and she led so "molt richement" [splendidly equipped] (line 4085) an army of four thousand soldiers that onlookers concluded that she was "tant ert prozet tant ert bele" [so brave and so beautiful] (line 4094).[51] The second *effictio* describing Silence differs from that of Camille because it avoids a parallel between the value of a knight's battledress and military prowess. Rather, the text addresses the goodwill of the king when it recounts the splendor of Silence's hauberk: "Que li rois de France ot tenu / En tel cierté qu'il nel donast / Por rien c'on li abandonast" [that the king of France had valued so highly that he wouldn't have exchanged it for anything anyone could have offered him] (lines 5338–40).

Whereas Stock, I think, is right in arguing that at this moment "both the receipt and the display of such armor would inestimably add to the . . . culturally valued esteem, renown, and worthiness of any male warrior," *Silence* makes no such conclusion obvious in its narrative.[52] Heldris instead both applauds and perpetuates the notion of largess described in the *Histoire des ducs de Normandie et des rois d'Angleterre*, which illustrates the goodwill of England's King John in his liberal distribution of clothing and gifts to the knights in his service at the beginning of the thirteenth century, so as to affirm a positive aristocratic image.[53] Similarly, Heldris underscores the necessity for the aristocracy to shun avarice by praising the largess of the king who gives Silence a helmet bejeweled with "Pieres i a et cercle d'or / Ki valent bien tolt un tressor" [precious stones and golden circles that were worth a fortune] (lines 5355–56): "Li rois de France li dona. / Bien ait quant il l'abandona" [The king of France gave it to him—may he prosper for his gift] (lines 5357–58). Despite the extended attention to Silence's dress, the *effictio* ignores the knight's own talents that might be most closely associated with attire. In this way, the poet reaffirms the stance he takes with respect to avarice in the prologue by demonstrating that a patron's munificence is more desirable than the chivalric skills of those who wear the gifted battledress.

Because the poem continually deems Silence "moult frans et honorables, / Cortois et pros et amiables" [so noble, honorable, courteous, valiant, and kind] (lines 5121–22), it is not surprising that the conclusion of the second *effictio* instead evaluates the ethical conduct of his retinue. Just as Heldris shows that material worth derives from the goodness of Silence's sponsor, rather than from the knight's own martial capabilities, so does he deflect questions of moral behavior away from Silence by figuring him apart from his followers. Indeed, the eponymous hero assumes the role of the leader who urges his fellow knights to mind their behavior in battle:

> "Or si vos voel jo moult requierre
> Que vos soiés ensi par vos
> Que nus ne puist dire de nos
> Orguel, oltrage, ne folie,
> Se il nel dist par droite envie.
> Jo sui a vos et vos a mi."
> (lines 5378–83)
> —
>
> ["Now I should like to urge you to conduct yourselves in such a way that none may accuse us of arrogance, excess, or folly unless they do it out of sheer envy. I am pledged to you and you to me."]

By using the second-person-plural pronoun, "vos," in his directive to his followers, Silence positions himself apart from the others. He registers, as does the narrative voice, that "si per ne valent a lui rien" [his peers were nothing compared to him] (line 5124). Yet, his entreaty that he does not want anyone to accuse "us" [nos] of sinful behavior suggests that his retinue's collective comportment ultimately impacts the entire group. Although Silence may appear to be perfect, his moral fiber risks damage by his knights, whose behavior may place the group's shared reputation at risk.

Although Silence includes himself as a member of the chivalric band, as evidenced by the commitment he pledges to his followers, his instruction suggests that only his followers may succumb to cowardice in battle—a transgression that, according to the narrative, results in the serious punishment of being excluded from entry to the church (lines 5371–74).[54] The narrative completes the *effictio* of the warrior by acknowledging Silence's golden spurs that expertly touch the flanks of his horse, but it continues to separate Silence rhetorically from his retinue by articulating neither his chivalric talents nor how he might inspire his followers. Instead, the text turns to the thirty French knights who follow their commander and notes that craven chivalric behavior results in a religious penalty. Such a consequence is important for two reasons. First, it applies only to Silence's retinue, a move that distances Silence's ethical conduct from that of his fellow knights. Second, exclusion from the church recalls an early penitential exercise that canon 21 reaffirms in 1215, whereby sinners were prohibited from entering their place of worship until they completed penance and were invited back into the Christian community.[55] In imposing a kind of religious exile as the penalty for martial pusillanimity, *Silence* demonstrates that certain chivalric behavior in battle is not without spiritual consequences. By extension, this threat of excommunication encourages knights to evaluate themselves in light of acceptable behaviors—whether chivalric in that Silence's men show no signs of cowardice, or religious in that no observer may accuse any of them of "arrogance, excess, or folly" (line 5380), or both.

The focus on the religious repercussions that Silence's retinue would suffer after an *effictio* that makes the leader's cross-dressing explicit may appear misplaced given the church's stance on transvestism. Deuteronomy 22:5 condemns women and men for wearing clothing of the opposite sex since "all that do so are abominations unto the Lord God," and the medieval biblical commentaries associated with that chapter and verse illustrate an understanding of transvestism as a sin against nature (*contra naturam est*).[56] As Ad Putter explains, such a position either against transvestism in general or on cross-dressing as a sin against nature was reaffirmed in early church councils and laws, from the Council of Granga (before 341) to Burchard's *Decretals* (ca. 1010). Furthermore, just as the transvestite knight makes his appearance in medieval romance, Hildegard of Bingen (ca. 1150) and cleric

Alexander of Hales (ca. 1240) condemn the practice in their writings.[57] Yet the *effictio* describing Silence's military outfit and retinue avoids any commentary both on transvestism and what might be considered Silence's sin against nature. Instead, it asserts the primacy of chivalric self-control so as to celebrate the moral virtue of the cross-dressed knight in battle.

While *Silence* does not name its protagonist's transvestism as a sin *contra naturam*, it does illustrate an extended debate between Silence and the two personifications, Nature and Nurture. These allegorical figures appear at two separate moments to dispute whether Silence should comport himself based on the biological fact that he is a woman or whether he should continue to behave like a man. When Silence turns twelve years old and Nature and Nurture pay him a visit, the adolescent acquiesces to Nature's admonishments and renounces the typically male practice of "fendre mes dras, braies calcier" [slitting garments and wearing breeches] (line 2560). In so doing, Silence reevaluates the behavior that Nature finds offensive by first questioning his transgression and then rejecting it in a nuanced consideration of cross-dressing. In jettisoning practices typically associated with men—a particular choice of dress, haircut, or activity at court—and thus espousing activities and appearances that pertain to women, Silence affirms that he has not deceived the public out of greed and finds solace in the idea of a munificent God who dispenses goods to all according to their nature:

> "Cis Dameldex qui me fist naistre
> Me puet bien governer et paistre:
> Queles! ja n'ai jo oï conté
> Qu'il est plains de si grant bonté
> Et done a tolte creäture
> Sofisalment lonc sa nature?
> Fu ainc mais feme si tanee
> De vil barat, ne enganee
> Que cho fesist par covoitise?
> Nel puis savoir en nule guise."
> (lines 2577–86)

—

[“The good Lord who created me will be my shepherd and my guide. Haven’t I heard it said that in his great goodness he dispenses of his bounty to each creature according to its nature? Was any female so tormented or deceived by such vile fraud as to do what I did out of greed? I certainly never heard of one!”]

Silence concedes that greed could have motivated him to perpetuate fraud through cross-dressing because his male appearance would secure his inheritance, yet the narrative rejects such a conclusion.

The question that Silence asks, “Was any female so tormented or deceived by such vile fraud as to do what I did out of greed?” bears crucially on the text’s position on transvestism with respect to both moral behavior and the narrative’s frame of avarice. In particular, the question’s syntactic structure displaces sin from Silence. Instead of continuing to position himself as the object of scrutiny, as he does in the previous two statements, which describe his fear of being discovered when undressing and his refusal to play games traditionally reserved for boys, Silence moves to a generalized subject and a passive verbal clause that questions whether “any female so tormented or deceived by such vile fraud” would have disguised herself, as Silence did. The diction and syntax indict not Silence but the “fraud” [barat] that acts upon “any female.” As a result, Silence shifts any judgment concerning his transvestism away from his own potential engagement with sin by asserting that he does not cross-dress out of greed.

The text, too, seconds Silence’s claim that avarice does not motivate his decision by linking his clothing to highly successful chivalric conduct. Heldris describes Silence’s valor in battle, from his enthusiasm to engage in armed combat, his perfect form during a joust, and his uncanny ability to unhorse his opponents (lines 5148–57) to the humiliation that a fallen knight would likely feel had he known

> Que feme tendre, fainte et malle,
> Ki rien n’a d’ome fors le halle,
> Et fors les dras et contenance,
> L’eüst abatu de sa lance.
>
>   (lines 5161–64)

[that a tender, soft, faint-hearted woman, who had only the complexion, clothing, and comportment of a man, could have struck him down with her lance.][58]

The poet draws upon the subtle relationship between "clothing and comportment" that he invokes through the assonance of "dras et contenance" (line 5163).[59] Silence may be a woman underneath masculine attire, but the garments do not bespeak aberrant behavior. Instead, transvestism allows Silence to win victories that would shame any of his opponents should they realize that he was a woman. As if to laud Silence's chivalric success as an example of appropriate behavior, the poet Heldris intrudes here to reveal the merits of refined manners and courtliness:

Bons us tolt moult vilonie
Et fait mener cortoise vie.
Car bons us a qui bone vie uze
Et vilonie le refuse.
                    (lines 5167–70)

——

[Good manners refine one's behavior and help one lead a courtly life. Proper behavior is the sign of a good life and of moral refinement.]

Afterward, the text segues to Silence. It ignores any moral commentary on transvestism and features the protagonist as the epitome of such proper behavior and moral refinement, because "chevaliers est vallans et buens" [he was a valiant and noble knight] (line 5179) and fights those who commit what the poem sees as the more important transgression of defying the king "par grant orguel et par derroi" [out of great pride and folly] (line 5190).

These examples and the conclusion of the poem, when Merlin reveals Silence's female sex, demonstrate the text's ambivalent stance with respect to clothing as a means to conceal. On the one hand, the narrative repeatedly asserts that clothing deceives the public into believing that Silence is a man: "Il est desos les dras mescine" [under the garments he is a maiden] (line 2479);[60] "Mais el a sos la vesteüre /

Ki de tolt cho n'a mie cure" [But what that boy has under his clothes has nothing to do with being male] (lines 2829–30); "Si est desos les dras meschine" [he is a girl beneath his clothes] (line 6536). On the other, this deception does not often appear problematic to anyone other than Silence's conscience and to Nature and Nurture because the text applauds the chivalric success that cross-dressing brings to both the transvestite knight and his king.

The ambivalence surrounding dress, disguise, and identity may point instead to a broader engagement that *Silence* has with medieval understandings of clothing. Tertullian (ca. 155–230) addresses women's attire and its illusory effect on a viewing public, arguing that excessive dress—the kind associated with either nobility or harlots—deceives. Such falsification appears problematic to Tertullian because he finds sin when women modify God's work:

> What a wicked thing it is to attempt to add to a divine handiwork the inventions of the Devil! . . . To lie in your appearance, you to whom lying with the tongue is not allowed! To seek for that which is not your own, you who are taught to keep hands off the goods of another! To commit adultery in your appearance, you who should eagerly strive after modesty! Believe me, blessed sisters! How can you keep the command-ments of God if you do not keep in your own persons the features which He has bestowed on you?[61]

Tertullian contends that clothing "lies." An illicit desire "for that which is not [one's] own" is sartorial "adultery." In espousing differ-ence through dress, the woman has transgressed divine authority by losing the "features" of her "own person." This particular position of Tertullian's at once looks back to the writings of Ovid in his *Remedia amoris* and forward to those of Peter the Chanter, an important secular cleric of the twelfth-century cathedral school of Notre-Dame at Paris, whose *Verbum abbreviatum* includes chapters "Against the Superfluity and Expense of Clothing" and "Against the Form of Clothes." Peter quotes Ovid's complaint: "We are won by dress; all is concealed by gems and gold; a woman is the least part of herself" (*Remedia*, lines 343–44); and he continues in the vein of both Ovid and Tertullian by noting that tailored attire adds to the body whatever Nature has denied it.[62] In these ways, both Classical and medieval writers illustrate an interest in dress as deception, falsification, and a means to communicate the desire to be something other than Nature intended—the last of which resonates with the prohibitions against cross-dressing in Deuteronomy 22:5 and runs counter to Lateran IV's canon 68, which stipulates sartorial measures to reveal human essence.

While examples in *Silence* demonstrate that dress may conceal and even deceive, the text registers very little concern with Tertullian's position that garments falsify truths (until the end of the poem, of course, and that is a point to which I will return). Instead, the narrative uses the moments at which Silence considers sartorial deception to explore appropriate conduct that would encourage individual advancement within social and spiritual realms. Such encouragement appears after Silence's heart reminds him that he cross-dresses to convince people that he is a boy despite having been born a girl. But rather than admonishing him, Silence's heart immediately articulates a practical concern: should the king die, women would inherit again. Silence should thus use his time in disguise to acquire a skill that would serve him as a woman.

What follows the observation, "Mais el a sos la vesteüre / Ki de tolt cho n'a mie cure" [But what that boy has under his clothes has nothing to do with being male] (lines 2829–30), is not an indictment of the demerits of transgressive sartorial falsification in the vein of Tertullian but rather an exploration of how a woman might be successful in a particular political regime. The text advocates minstrelsy as a logical choice of art, since both men and women can learn and practice this skill.[63] This conclusion motivates Silence's decision to abandon the safety of his guardian's home, disguise himself further (by darkening his face) as a man of low social standing, and follow travelling *jongleurs* who have stayed with his guardian so that he may learn their trade. Silence succeeds so well at his apprenticeship that he quickly surpasses his masters' talent and finds, not surprisingly, "much greater favor at court than they ever had" [Et por cho qu'il a gregnor grasce / Que il nen aient mais en cort] (lines 3146–47). Robert S. Sturges reads Silence's masquerade and pursuit of minstrelsy as a moment that exemplifies Marjorie Garber's argument that transvestism signals crisis in a category other than gender, namely, class and economics.[64] The narrative subsequently comments on the economic successes and challenges that Silence encounters as an itinerant musician. Yet, in addition to bespeaking a crisis in class and economics, as Sturges has shown, Silence's transvestism precipitates another "category crisis," to borrow Garber's term, when it turns to an examination of those persons who interact with the cross-dresser.

What began as a sartorial crisis in Silence's heart thus evolves into not only a commentary on class and economics, as Sturges asserts, but also an exemplum of sound moral comportment when the avaricious masters who have trained Silence in minstrelsy plot his death. Arguing that Silence "nostre damages doblera, / Car nostre avoir enportera" [will more than double (their) losses because he will take away (their) earnings] (lines 3277–78), the two men conspire to kill their apprentice. Silence, well aware of their evil machinations, thwarts their plan by refusing to travel with them any longer. As Silence explains his decision to stay behind because he fears that he will be worse off should he continue with his fellow *jongleurs*, he opts not to accuse them but rather tells them to continue alone on their journey "com prodome / et bone gent" [like upright and honest men] (lines 3462–63). "Prodome" functions as an important descriptor here in that it conveys, as John W. Baldwin notes, that "the supreme virtue for the solitary knight was prowess (*proece*; adj., *preus*)." The "prodome" thus exists as an "ideal knight" who exhibits virtues of chivalric combat—from strength and endurance to courage and valor—and of moral perfection.[65] There is both irony and a lesson in Silence's encouragement to the *jongleurs* to behave like "upright and honest men." The irony is that Silence, not the *jongleurs*, appears as the exemplar of virtue in this exchange. Moral restraint both squelches sinful desires and encourages the hasty departure of the *jongleurs* once they realize that Silence has thwarted their plot.

The end of the poem interweaves threads of largess, avarice, and morality into Heldris's consideration of transvestism as deception or as an act *contra naturam*. Silence finds himself at Ebain's court after having captured Merlin, an act that has intrigued the king's nobles because of the prophecy that only a woman would bring the sorcerer out of the wilderness. When Merlin promises to tell the king how he was captured and that there are, in fact, two people who deceive the court with "fainte vesteüre" [false clothing] (lines 6485, 6520),[66] Silence invokes two central issues that have impacted the poem's attention to cross-dressing: his inheritance, and his behavior *contra naturam*. Not motivated by any pleasure that he has garnered by passing as a man, Silence expresses his primary concern that he will no longer be able to realize his father's wishes to inherit the family's wealth. His immediate reaction to bringing Merlin to court—"C'or ai jo tel coze bastie / Dont g'iere tols desiretez!" ["For now I have fixed things so that I will be disinherited!"] (lines 6446–47)—leads him to articulate the second issue that initially had emerged in the debates between Nature and Nurture. Echoing Deuteronomy 22:5's stance on transvestism and Tertullian's position on dress for women, Silence concedes that what he did was "contre nature" [against nature] (line 6456). Despite this admission, the text nevertheless refuses to consider the immoral implications of transvestism. Instead, it figures Silence's conscience ignoring his unnatural act and instead reflecting on the impending punishment that Queen Eufeme will undergo as a result of her treachery.

Merlin's account of how the queen, her nun, and Silence have deceived Ebain suggests that Heldris's world of medieval Arthurian romance does not concern itself with the moral ramifications of cross-dressing in the same ways as did the church. Instead, the romance's rather complex stance on transvestism draws upon the church's position in its usual condemnation of the act while also reshaping it. I quote the passage at length, when Merlin addresses the king:

"Sire rois, c'est la verté fine
Que honi vos a la roïne.
Si sarés bien coment, ains none.
Cil doi, Silence et la none,
Sont li doi qui gabés nos ont,
Et nos li doi qui gabé sunt.
Rois, cele none tient Eufeme.

Escarnist vos ses dras de feme.
Rois, or vos ai jo bien garni.
Silences ra moi escarni
En wallés dras, c'est vertés fine,
Si est desos les dras meschine.
La vesteüre, ele est de malle.
La nonain, qui n'a soig de halle,
Bize, ni vent, ki point et giele.
A vesteüre de femiele.
Silences qui moult set et valt,
Bials sire rois, se Dex me salt,
Ne sai home qui tant soit fors
Ki le venquist par son efforss."
(lines 6525–44)

———

["My Lord King, the truth is that the queen has dishonored you. You shall know how before noon. These two, Silence and the nun, are the deceivers; you and I are the deceived. King, this nun is Eufeme's lover; his woman's dress deceives you. Now I've spoken plainly enough, King. Silence on the other hand, tricked me by dressing like a young man: in truth, he is a girl beneath his clothes. Only the clothing is masculine. The nun, who has no need to fear the scorching sun or the north wind's blast that stings and freezes, is a woman in clothing only. Silence is wise and valiant, good Sir King, so help me God, I don't know any man, however strong, who could have conquered him in combat."][67]

Like Tertullian, Merlin conceives of dress as a means of falsification [fainte vesteüre] (lines 6484–85, 6520). But whereas Tertullian indicts the deceiver for attempting to change God-given natural characteristics, Merlin makes no such move. Instead, he critiques adultery and disloyalty by revealing the queen's betrayal. His refusal to condemn Silence's sartorial transgression contributes to Heldris's larger project of depicting transvestism as a morally acceptable act as long as it allows social advantages (in this case, Silence's obedience to his father).[68] In qualifying Silence's deception by praising the knight's wisdom and martial valor, Merlin suggests that his innate sagacity and chivalry trump any artifice that Silence could use to influence his public persona. As such, even in Silence's literal unveiling, he remains a paragon of virtue, whose evaluation by the king as a "prols / Bials chevaliers, vallans et buens" [very valiant, courageous, and worthy knight] (lines 6579–80) is confirmed by Merlin.

Modern theories of cross-dressing may enhance interpretations of Merlin's consideration of transvestism. In *Fetish: Fashion, Sex, and Power,* Valerie Steele argues that transvestism as a behavior is not particularly significant. Highlighting the cross-dresser's "feelings" and "motivations" as integral for understanding the effect that transvestism has on a viewing public, Steele asserts that "the meaning the behavior indicates" becomes important.[69] Cross-dressing itself does not pose a problem; rather, the desires that motivate such a decision do. Garments thus appear as icons of intention. In the words of Charlotte Suthrell, "the material aspect of transvestism has the capacity to make inner states and behaviours material and observable," especially for transvestites who seek to relieve anxieties about sex and gender definition through wearing clothing normally reserved for the opposite sex.[70] In the case of *Silence,* a crisis in sexuality or gender construction does not appear to precipitate the cross-dressing. The first instance of transvestism results instead from a paternal desire to control the disposition of wealth. At the moment of Silence's unveiling and the revelation that the queen has a male lover passing as a nun, cross-dressing again does not appear to derive from psychological concerns with sexual difference. In the case of Eufeme's attendant nun, wearing women's dress is by no means an extension of any desire to emulate or even become a woman of the cloth. The man disguised as Eufeme's female religious advisor uses garments to deceive others and gain sexual satisfaction.[71] Merlin furthermore reiterates the point that both the nun's and Silence's transvestism does not derive from a particular femaleness or maleness rooted within the self. Clothing alone bespeaks gender identity: in terms of the nun, she is "a vesteüre de femiele" [a woman in clothing only]; and for Silence, "la vesteüre, ele est de malle" [only the clothing is masculine].

This is not to say that Suthrell's argument of dress manifesting inner states and behaviors is completely inappropriate for *Silence*. On the contrary, it may explain why the nun is punished and Silence is not. The nun's motivation for cross-dressing results in adultery, lust, and cuckoldry, while Silence cross-dresses out of loyalty to his father. Consequently, Merlin's praising of Silence's wisdom and valor on the battlefield suggests that the knight's iconography of transvestism demonstrates inner states not of gender confusion, but of virtuous behavior. In this way, the text illustrates another moment where modern theories of cross-dressing appear incompatible with the medieval text: transvestism enables a kind of transformation for a different life, as Suthrell would have it,[72] but the act of passing does not precipitate the adoption of a different set of values. In *Silence*, cross-dressing affirms values of generosity and loyalty that Heldris lauds persistently throughout the text, from its prologue to its conclusion.

Unlike the cross-dressers in Suthrell's and Steele's respective studies, or those in the medieval transvestite romances who cross-dress of their own volition,[73] Silence's passing does not stem from his own questions of gender or sexuality. Instead, he cross-dresses in order to continue the disguise instituted by his parents and then to maintain filial loyalty. To be sure, Silence's transvestism does not appear in the narrative as a choice that the knight voluntarily makes. We might recall that upon the birth of a daughter, Silence's parents devise a plan so that their child may inherit their wealth despite the king's decree that women will no longer have such a privilege: Cador "faire en voel malle de femiele" [wishes to make a male of a female] (line 2041) and thus "devant le ferai estalcier, / Fendre ses dras, braies calcier" [will have her hair cut short in front, split her garments, and dress her in breeches] (lines 2055–56).[74] Furthermore, Silence defends his transvestism as deriving from a loyal commitment to his father:

"Et por mon iretage quierre
Me rova vivre al fuer de malle,

Fendre mes dras, aler al halle,
Et jo nel vol pas contredire."
(lines 6598–601)

——

["And in order to claim my inheritance, he asked me to live like a man,
to wear men's dress and not protect my complexion. I didn't want to go
against him."]

Silence's sartorial deception thus becomes the most visible means of
expressing filial honor and integrity rather than questions of gender
and sexuality.

I turn now to the question of spirituality because the ending of the poem reiterates Silence's laudable behaviors in his loyalty to
his father, his king, and his God through a quasi-confessional moment. Though not a sacramental confession because Silence speaks to
a layman, the circumstances surrounding his public divulgence suggest that Silence's actions would accord with the goals of confession
in the thirteenth century: to reveal an intense psychological discomfort
with what has occurred.[75] King Ebain prepares the stage for a confession at court by invoking "le foi / Que tu dois Dameldeu et moi"
[the faith that you owe God and me] (lines 6582–83) as the reason
for divulging the knight's motivations for cross-dressing. Silence iter-
ates all that he has done that may have been sinful, from perpetuating
a sartorial disguise to withholding the truth for fear that the queen
would reveal his "nature" (line 6606) as a woman. In an exhausting
moment, Silence abandons any further disguise and concedes defeat.
He tells Ebain that he will no longer uphold the promise he made to
his father:

"La vertés nel puet consentir
Que jo vos puissce rien mentir,
Ne jo n'ai soig mais de taisir.
Faites de moi vostre plaisir."
(lines 6625–28)

——

["Truth does not permit me to keep anything from you, nor do I care to keep silent any longer. Do with me what you please."]

Critics of the poem have read this ending as one that admits defeat for women. Feminist scholars, in particular, are troubled by the plot turn, which has Silence "disappear into the role of Queen."[76] By "keeping silent" [taisir], Simon Gaunt argues that Silence "suppresses any threat she might pose," while Sarah Roche-Mahdi suggests that her last words convey "traditional female submissiveness."[77] In short, "the king's authority depends on the exclusion of women."[78] While Heldris's circumscription of Silence, and by extension all women, is indeed troubling, I wish to suggest that gender discourse is not the only lens through which readers may look to find significance in the poem's ending.

Much like Heldris uses transvestism, which so often invites readings informed by sex and gender studies, to draw readers instead toward considerations of moral conduct, so does he take this ending as an opportunity to examine spiritual practice and its consequences. The weight of the burden of loyalty to Silence's father's wishes proves too heavy to bear any longer. Silence reveals not only a dolorous response to his own actions but also voluntarily chooses to abandon any further tendency to falsify himself. Such dispositions echo ideal penitential behavior according to twelfth- and thirteenth-century theologians.[79] Despite Silence's apparent forsaking of the promise to his father, his public confession to a layman communicates virtue. Thomas Tentler describes scenarios in which penitents confess to laymen and notes that such action is a "work of virtue" that accentuates the piety of the confessant, especially since there was no guarantee for absolution in that kind of verbal articulation.[80] The line-ending rhyme describing the "price of [Silence's] loyalty" [Miols valt certes ta loialtés] (line 6631) as "far above that of [the king's] royalty" [Que ne face ma roialtés] (line 6632) at once communicates Silence's enduring commitment as a loyal child while simultaneously connecting aristocratic wealth to a loyal subject, thereby returning to the initial moral concern of avarice stated in the poem's prologue.

Heldris begins *Silence* by condemning the greed that permeates the court, especially that of the king of France. In crafting a narrative that takes as its subject an English cross-dressed knight who is described as the "mireöirs del mont" [mirror of the world] (lines 3063, 3116)—a term that recalls titles of didactic moral texts on virtue and vice as well as the "mirror for princes" genre that seeks to model superlative political and social behaviors—Heldris reflects myriad moral ideals in the figure of Silence.[81] It may be argued that Silence's return to womanhood in both face and fashion (lines 6669–76) and her subsequent acceptance as Ebain's queen present a contradiction in the terms of this chapter: as a transvestite, Silence revealed a crisis in morality at court, yet as Ebain's queen her own integrity remains intact despite being subsumed into a place of moral decay. Ebain's court, however, is not the same as that of the "king of France," which Heldris derides in the romance's prologue as one marked by avarice, dishonesty, and shame. Moreover, Heldris continually maintains that Silence should be praised throughout the end of the poem: "Maistre Heldris dist chi endroit / C'on doit plus bone feme amer / Que haïr malvaise u blasmer" (lines 6684–86) [Master Heldris says here and now that one should praise a good woman more than one should blame a bad one]; and despite blaming and censuring Eufeme, Heldris has "Silence plus loëe" (line 6698) [praised Silence more]. Her purity of heart and loyalty to home and hearth outweigh any sartorial deception. Any instance of transgression in dress described in the romance instead points to morality (or lack thereof) at court: transvestism prompts consideration of either proud, arrogant behaviors in Silence's knightly retinue, or royal largess with respect to the gift of Silence's magnificent armor, or the gravity of adultery realized by disguised attire.

In gesturing to questions of morality and disguise, Heldris de Cornuälle positions a discourse of cross-dressing within a larger cultural field informed by sartorial mandates in Lateran IV that promote moral discipline and the revealing of human essence. By presenting a transvestite as one who both hides her essence while expanding readings of moral conduct to a larger public, Heldris, in fact, illustrates that transgression in attire need not necessarily be immoral. The private morality of one unlikely heroine gives rise to a public morality.[82] Transvestism, while a charged iconography, allows Heldris to position his protagonist as a mirror of both ideal female beauty and male chivalry, effectively using dress to interrogate as its primary goal not questions of gender but those of morality—a topic that preoccupied this thirteenth-century writer as well as the fourteenth-century poets of *Sir Gawain and the Green Knight* and the *Canterbury Tales*, as the following chapters will show.

CHAPTER THREE

The *Gawain*-Poet
Fashioning Penance in *Sir Gawain and the Green Knight*

The goods of fortune are adornments, honors, riches, pleasures, and pros-

perities; and in these, men sin in many ways by vainglory. For when a man is

raised so high in prosperity, he thinks first in his heart about his great dignity,

and afterwards on his wealth, riches, bodily pleasures, the great fellowship that

follows him, the many attractive people who serve him, his manors and castles,

the handsome horses and horsemen that remain with him, his beautiful robes

and expensive clothing that are of strange fashion and in great number.

—*The Book of Vices and Virtues*

The epigraph to this chapter draws from the late fourteenth-century *Book of Vices and Virtues* (ca. 1375), a vernacular penitential manual that provides clergy and laity with lessons on the Articles of the Faith, the Cardinal Sins and Virtues, and the tripartite structure of penance, which includes an explanation of contrition (sorrow in heart), confession (private, individual expression of sin to a priest), and satisfaction of sin (works designed to reconcile the penitent both with God and his or her immediate Christian community). In describing the gravest of the seven deadly sins, pride, with particular attention to its fifth branch, "vainglory," the *Book* asserts that vain men and women transgress because they glorify their "goods of fortune" more than God. Indeed, the *Book* continues, a man raised so high further thinks of:

> the arrangement of his house, housewares, bedding, and other furnishings that are attractive and valuable, great presents and gifts and the great feasts that men hold for him all around, and his good reputation and commendations that spread and vanish all around. Concerning these things, he comforts and glorifies himself as a wretch in his heart, so that he does not know he is a man. These are the twelve kinds of vainglory; that is to say, twelve varieties of temptations and more, of vainglory that they, who are of great estate in this world, have, whether they be religious, cleric, or unlearned man.[1]

All Christians are equally prone to this sin, of course, but the *Book* makes it clear that vainglory tempts especially those persons of high rank, whether religious or lay.

These temptations are also the very elements used to characterize the aristocracy in romance, as Marie de France and Heldris de Cornuälle have shown in their respective twelfth- and thirteenth-century poems. As one of the purportedly finest romances of the fourteenth century, *Sir Gawain and the Green Knight* (*SGGK*, hereafter) exhibits the tensions evoked when showcasing ornate fineries as important signs of courtliness within a Christian aristocratic milieu. Like other critics, Wendy Clein comments upon the conjunctions and disjunctions of worldly and divine systems of knightly behavior that color fourteenth-century experience. Knighthood was both "celebrated by heralds as a cultural ideal and upheld by moralists as an example of vice" because, as the *Book of Vices and Virtues* reflects, much that romance celebrates is condemned as the sin of pride.[2] Such a denunciation by the moralist depends upon understanding the lavish environment at court as an example of man's tendency toward excess and his subsequent degraded state of being. As the *Book* reminds us, to be seduced by these luxuries signifies a lack of self-knowledge, for the aristocrat of "great estate" is a "wretch in his heart, so that he does not know he is a man."

By the fourteenth century, men's and women's fashion became notably more distinctive due to the advent of plate armor. The thick unfitted tunics that were worn under the heavy chain mail characteristic of the Anglo-Saxon era gave way to snug padded suits tailored by linen-armorers, who followed the lines of the male physique through curved seams and rounded armholes.[3] Those styles, initially designed for ease of movement under armor, gradually became popular for aristocratic wear outside of combat, as exemplified historically by the *pourpoint* worn by Charles de Blois (1319–64), duke of Brittany and nephew to France's King Philippe VI (see fig. 2), and illustrated literally by the Green Knight, who enters Arthur's court wearing "[a] strayt cote ful stregt þat stek on his sides" [a close-fitting, constricting coat that clung to his sides] (line 152) and "[h]eme wel-haled hose of þat same grene, / Þat spenet on his sparlyr" [neat, well-drawn hose of that same green that clung to his calves] (lines 157–58).[4]

The *Gawain*-poet's engagement with popular styles and luxury garments as they appear in Arthur's and Bertilak's respective courts extends to his protracted consideration of the highly wrought, embroidered belt that bridges Camelot with Hautdesert and the chivalric with the spiritual. No less important than the novel sewing techniques that produced form-fitting dress in the mid-fourteenth century, intricate and imaginative embroidery on clothing and belts has been included as part of "the most startling manifestation of a completely new fashion" that marked the end of the 1350s in England and in France.[5] This chapter takes as its subject a small accessory that nevertheless serves as a great sign of a change in fashion and a change in conduct. In particular, I argue that Gawain's elaborate girdle enacts spiritual rehabilitation within courtly communities despite its excessive ornamentation and great values. Drawing upon a variety of histories, chronicles, and vernacular penitential manuals that view expensive attire in general and belts in particular as evidence of pride, I suggest that the *Gawain*-poet negotiates the generic demands of romance with spiritual concerns of penance. He recasts the girdle as a catalyst for religious conversion by positioning it as a penitential

Figure 2 Doublet, or *pourpoint*, of Charles de Blois. MT 30307. France, late fourteenth century. Musée des Tissus de Lyon. Photo Stephan Guillermond.

garment worn as the means to reconcile the individual to God and to the Christian community. In this way, the girdle, much like the penitential hairshirt, reminds sinners of past transgressions and prompts morally sound behavior.

Readings of the girdle run a wide gamut, from an article of clothing with magical life-saving properties to a love-token signaling sexual conquest, and I seek to contribute to these readings through an examination of the expensive, bejeweled girdle as a penitential garment that urges spiritual reform.[6] Embroidered and ornamented belts like Gawain's would often invite condemnation because clerics believed that they signified pride in attire and investment in worldly goods, as the following pages will show. Yet Gawain presents a unique view of the belt that rejects its monetary value and instead embraces both its life-saving properties and its penitential function to encourage contrition. The girdle marks Gawain's pride in himself (rather than his pride in objects) because he values his life more than any self-respecting knight should, yet he chooses not to reject the garment but rather to elevate its status to an expression of public penance that continually humbles his heart.

Some scholars have previously noted the penitential value of the girdle, but none has yet to read the belt as an important symbol of courtly life that nonetheless resonates with the popular expiatory practices defined in the vernacular spiritual guides and manifested in contemporary medieval literature.[7] John A. Burrow may be considered an exception to this claim because he argues that the girdle operates within "the traditional iconography of penance."[8] While Burrow notes that it resembles the penitential halter that sinners wear during public demonstrations of sin, he ultimately concludes that "the belt bears little resemblance to any of the accepted medieval 'arms of shrift'" and understands it simply as a "reminder" of Gawain's adventure.[9] The girdle certainly serves as a reminder, but it also emblematizes a complex intersection between expensive, highly wrought aristocratic items and Christian morality.

In figuring an object so strongly associated with courtly excess as a tool that expresses penance, the *Gawain*-poet demonstrates that courtly life and its symbols need not be jettisoned but rather reinvested with new, spiritually sound meaning. Indeed, this chapter argues that Gawain finally wears the girdle as a penitential garment, and in so doing his sartorial maneuver positions contrition, confession, and the satisfaction of sin in the same material register conventionally condemned by clerics. Such a strategy, which is not unlike Marie de France's (as explored in chapter 1), challenges the contemporary clerical view of clothing as an invitation to sin and recognizes proud attire—that is, dress that moralists see as luxurious and Gawain understands as a mark of pride—as both a means to encourage contrite and spiritually sound behavior and, when understood in this way, as a justification for lavish consumption.

A late fourteenth-century aristocratic audience of *SGGK* would have been quite used to the extravagances found in romance since its own milieu was likely punctuated with sumptuous displays similar to those of the notoriously rich court of Richard II.[10] In order thus to educate the nobility to conceive of worldly possessions in ways that would not exemplify pride, the *Gawain*-poet positions the girdle as a tool available to lay aristocrats as they attempt to find spiritual progress through material luxuries. No longer a mere lady's love-token— a common sign of fidelity between lovers in medieval French and English romances—the girdle becomes a religious sign of the penitential work known as satisfaction that bespeaks a contrite and absolved soul. In this role, the secular girdle appropriates sacred qualities, thus becoming a sartorial contribution to Malcolm Vale's notion of "the increasing sacralization of the secular."[11] This novel understanding of aristocratic attire, in turn, becomes a part of the *Gawain*-poet's "aristocratised theology," which teaches Christian doctrine by appealing to the interests and desires of readers who may have not only seen themselves "flatteringly embodied" in the nobility of *SGGK* but also owned a girdle as stunning as Gawain's.[12]

Gawain's Girdle: Item of Luxury or Sign of Pride?

Positioning *SGGK*'s ornate girdle as an article of pious behavior may seem to run counter to medieval views of luxurious belts as valuable accessories that usually express excessive wealth, pride, or martial weakness. Girdles or belts became standard features of late medieval attire for men and women, but while the laboring population wore belts made of leather, the rising gentry and aristocracy dressed in silk girdles more elaborately embroidered, bejeweled, and decorated with gold or silver than ever before.[13] Often read as indicators of social status, expensive belts appear as noteworthy sartorial accessories in England's 1363 sumptuary statute, one of several attempts to regulate particular styles for certain populations. For example, craftsmen and yeomen could wear neither "girdle, ring, garter . . . nor no such other things of gold nor of silver, nor no manner of apparel embroidered, aimeled [enameled], nor of silk by no way." Squires and gentlemen below the rank of knight had similar restrictions depending on their land wealth. They, too, could wear "no manner of clothing imbroidered . . . nor . . . girdle . . . of gold nor of silver."[14] Thomas Walsingham finds a similar restriction in the 1382 statute worthy of mention in his *Chronica maiora*. He finds especially pertinent the "prohibition of fur and silver workmanship in belts, etc., used by commons of inferior status" [de abrogacione pellure et apparatus argenti in zonis etc., a communibus status inferioris].[15] These various Acts of Apparel acknowledge that lawmakers sought to reserve gilded, silvered, embroidered, or ornamented girdles for wealthy aristocrats such as John of Gaunt and his nephew, King Richard II, whose account books reveal an interest in upholding social status through visual markers. For instance, John's 1381 entry notes payment to "Herman Goldesmyth" for a gold belt decorated with the letter "J" and a variety of metal links, while Richard's 1393–94 wardrobe expenses name the cost incurred by "Wynald Aurifaber" for gilding and decorating a variety of girdles.[16]

The finery that John of Gaunt and Richard II order from goldsmiths resonates with those rich textiles that appear as expressions of aristocratic wealth in *SGGK* and as signs of sin in late medieval sermons and penitential guides. At Hautdesert, Bertilak's wife gives Gawain a belt "gered . . . with grene sylke and with golde schaped, / Noȝt bot arounde brayden, beten with fyngrez" [adorned . . . with green silk, mounted with gold, embroidered around the edges, and inlaid with handiwork] (lines 1832–33). Much like the metal links that adorn John of Gaunt's belt, Gawain's girdle features "syde pendaundes" [side pendants] (line 2430) hanging from the belt's edges. These gems contribute to the belt's worth as a veritable "juel" [jewel] (line 1856) of clothing, a description that highlights the girdle as a "highly wrought art-object" valued for "þe costes þat knit ar þerinne" [the qualities that are knit therein] (line 1849), which include "golde" (line 2430), "sylk" (line 2431), "wlonk werkkez" [splendid handwork] (line 2432), and, perhaps most important to Gawain, protecting the wearer from harm.[17] This girdle, in addition to Bertilak's magnificent "enbrauded" [embroidered] (line 879) outer coat trimmed with fur (lines 878–81), and the "ryche robes" characterized memorably by flowing, "saylande skyrtez" [sailing skirts] (line 862) that Bertilak's men provide for Gawain to wear, bespeak a luxurious way of living that romance deems appropriate for courtiers, but that religious guides condemn as prideful indulgence.

A variety of fourteenth- and fifteenth-century religious guides destined for clergy and lay aristocracy typically situate luxurious dress, like the garments described by the *Gawain*-poet, as a sign of pride because those who clothe themselves in such finery wish to appear more worthy than others. The fifteenth-century English translation of *Speculum Christiani*, a fourteenth-century Latin compilation of Christian teachings, positions garments, in particular, as the first physical manifestation of prideful behavior when man "stryueȝ of hyer place" [strives for a higher rank]: "Euery proude man es intollerable, for hys clothynge es to ouere mych, hys goynge es proude, hys haterel vp-raysede, then proude loken and scorneful" [Every proud man is intolerable because his clothing is too excessive, his gait is proud, and with the crown of his head upraised, he looks around as if proud and scornful].[18] Where the *Speculum Christiani* condemns the superfluous excess of "ouere mych" garments, the *Memoriale Credencium* denounces "fair clothing." This fourteenth-century penitential manual, largely derived from William of Pagula's popular *Oculus sacerdotis* (ca. 1332), targets a privileged audience in its definition of pride: the sin occurs "whan a man holte himself more worthe þan eny oþer of his euen cristen and hit wexiþ in a mannes hert for dyuerse þyngus" [when a man believes himself to be more worthy than any other Christian, and pride grows in man's heart for a variety of things], which include knightly "strengþe of body," "noblesce of blode," "ricchesse," "grace and fauour of men," and *"faire cloþyng."*[19] So, too, does the late fourteenth-century analogue to Geoffrey Chaucer's *Parson's Tale,* the *Clensying of Mannes Sowle,* implicate a noble audience when highlighting vanity in man's desire for aristocratic trappings that include "temporel godes, . . . londes, . . . rentes, . . . gay housynge and *gay apparail* and worldely richesse."[20]

The notable early fifteenth-century unpublished penitential handbook, St. John's College, Cambridge, MS S 35, speaks to the social realities experienced by aristocrats and provides a view of how priests might interrogate the penitent's motivations for acquiring worldly goods that would, in turn, reflect high social standing. In the first section of the well-worn manual, which treats each of the seven deadly sins, beginning with pride, the text asks its reader: "Haue ȝe be proude alsoo of apparaile of your bodie and araid ȝe þe more gailye to haue a name and worchip of þe worlde[?] [Haue ȝe be proude also] of cloþinge, housinge, [and] possessione meyne[?]" [Have you been proud also of your clothing and dressed yourself more gaily in order to make a name for yourself and show that you worship worldly goods? Have you been proud also in dress, housing, and in having many possessions?][21] In posing such questions, these Middle English penitentials insist that fine apparel emblematizes vice, a position that the *Gawain*-poet, too, will initially espouse but ultimately reject as he transforms the girdle from an article that would indicate sin to one that prompts contrition.

As pedagogical tools, religious guides as well as sermons attempt to restrain the social behavior of individuals who wear fashionable dress by insisting on sartorial reform as a precursor to moral reform. Just as vernacular religious guides maintain that "faire cloþyng" evokes sin, so do a variety of homilies find excessive expenditures on aristocratic attire as equally transgressive. A late fourteenth-century clergyman bemoans "the estaat of knyȝthode" that participates in "this foule synne of pride" because knights require even their least experienced page to be outfitted in clothing decorated with pearls and fur, which costs more than half of the knight's income in one year.[22] The concern over extravagant expenditures also appears in the sermons of Robert Rypon, who preaches in the time of the *Gawain*-poet and cites particularly costly textiles that express wealth and moral degeneracy: "as their pride grew, men used . . . silken garments which are fashioned from the entrails of worms . . . [more] for vain-glory and worldly pomp than for the necessity of nature, diversely decorated as it were in an infinite variety of ways."[23] For an anonymous sermonist preaching about penance on Ash Wednesday, "garments with decorated edges, pointed shoes, short clothes that hardly cover their loins" mark the fashions of those serving a house steward personified as Pride.[24] These embellishments, just like those in Rypon's sermon, become the focus of Chaucer's Parson's disapproval of the economic implications of dress in *The Canterbury Tales*. When describing pride "in superfluitee of clothynge," which should ultimately be abandoned, the Parson criticizes

> nat oonly the cost of embrowdynge, the degise endentynge or barrynge, owndynge, palynge, wyndynge or bendynge, and semblable wast of clooth in vanitee, / but . . . also costlewe furrynge in hir gownes, so muche pownsonynge of chisels to maken holes, so muche daggynge of sheres. (X.417–18)
>
> —
>
> [not only the cost of embroidering, the ostentatious notching of the borders or ornamenting with decorative strips, undulating stripes, vertical stripes, folding, or decorative borders, and similar waste of cloth in vanity, but . . . also [the] costly fur trimming on their gowns, so much punching designs with blades to make holes, so much slitting with shears].[25]

By condemning as wasteful the unnecessary decoration of cloth, the money used to purchase the fabric, and the manpower to create the garment, the Parson indicts the aristocracy for their extravagance.

The aforementioned concerns that appear in medieval literature derive in part from contemporary events described in historical documents. Kay Staniland cites an instance in Edward III's Great

Wardrobe account of the years 1350–52, where the king ordered the work of over eighteen craftsmen and women to create an outfit for the feast of Saint George. She notes that it took over 403 working days to create two sumptuous supertunics and one tunic and to embroider meticulously a cloak with "silver clouds and eagles of pearls and gold—that is, under every alternate cloud an eagle of pearls, and under every other cloud an eagle having in its beak a garter embroidered with the words of the King's motto *hony soit qe mal y pense* [shame to him who thinks evil of it]."[26] Such superfluity in attire becomes the focus of the moralists' reading of excessive pride. Richard Lavynham, a Carmelite friar contemporary with Chaucer, worries in his *Litil Tretys on the Seven Deadly Sins* that the extravagantly dressed individual "þenkyth þat alle oþer men scholde hym worschipe" [believes that all other men should worship him] instead of focusing his energies on his devotion to God.[27] Likewise, the *Memoriale Credencium* reminds its readers that individuals indulge in sin when they present themselves "with pompe and vayne glorie with nobul atyre þe more for to be byholde of þe puple þan for deuocioun to god" [with pomp and vainglory with their noble attire, worn more for people to behold, rather than for devotion to God].[28] Penitent individuals, so the guides assert, should jettison "superfluitee" [excess] in clothing in favor of metaphorically clothing the soul with good works.

The concern that luxurious attire bespeaks an inordinate concern for personal worth is part of a larger understanding of prideful garments—like the belt Gawain accepts from Bertilak's wife because he believes it will save his life—as indicators of spiritual infirmity that jeopardize the national welfare. In a variety of clerical histories, ornamented girdles play a particularly important role as an accessory that indicates immoral tendencies. Worn by nobles bound to military service, expensive belts convey a knight's martial weakness rather than his privileged status. For instance, the "Complainte de la bataille de Poitiers," a ninety-six-line poem written by a clergyman at the cathedral of Notre-Dame in Paris, describes a belt in its recounting of the humiliating defeat suffered by the French in 1356 when their king, John II, was captured by England's Edward the Black Prince. Since John had mobilized the best of his army and still lost the battle, contemporary accounts speculate that the king was betrayed by his own men. The "Complainte" endorses such a position and notes, in no uncertain terms, that John's knights channeled too much energy into their appearance and not enough into defending the realm:

> Bonbanz et vaine gloire, vesture deshoneste,
> Les ceintures dorées, la plume sur la teste,
> La grant barbe de bouc, qui est une orde beste,
> Les vous font estordiz comme fouldre et tempeste.
> Tels gens ou reigne orgueil qui est si vil péché
> Sont de touz mauvais vices et d'ordure entéché;
> Touz temps seront traistres, puis qu'il sont aléché,
> Car touz les bens de grace sont en euls asséché.
> Or voient comme orgueil et leur grant surcuidance
> Et leur haute manière en honeur les avance!
>
> (lines 25–34)

———

[Arrogance and vainglory, improper clothing, golden belts, feathers on heads, (and) a large beard of a goat, which is a filthy beast, stuns you as (if hit by) lightning and a storm. Such people, in whom reigns pride, which is such a sordid sin, are marked by all bad vices and filth. They will be traitors all of the time, since they are seduced, because all of the goods of grace are dried up in them. Now they see how pride and their great presumption and their haughty airs of honor push them forward.][29]

Citing "vesture deshoneste" [improper clothing] and "ceintures dorées" [golden belts], the cleric figures these knights as "traistres" [traitors] because they do not adequately defend their king from the English. Their pride, presumption, and airs, which the poet expresses visibly by dress, in general, and belts, in particular, evoke sin that not only endangers the well-being of the soul but also that of the realm.

Whereas the writer of the "Complainte" stresses the prideful effects of dress, Carmelite friar Jean de Venette (ca. 1307–70) notes that bejeweled girdles encourage idle and lustful comportment in his *Chronicle* (ca. 1359–60) of contemporary events in France. The offending aristocrats, who "wore pearls . . . on their gilded and silver girdles and elaborately adorned themselves from head to foot with gems and precious stones," were not interested in martial pursuits, but rather "by night they devoted themselves immoderately to the pleasures of the flesh or to games of dice; by day, to ball or tennis."[30] The concern expressed by the French clerics finds a counterpart in England, where the Monk of Malmesbury conveys similar anxiety in 1362 about "the whole English community [that] is turned in such frenzy and elation, raging in physical accoutrements" [tota communitas Anglicana versa est in tantam rabiem et elationem in ornamentis corporeis sæviendo], which include "gilded and silvered belts of great price" [cingulas aureas, argenteas, magno pretio]. More attuned to fine physical appearance than engagement in military exploits, those men who wear such belts "are judged more to be scamps and idlers than barons, more actors than soldiers, more mimes than arms-bearers" [potius judicantur citherones et nebulones quam barones, histriones quam milites, mimi quam armigeri]. Furthermore, the Monk of Malmesbury warns, these same belted individuals may fall prey to the seven capital vices, especially wrath, pride, lust, and gluttony.[31] In England and on the Continent, the predominant clerical position articulated in various chronicles suggests that the nobility's interest in expensive girdles places at risk the spiritual salvation of the individual and, by extension, the security of one's country. These texts provide a moral backdrop to medieval romance that casts a shadow on the elegant clothing that the genre demands for its protagonists.

A turn now to vernacular books of chivalric conduct may shed light on other equally important readings of aristocratic attire because these texts, like romances, consider belts as an indispensible accessory to knights as they defend their lords and lands. Ramon Llull's *Book of the Order of Chivalry* (*Libre que es de l'ordre de cavalleria*, initially composed in Catalan ca. 1280) became the most popular vernacular manual for knights and served as the source for Geoffroi de Charny's early fourteenth-century *Livre de l'ordre de chevalerie* and William Caxton's fifteenth-century Middle English *Ordre de Chyualry*.[32] Drawing on the notion of arming oneself against vice with the virtue of faith in Christ, as Paul articulates in Ephesians 6:10–17, all three texts describe battle gear and weaponry as having spiritual import: a knight's sword defeats enemies of the Cross, while the helmet signifies modesty and the hauberk protects him from vice.

Geoffroi's *Livre*, however, stands out as a notable text among these three with respect to *SGGK* for several reasons. First, French historian Jean de Froissart, who was employed at England's royal court and heard firsthand accounts about the Battle of Poitiers where Geoffroi lost his life, commends him as "the most worthy and valiant [knight] of them all" [le plus preudomme et le plus vailant de tous les autres].[33] Second, Geoffroi views medieval chivalric practices from the perspective of an arduous fighter called to defend his king, much like Gawain is summoned to serve Arthur. Third, Geoffroi writes as a layman, and he thus elaborates on worldly chivalric behavior in ways that do not concentrate predominantly on the religious symbolism of knighthood, unlike Ramon Llull's work, which addresses the customs of a knight largely in terms of faith, hope, and charity.[34] And fourth, the *Livre* includes a particularly social understanding of attire in its description of the knighting ceremony, while Llull's *Book* and its French and English translations do not—a point that is significant for *SGGK* because it too, I argue, seeks to reach a lay audience that embraces aristocratic accoutrements as essential to appropriate knightly behavior.

Likely composed in the mid-fourteenth century around the time of John II's founding of his Company of the Star (a chivalric order of which Geoffroi was an initial member), which was created to rival Edward III's Order of the Garter (whose motto appears at the conclusion of *SGGK*), Geoffrey's *Livre* posits foremost a direct correlation between repentance of sin, dress, and a community of knights. For Geoffroi, the connection between virtue, dress, and knightly brotherhood begins with bathing and dressing novice knights before their induction:

> Then the knights should come to the beds to dress those to be knighted; the stuff in which they dress them, the linen and all that goes with it should be new: this signifies that just as the body of each one should be cleansed of all the impurities of sin, so should it be clothed

in new, white, and clean material, signifying that they should all from henceforth keep themselves pure and free from sin.

—

[Puis doivent venir les chevaliers au lit pour vestir yceulz et les doivent vestir de neufs draps, linges et toutes choses neuves qui y appartiennent en segnefiant que, ainsi comme le corps de celli doit estre nettoiez de toute ordure de pechié, le revest l'on des draps blans et neufs et nez en segnefiance que des lors en la se doivent tenir nettement et sanz pechié.]

Outward markers of the inductees's physical continence complement these white garments, worn next to the body and thus unseen. Novices wear "a white belt" [une courroie toute blanche] to indicate "chastity and purity of the flesh" [de chasteté et de netteté de corps] around a red tunic, which signifies "that they are pledged to shed their blood to defend and maintain the faith," and black hose, which serves as a reminder that they will return to the earth in death.[35] Geoffroi illustrates the primacy of community, both religious and aristocratic, by having veteran knights dress the inductees, bringing white linen, a red robe, and black hose to each new brother in arms. They gird the novices in their white belts; they lead them to mass; they then shepherd the group to the ceremony. In the hands of more experienced knights, chivalric attire functions as a metonym for the novice's sacred commitment in two distinct realms: the more immediate community of his fellow knights, and that of the larger Christian world.

Despite figuring a knight's belt, tunic, and undergarment as sacred signs of service to one's chivalric and Christian community, Geoffroi is not unaware of the temptations that these worldly delights could pose to knights. Consequently he articulates the very concerns that appear in the penitential manuals regarding dress by warning those with financial resources who

want to spend it all on adorning their wretched bodies and on decking themselves out with precious stones, pearls, fine work, and embroidery, which cost so much and are worth so little, and on buying the rings on their fingers and great belts of gold and silver of which the

workmanship costs many times more than the gold or silver of which
they are made.

———

[il veulent mettre en leurs povres corps aourner et parer de pierres, de
perles, d'ouvrages et de brodure qui tant coustent cher et si po valent,
et les aneaux en leurs dois et les grosses courroies d'or ou d'argent, dont
li ouvraiges coustent plus moult de foiz que ne fait l'or ou l'argent de
quoy elles sont faites.]

Geoffroi explains that adorning their "wretched bodies" with gems,
pearls, and large silver or gold belts distracts knights from considering
their chivalric responsibilities of service, humility, and honor:

> the excessive adornments with which they deck themselves out make
> them neglect to perform many great deeds; and there are many who for-
> get all shame, and just as they forget all shame, so is all honor forgotten;
> this can be seen in various forms of behavior, which is a great pity.
>
> ———
>
> [les outrages des ornemens dessus diz qu'il mettent sur eulz leur font
> oublier moult de biens a faire, et maintes en y a qui oublient toutes hon-
> tez; et ainsi comme il oublient toutes hontes, ainsi sont obliez toutes
> honnours, et bien peut apparoir en pluseurs manieres, dont c'est pitiez
> et domages.][36]

Despite Geoffroi's condemnation, he concedes that there is no reason for young men not to be dressed "decently, neatly, [and] ele-
gantly," as long as they do so "with due restraint" [faitissement et
joliement sanz grant outrage]. As if to recall the sartorial strategy of
Marie de France, described in chapter 1, Geoffroi promotes elegant
dress, as long as knights temper their desires for fashion with the performance of virtuous deeds while remaining mindful of God:

> for it is right that people should behave, each according to their years,
> provided so much be not devoted to adornment of the body that the
> more important things remain undone, that is to say, great and good
> deeds. And if anyone is thus elegantly dressed and in good fashion, as

befits a young man, it should not be done through pride nor should Our Lord be forgotten; but be careful not to spruce yourself up so much that you do not remember God.

—

[car raisons est que l'on se gouverne selon les ages, mes que l'on ne mette mie tant sur le corps de li que li plus demoure a faire, c'est a entendre le bien. Et s'il est ainsi que l'on soit jolis ainsi et en bonne maniere comme il affiert a joennes gens, si ne le doit l'en mie faire pour orgueil ne oublier Nostre Seigneur, mais garder de tant cointir que Dieux vous face oublier.][37]

As a practitioner of chivalric duty and honor himself, Geoffroi is well aware of the secular and spiritual demands placed on a man-at-arms, and for that reason he supports fashionable dress as long as it is worn without pride, with commitment to community, and while thinking of God.

Geoffroi's *Livre* becomes an important text to read alongside *SGGK* because it serves as a foundation of ideal chivalric and spiritual behaviors that the romance builds upon. In particular, *SGGK* expands Geoffroi's multivalent understanding of a luxurious belt that expresses both spiritually sound behavior and an individual's reinsertion into the community by using it as a tool to prompt Gawain's introspective turn. Rhetorically, the *Gawain*-poet accomplishes such a broadening of Geoffroi's position by first asserting a fundamental relationship between Gawain, the girdle, and the concept of "vylany." An important word in Arthurian literature—from *Arthur and Merlin* in the early fourteenth century to Thomas Malory's *Morte d'Arthur* in the fifteenth century—"vylany's" definition bridges missteps in courtly manners with immoral behavior.[38] It denotes both "the state and condition of being a thrall to sin" and "discourtesy," the latter of which would be first expressed if Gawain were to rise and meet the Green Knight's initial challenge without consent from his king.[39] Instead, Gawain respectfully requests permission from Arthur to answer the Green Knight's call to a beheading game. His appeal to Arthur, "Bid me boȝe fro þis benche and stonde by yow þere, / Þat I wythoute vylanye myȝt voyde þis table" [Let me come from this bench and stand by you there so that I may leave this table without villainy] (lines 344–45), thus exemplifies an awareness of chivalric responsibility.[40]

The meaning of "vylany" as chivalric dishonor soon shifts to a sense of moral failure when the poet deploys the term to examine two entities that appear as "juels" in the text: Gawain, and the girdle. At the end of the *effictio* describing the arming of the warrior, a simile likens Gawain to a precious metal as he prepares to leave Camelot in search of the Green Knight: "Gawan watz for gode knawen and, as golde pured, / Voyded of vuche vylany, with vertuez ennourned" [Gawain was known for his goodness and, as refined gold, he was void of every villainy, adorned with virtues] (lines 634–35). The text depicts Gawain dressed in "godlych gere" [fine gear] (line 585), "with vertuez ennourned" [adorned with virtues], thus correlating ethically sound chivalric conduct with magnificent ornament. Like refined gold, Gawain's virtue is free of dross and thereby bespeaks the moral perfection associated with "purity."[41] The poet further affirms this spiritual excellence by using "vertuez" as the last alliteration to expand the appositive "Voyded of vuche vylany." Gawain, analogous to "pure" gold, thus appears as a prized object, with virtue rhetorically adorning his body.[42]

In the second instance where "vylany" appears with respect to the girdle, Gawain evaluates his behavior in ethical terms that connect spiritual shortcomings with sartorial sin. Gawain finds himself face to face with the Green Knight, who has revealed himself as Bertilak, the husband to the woman who persistently tried to seduce Gawain and the architect of the plan to test Gawain's chivalric and moral worth. In a moment commonly referred to as the second confession scene, the first of which occurs after Gawain accepts the girdle from Bertilak's wife but before he leaves Hautdesert to meet his death by the Green Knight's axe,[43] Gawain displays contrition as he "schrank for schome" [flinched on account of shame] (line 2372) and acknowledges that his moral fiber has been compromised by cowardice and covetousness, in which are villainy and vice:

> "Corsed worth cowarddyse and couetyse boþe!
> In yow is vylany and vyse, þat vertue disstryez."

Þenne he kaȝt to þe knot and þe kest lawsez,
Brayde broþely þe belt to þe burne seluen:
"Lo! Þer þe falssyng—foule mot hit falle!"
(lines 2374–78)

———

["Cursed be cowardice and covetousness both! In you are villainy and
vice, that destroy virtue." Then he took hold of the knot and loosened
it, flung the belt violently towards that man: "Lo! There is that false
thing—let it fall into vileness!"]

Following the Green Knight's accusation that Gawain "lufed [his]
lyf" (line 2368), and Gawain's subsequent "greme" [anger] that he
feels "withinne" (line 2370), Gawain draws upon both chivalric and
moral contexts in his outburst, "In yow is vylany and vyse, þat vertue
disstryez." This bitter accusation may also be read as directed at Gawain himself: because he has coveted his life, and because covetousness was regarded in the later Middle Ages as one of the capital sins,
Gawain's villainy registers morally.[44] Since he has withheld the girdle
from Bertilak and betrayed their covenant to exchange all goods received during each of their three days at Hautdesert, Gawain's villainy
appears uncourtly. By following the condemnation of cowardice and
covetousness with a description of Gawain's violent rejection of the
girdle and his subsequent denunciation of it as false and vile, the poet
suggests an understanding of the girdle as a bridge between the moral
and the chivalric. Consonant with contemporary views of luxurious
belts that connect sumptuous attire with pride, as in the "Complainte
de la Bataille de Poitiers" and the histories of Jean de Venette and the
Monk of Malmesbury, the *Gawain*-poet positions Gawain's girdle as
an index of chivalric frailty that eventually gives way to sin. Covetousness and cowardice may be human characteristics that destroy virtue
but so, too, are they linked with the very object that Gawain has accepted from Bertilak's wife. In his disapproval of the girdle, Gawain
registers a similar self-understanding that sumptuous attire and what
it represents may destroy a knight's virtue.

Such a view of luxurious attire has not to this point been of interest to Gawain, for he has a unique understanding of the belt that

has nothing to do with fashion and everything to do with saving his own life. The origins of Gawain's self-indictment as villainous and vice-ridden depend on the knight's initial misinterpretation of the girdle's value for its life-saving properties. During Bertilak's wife's third attempt at seducing Gawain, she offers him a ring, which the knight refuses because he has nothing of equal value to give in exchange. Because she knows that Gawain will decline any gift that seems too rich (line 1827), she downplays the value of her belt, qualifying her offer of a second gift as "vnworþi" [unworthy] (line 1835), "symple" (line 1847), and "littel" (line 1848) despite its green silk, gold decorations, and extensive embroidery (lines 1832–33). Instead, she highlights the belt's "qualities knit therein" (line 1849) [þe costes þat knit ar þerinne], namely, its life-saving properties that appear so attractive to Gawain. He accepts the girdle in the hope that it will protect him when he bares his neck before the Green Knight's axe:

> Þen kest þe knyȝt, and hit come to his hert
> Hit were a juel for þe jopardé þat hym jugged were:
> When he acheued to þe chapel his chek for to fech,
> Myȝt he haf slypped to be vnslayn þe sleȝt were noble.
> (lines 1855–58)
>
> ——
>
> [Then the knight reflected and it came to his heart that the girdle would be a jewel for the hazard assigned to him when he reached the chapel to receive his doom; could he escape not killed, the skill would be noble.]

Gawain's decision to take the belt appears heartfelt. Yet his understanding of the girdle as a life-saving talisman reveals a grave misstep in chivalric conduct, which deems desire for life and fear of dying dishonorable.[45]

Gawain's acceptance of the belt for its life-preserving properties affirms what scholars have suggested is either his greed or his pride for life.[46] As a branch of avarice, the covetousness that Gawain invokes when he realizes his missteps at the Green Knight's chapel (and that the poet invokes on several other occasions) may be understood as a result of Gawain's fear of death and thereby greed for his life, as Richard Newhauser has convincingly argued.[47] Yet the text also persists in identifying pride and its branch, "sourquydrye" [presumption], as defining traits of the Knights of the Round Table. When the Green Knight finds Arthur's knights unresponsive to his invitation to exchange axe strokes, he questions their "sourquydrye" (line 311) and "gryndellayk" [ferocity] (line 312). Toward the end of the narrative, after the Green Knight has revealed himself as Bertilak, he tells Gawain that Morgan la Faye prompted him "to assay þe surquidré" [to test the presumption] (line 2457) of the Round Table. In between these two moments that bookend the poem, Arthur's court bemoans the knight's impending death, citing Gawain's "angardez pryde" [arrogant pride] (line 681) as the reason for his departure to find the Green Knight. That both the poem and its critics move between pride and avarice to identify Gawain's fault may attest to a medieval awareness of the variable and fluid relationship between these sins.[48] While avarice may have been supplanting pride as the deadliest of sins, *SGGK* nonetheless consistently engages pride and its subcategory, presumption, in both its chivalric ethos and its reliance on the luxurious girdle that persists as evidence of pride in contemporary medieval literature.

By reading the girdle as a metonym for Gawain's pride for life, the poet first situates Gawain's behavior within a long-standing clerical tradition concerning dress and pride that is punctuated by works such as Gregory the Great's *Homiliae in Evangelia*, Thomas Aquinas's *Summa theologiae*, and the *Book of Vices and Virtues*. Gawain's behavior is similar to that which Gregory the Great (ca. 590) warns against, but with an important distinction. Gregory writes: "Nobody, of course, seeks special garments unless he seeks glory in relation to vanity, namely, in order that he may be seen to be more honorable than others."[49] *SGGK* has Gawain seeking glory by escaping the Green Knight's axe unharmed, an act that Gawain considers a "noble sleȝt" (line 1858) and that would certainly command the honor of Camelot. Gawain's indulgence in fashionable excess thus appears motivated by the kind of pride for life acknowledged by Thomas Aquinas: "the inordinate desire for goods, which involves overcoming an obstacle, belongs to the pride of life, in the sense that pride is an inordinate attraction for some kind of superiority."[50] Might it be that Gawain, Arthur's envoy who represents Camelot, believes that he must show himself superior to the Green Knight's axe so as to answer Morgan la Faye's testing of the Round Table's "surquidré?"

While the poem may not articulate Gawain's superiority, it arguably demonstrates it through the knight's self-sacrificing decision to play the Green Knight's decapitation game and through the public's tearful farewell to the "semly syre" [fair lord] (line 685) in full battle regalia as he leaves the court. These demonstrations of superiority become a personal manifestation of Gawain's pride when he accepts the lady's girdle because it would help him overcome the obstacle posed by the Green Knight's axe. Eventually, though, Gawain will come to understand the girdle as a sign of his own transgressions, which the Green Knight emphasizes when accusing him of having both "lakked a lyttel" (line 2366) and "lufed [his] lyf" (line 2368). If Gawain sins because he esteems his life over another man's, which is the way in which the *Book of Vices and Virtues* defines pride, then one remedy would involve first relinquishing the garment and then clothing oneself metaphorically in humility and in service to God.[51] Gawain, however, chooses not to give it up. Understanding full well that lay folk, unlike monks, cannot jettison the signs and symbols of courtly life, the *Gawain*-poet instead repositions the girdle in a different interpretive paradigm. He shows that the aristocracy can reinvest courtly dress with new spiritually sound significances, which is exactly what Gawain will do after leaving the Green Knight and Hautdesert.

The Girdle as a Penitential Garment

In a move that describes the extreme luxury and value of the girdle, the poet does not allow it merely to represent the evils of extravagant aristocrats that clerics would highlight or the proper standard of attire in a literary trope that a romancier would employ. Instead, as a vernacular theologian, the *Gawain*-poet keeps elements of both while recasting the girdle's significance to one of penance:

"Bot your gordel," quoþ Gawayn, "—God yow forȝelde!—
Þat wyl I welde wyth guod wylle, not for þe wynne golde,
Ne þe saynt, ne þe sylk, ne þe syde pendaundes,
For wele ne for worchyp, ne for þe wlonk werkkez;
Bot in syngne of my surfet I schal se hit ofte,
When I ride in renoun remorde to myseluen
Þe faute and þe fayntyse of þe flesche crabbed,
How tender hit is to entyse teches of fylþe.
And þus, quen pryde schal me pryk for prowes of armes,
Þe loke to þis luf-lace schal leþe my hert."

                                        (lines 2429–38)

———

["But for your girdle," said Gawain, "God repay you for that! I will accept it with good will—not for its precious gold, nor the girdle itself,
nor the silk, nor the side pendants, nor the honor it confers, nor for the
splendid handwork. But I shall look on it often as a sign of my excess
and, when I ride to be esteemed by others, recall with remorse the fault
and the corruption of the perverse flesh—how tender it is to attract
spots of filth. And thus, when pride shall prick me for prowess in arms,
a glance to this love-lace will humble my heart."]

Gawain accepts the garment gratefully but rejects its association with
riches and honor, instead adopting it so that he may look at it often
as a sign of his "pryde" when he "ride[s] in renown." His reasons for
rejecting it resonate with an exemplum in an important fourteenth-
century penitential guide, *Speculum Vitae*. Like Gawain, *Speculum Vitae*'s
Queen Hester distances herself from the opulence of "riche robes"
(line 10,593) associated with her office: she has

    . . . na lykyng in riche apparaylle
    Of precious stanes ne of gold rede,
    Nouthir on body ne on hede.
    Bot it es to [her] abhomynable,
    For it may make mens hertes vnstable.

                                        (lines 10,604–8)

———

[no desire for rich apparel, for precious stones, nor of pure gold, neither on the body nor on the head. But it is to (her) abominable because it may make men's hearts unstable.][52]

Since she sees such adornment as evidence of "þe tokenyng of Pryde" (line 10,602), much like Gawain will later conceive of his garment as a "token of vntrawþe" (line 2509), Hester puts "hir riche apparaylle away, / When sho bifore Godde come to pray" (lines 10,597–98). The abomination that she finds in adornment ceases to be a factor for Gawain, for where Hester distances herself from luxury, Gawain fastens it tightly across his body. In this way, the *Gawain*-poet embraces sartorial splendor as a means of prompting self-reflection in light of sin: a "look to the girdle will humble his heart." This moment of introspection is more poignant and important than the first time a consideration of the belt "c[a]me to his hert" (line 1855) in the company of Bertilak's wife. In this second instance, the poet places the reflexive turn in the first person, rather than in the third, which initially announced the girdle as a "jewel for the jeopardy" (line 1856) that Gawain was to experience.

This shift of voice mirrors a move to Gawain's self-consciousness as he grapples with ethical questions of courtly behavior that arise when considering the impact of his private affair on his public persona at Hautdesert.[53] After realizing his missteps at the Green Knight's chapel, Gawain first acknowledges his pride and then situates the girdle as a remedy for the sin that clerics often associate with sumptuous attire. As a result, the poet solicits a reinterpretation of Gawain's initial understanding of the belt as a "juel for þe jopardé," for which he is judged by the Green Knight. Alliteration underscores the earthly quality of the belt as a "juel," its connection to danger ("jopardé"), and the Green Knight's judgment of Gawain's pride for life. The girdle's elegance announces the danger that Gawain's pride invites, but in looking to the girdle to humble his heart, Gawain recasts this sign of extravagance into one of virtue. Aristocratic wealth in attire may be the means to penitential ends.

Late medieval penitential practices provide a framework that informs Gawain's innovative use of courtly attire. After hearing Gawain's confession, Bertilak pardons him and assigns him "public penance" by nicking his neck with his axe:

"Þou art confessed so clene, beknowen of þy mysses,
And hatz þe penaunce apert of þe poynt of myn egge,
I halde þe polysed of þat plyȝt and pured as clene
As þou hadez neuer forfeted syþen þou watz first borne."

(lines 2391–94)

———

["You have so cleanly confessed, admitted your faults, and have public penance from the edge of my sword. I declare you absolved of that offense, and washed as clean as if you had never transgressed since you were first born."]

This "penaunce apert" has not always been acknowledged by modern translators of the poem: James Winny calls it "honest," Marie Borroff understands it as "plain," and some choose not to recognize it at all.[54] Given the context of confession, "apert" denotes public penance in particular, as opposed to the private penance that became increasingly popular after the Fourth Lateran Council of 1215. In the early Christian church, public penance existed as a dramatic ritual of purification performed once in a lifetime when sinners would voluntarily don sackcloth and ashes and walk barefoot until they were welcomed back into the church and absolved.[55] The severe and rigid nature of this public penance, which was termed solemn or canonical, and the consequence that penitents could never marry, hold public office, or become clerics arguably led to a decline in this practice.[56] Canon 21 of Lateran IV further accelerated the shift from public to private penance because it mandated annual auricular confession for all people, under pain of excommunication. Despite the emphasis on private penance after 1215, public penance remained a means of expiation well into the fourteenth century: penitents could refuse communion (they were forbidden to partake of the Eucharist in a state of sin), go on pilgrimages (like the pilgrims in Chaucer's *Canterbury Tales*) so as to become reconciled to the church, or wear garments such as goatskin, sackcloth, or hairshirts as physical reminders of the spiritual torments of sin.[57]

In describing Gawain's neck gash, the Green Knight provides Gawain with a particularly public punishment that resonates with a literary rendition of penance as a figurative prick in the flesh from a pick-axe in Henry of Lancaster's *Livre de seyntz medicines,* a sequence of confessions and devotional writings that the highly esteemed knight produces in 1354 for his friends and perhaps a wider readership. In his exposition on repentance, Henry writes: "adonqes covient le pik q'est ou diaux poyntz: l'un poynt si doit ferir en terre, c'est en ma char par poignantes penances; et l'autre, par dout de la peyne d'enfern" [therefore the pick-axe, which has two points, promises one point which must hit the earth, that is to say in my flesh with prickly penances; and the other, without doubt is the pain of hell].[58] Henry describes a symbolic wound that the *Gawain*-poet literalizes on his hero's neck: the Green Knight "homered heterly" [struck fiercely] (line 2311), but "hurt hym no more" except where he "seuered þe hyde" [severed his skin] (line 2312). Henry's *Livre* provides a valuable context for *SGGK* because of its dramatization of orthodox Christianity and chivalric life. Like the well-reputed Sir Gawain, Henry of Lancaster is, according to chronicler Jean Froissart, "si bon chevalier et si recommandé" [such a good knight and so highly recommended], "moult noble et très gentil de cœur" [most noble and very gentle of heart], "aimé de tous ses amis et ressoingné de tous ses ennemis" [loved by all his friends and respected by all his enemies].[59] Not without an awareness of his sinful nature, this noble and gentle-hearted knight features himself as a character in a vernacular penitential manual designed to instruct its aristocratic readers on the seven deadly sins, which manifest themselves as figurative bodily "wounds" [plaies] (line 210), and their remedies.[60]

In teaching his audience about the cardinal sins by describing chivalric excesses in feasting and attire as occasions for transgression, Henry presents a disjunction between the generic conventions of romance and the penitential that the *Gawain*-poet would likely not find problematic. According to Clein, "Where romance emphasizes visual spectacle and culinary refinement, the penitent dwells on excess."[61] Henry believes that the transformation from chivalric to spiritual knighthood must necessarily entail a rejection of courtly finery, a position that remains orthodox teaching in vernacular penitentials. In negotiating demands of romance with clerical didacticism, the *Gawain*-poet proposes an alternative way of dealing with aristocratic luxury in light of Christian ideologies. Material signs of courtly life in *SGGK* need not be jettisoned but simply reinterpreted. Take, for instance, the nick in the neck that Gawain receives because he transgresses. Unlike Henry's figurative pick-axe wound that represents sin, Gawain's expresses the sacrament— penance—that rehabilitates the soul. After his wound heals, Gawain repositions the girdle as a garment with rehabilitative properties.

Now with the belt as a public manifestation of satisfaction, the *Gawain*-poet manipulates sartorial motifs much like Henry of Lancaster, but to different ends. Where Henry draws on one of the Seven Joys of the Virgin as a means to infuse his figurative bodily wounds with the holy medicine of joy to heal sin, Gawain incorporates Marian iconography in conjunction with the popular understanding of belts as signs of faith. The *Gawain*-poet invokes Mary as Gawain's protector, most obviously by featuring her image on the inside of his shield. Yet the Virgin's presence persists in a more subtle way by her association with belts and, by extension, with Gawain's girdle. Richard Firth Green notes a medieval iconographical tradition likely known by the *Gawain*-poet's audience that depicts the Holy Mother leaning from heaven and giving Saint Thomas her girdle in order to resolve any doubt in his mind about the miracle of her Assumption.[62] Like Mary's belt, which fittingly appears green and bejeweled in a fourteenth-century stained-glass window in Beckley, Oxfordshire (see fig. 3, facing p. 122), Gawain's girdle operates as a transformative, penitential garment. It promotes works that restore the soul to its unblemished state, thus reconciling the penitent to both God and his or her community.

Though his wound eventually disappears, the public nature of Gawain's penance does not. Rather, the healing of his wound coincides with his learning to read sartorial markers of courtly life in appropriate ways. Specifically, Gawain conceives of the girdle as a peni - tential garment that expresses satisfaction of sin. Vernacular guides of medieval penance most often describe elements of satisfaction as prayer, fasting with respect to food and sex, and the giving of alms. However, at least two penitentials, the *Clensyng of Mannes Sowle* and Chaucer's *Parson's Tale*, feature "bodily peyne" (*Parson's Tale* X.1038) derived from the harshness of penitential clothing on bare skin. Understood as the means "to put awey or voide þe cause of synnes, & to take none hede of here sugestiouns" [to put away or abstain from the cause of sins and to ignore their suggestions] (the *Clensyng*) and to convey "a pitous wyl of herte, that redresseth it in God and expresseth it . . . outward" [a pious will of heart that directs itself to God and expresses it . . . outward] (*Parson's Tale* X.1039), sartorial satisfaction functions in two ways: first, as the humiliating impetus to "put awey" sin; and, second, as an outward expression of a pious heart.[63] As such, both the *Clensyng* and the *Parson's Tale* embody the dual sense of the Latinate definition for penance (*penitentia*), which comprises acts of feeling both "sorwe for . . . synne" (*Parson's Tale* X.85) and "peyne for . . . giltes" (*Parson's Tale* X.86) or, as Mary Mansfield puts it, "both the sinner's saving contrition and the satisfactory penalty imposed."[64]

In vowing to wear the girdle as a "sign of his surfeit" [Bot in syngne of my surfet I schal se hit ofte] (line 2433), a glance to which will humble his heart [Þe loke to þis luf-lace schal leþe my hert] (line 2438), Gawain exemplifies a similar two fold conception of satisfaction. Though he still insists on referring to the girdle by its courtly name, "luf-lace," thereby recalling its origin as a lady's love-token, Gawain has learned to read the girdle as both a reminder of his transgression and an encouragement to humility. Such self-effacing conduct could not be more opposite to Mark C. Amodio's assertion that "Gawain's interiority and subjectivity, essential components of confession, . . . displace the divine from the center of his contemplation and replace it with the self."[65] In fact, Gawain's satisfaction more closely resembles the definition advanced by the *Clensying*: if the knight "will clerely be clensed, [he] most gladly [will] suffre correccioun and receyue [his] purginge as for satisfaccion."[66] Gawain has been "polysed of þat plyȝt and pured as clene" (line 2393), suffered correction in the "penaunce apert of þe poynt of [the Green Knight's] egge" (line 2392), and has purged his sinful state by rendering it visibly and permanently in the form of the green girdle. He reinvents the green belt

Figure 3 Fourteenth-century stained glass with Mary bestowing her belt on Saint Thomas. East window, St. Mary's Church, Beckley, Oxfordshire, England. BB92/07700. © Crown copyright. National Monuments Record.

Figure 5 Pride at apex of Tree of Vices. St. Ethelbert's Church, Hessett, Suffolk, England. Photo Michelle Duran.

The monumental *Speculum Vitae* (ca. 1350–75), an important ver-sification of Lorens's *Somme* and "a ceaseless inspiration for Middle English translators,"[51] articulates in no uncertain terms a relationship between fashion and vision that is missing in the *Parson's Tale*. In po-siting the dangers of looking at "ryche apparaylle and . . . clethyng" (line 15,628), the *Speculum* asserts that the primary peril in dress is one that can "maas [amass] grete outrage in mens sight" (line 15,630). Drawing on the notion of "curiouste" (line 15,632), as the *Clensyng* does, the *Speculum Vitae* maintains that "enchesouns [reasons] of synne may be / In othir men, als men may se" (lines 15,635–36), a stance clearly taken by the writer of another late medieval spiritual guide that bears some resemblance to the *Parson's Tale*, the *Weye of Paradys*. Where the *Parson's Tale*'s repetition of "showing" and "notifying" merely im-plies the sinfulness of those who look, the *Weye* openly states that viewing sinful practice can lead to sinful practice: "A man may drawe other to synne and do hem senne in many maneres, this is to seyn by word, by ensample, be consentement, be towchyng, by seyng."[52] The *Weye* remarks that the five senses are responsible for allowing sin into the body, but "especially" pertinent is "foolish beholding" because sin impacts both the viewer and the body being viewed.[53]

Late medieval homilists concur that visual acts can transmit sin between subject and object. For instance, Dominican friar John Brom-yard incorporates similar discourse into his massive *Summa Praedican-tium* (ca. 1346–48), an encyclopedic collection of articles arranged alphabetically that pertain to preaching and the care of the soul. Ex-isting "mainly as a witness to popular views on sex in the England of Chaucer's own day," as Richard Firth Green has recently shown,[54] Bromyard's *Summa* describes the sinfulness of both the women who wear revealing clothing and "those who behold them," since looking at "wantonly adorned women" exposes the spectator to "lascivious and carnal provocation."[55] Whereas Bromyard focuses on the effects of women's attire, Robert Rypon, a preacher contemporary with Chaucer, observes the repercussions of men's dress. He notes that men seek admiration from others and derive "sensuous pleasure" from dressing fashionably: "men wear garments so short that they scarcely hide their private parts (*et certe ut apparet ad ostendendum mulieribus membra sua ut sic ad luxuriam provocentur)*" [and certainly it appears that they do this for the purpose of exposing to view their members to women in order that likewise they are provoked to lust].[56] Rypon's preaching echoes the Parson's understanding of individual motivations to dress fashionably. According to Rypon, men wear tight hose and short jackets for two reasons: to reveal the form of their genitalia, and to encourage either their own lascivious behavior or that of those who behold them, an ambiguity rendered by the unarticulated subject of the verbal clause, "ut sic ad luxuriam provocentur." Though the direct antecedent for the final clause is the women (mulieribus) who behold the fashionable male, the subject of the verb—those who are provoked to lust—could also be understood as the men who provoke themselves to lust when they reveal their genitals (membra sua) through tight dress. In this way, the homilist affirms the viewer's complicity in sin. Pride, the capital offense that Morton Bloomfield cites as one "of exaggerated individualism," appears not to be so individual after all. [57] It is, in fact, contagious.

Sexual Repercussions of Sartorial Expression

Medieval notions of vision specify interactions between the curious observer and a viewed object that are similar to the ways in which penitential guides understand paradigms of spectatorship. A major authority in medieval Christian thought, Saint Augustine, writes in *De Trinitate* that "vision is produced both by the visible thing and the one who sees, but in such a way that the sense of sight as well as the intention of seeing and beholding come from the one who sees, while that informing of the sense, which is called vision, is imprinted by the body alone that is seen, namely, by some visible thing."[58] Visual perception, in Augustine's terms, is one of "intromission"; it happens when an object imprints an image of itself on someone who intends to see something. Though Augustine stipulates that two entities are needed in order for vision to occur, he privileges the person or thing viewed as the entity responsible for sight. This idea of intromission would appear in the thirteenth century through an Arabic text, written by a natural philosopher known as Alhacen (Ibn al-Haytham) and translated into Latin under the name of *De aspectibus,* which in turn drew from the Aristotelian defense of intromission theory.[59]

The thirteenth-century scholastic philosopher, Roger Bacon, who was considered one of the most important pioneers in medieval science, drew heavily from Alhacen's work and complements Augustine's stance in his *Opus Majus.* Bacon affirms the visible object's activity in his support of intromission: the object actively generates images of itself along light rays emanating from its surface and connecting with a passive spectator.[60] Bacon, however, does not completely reject intromission's opposite, "extramission," which predicates the viewer as the one who sees. He eventually concedes that "vision is active and passive. For it receives the species of the thing seen, and exerts its own force in the medium as far as the visible object."[61] Thus, while the object is responsible for conveying itself to the eye, the beholder does not remain completely passive. This theory of vision does not reserve the active position entirely for the spectator and the passive role for the object, which is how modern theories of spectatorship have tended to delineate the economy of looking.[62] Rather, it allocates a certain amount of agency to the viewed object.

Despite the agency that viewed objects can potentially exercise in the theory of intromission, the clothed figure in the *Parson's Tale* os - cillates between active subject and passive object. On the one hand, Chaucer figures the sartorial subject as an active agent who threatens to encourage simulation by "shewing" himself. On the other, Chaucer presents his Parson as quite concerned about this same body's passivity when the tale-teller likens a man's posterior to "the hyndre part of a she-ape in the fulle of the moone" (X.424). At this moment, the implications of spectatorship converge with transgressive tendencies: by witnessing a fashion-savvy man, the male spectator positions himself as a potential participant in a homoerotic dynamic. Beryl Rowland notes that simian sexuality addresses human behavior in the *Parson's Tale:* "the man of fashion, like the ape, flaunts his posterior for the purpose of sexual gratification." Rowland sees the imaginative simile working to highlight the "flagrantly provocative" nature of the clothed body, which mimics the "sexual skin changes and enlarged pudenda" of the she-ape awaiting copulation.[63] Significantly, the simile also situates the well-dressed man as a submissive object of scrutiny. Having suggested a kind of sexual gratification in which the posterior functions as the locus of sexual pleasure, the Parson positions the fashionably dressed man as passive. In Rowland's opinion, the simile points toward a natural coupling between the she-ape in estrus and the stimulated male ape. Yet it also endorses a more unnatural relation: by likening the fertile she-ape awaiting her stimulated mate to a fashionable aristocrat, the Parson suggests that the well-dressed man makes himself available for penetration.

The *Parson's Tale* is not unique as a fourteenth-century text that incorporates sexual repercussions of sartorial expression into readings of morally sound behavior. For instance, the *Eulogium* echoes the Parson's hostility for passive men by also condemning the "silken garments called 'paltok' by the vulgar" [indumentum sericum quod vulgo dicitur "paltok"] and the "hose divided in two" [caligas bipartitas] as the reasons for which fashionable aristocrats are "judged rather like women than men" [potius mulieres quam mares judicantur].[64] The *Tale* and the *Eulogium* find similarity in their focus on aristocratic vogues specific to the fourteenth century as a means to condemn effeminate men. But where the *Eulogium* warns men against becoming objectified by dress and therefore feminized, the Parson makes no such caveat. Instead, he finds that the boundaries between sartorial social transgression and sexual indiscretion are not so distinct. His proud, stylish subject functions not only as an example of sin but also as a figure in a complex system of pleasure in which the tale-teller and the reader may inadvertently derive delight from erotic descriptions in confessional guidelines.[65]

The repetitive description of men's attire reveals that pleasure exists first in the narrative of the body's "shewing" and then in the paradigm of visual spectatorship that figures a momentary erotic look between the Parson and his sartorial subject. By repeating an anatomical catalogue of the male lower torso twice, the Parson underscores its figural display. And in his exposition of the sinfulness of scanty attire, the Parson telescopes his readers' attention to the revealing contours of the male physique. Despite clothing's most obvious function as a covering for the body, the Parson employs dress as a means to expose it further.

Narrative theories proposed by Roland Barthes and R. Howard Bloch, respectively, address the *Tale*'s oscillation between inner and outer descriptions as the Parson turns from an image of raw genitalia to the overall silhouette accentuated by fitted attire. Barthes argues in *The Pleasure of the Text* that "the word can be erotic on two opposing levels, both excessive: if it is extravagantly repeated, or on the contrary, if it is unexpected, succulent in its newness."[66] In short, "the unfolding narrative is the site of bliss," or, as Carolyn Dinshaw puts it, "extravagant repetition" titillates.[67] Thus, in its anatomical catalogue that occurs twice, the *Tale* offers the exact repetition with variation that Barthes describes as erotic. That the Parson's narrative focuses primarily on parts of the body, rather than on the whole, suggests an engagement with the male figure that pertains to sexual desire, especially in light of Bloch's argument that "narrative fixation upon the partial object . . . [is] at the origin of desire."[68] If Bloch is correct, then the Parson's repeated interest in a specific area of the male body could convey textual and sensual delights: each succulent reiteration of the "swollen membres" reveals an increasing fascination in narrative that both generates eroticism in the text and bespeaks an engagement with pleasure that appears transgressive.

The Parson's consideration of prideful dress becomes progressively imbued with sexual suggestivity. In maintaining an emphasis on "shewing," he establishes pleasure in a paradigm of visual spectatorship, which in turn emphasizes looking at the fashionable body and that same body's status as a visual object. Such pleasure may appear to compromise the Parson's status as one of the spiritually sound clerics of the *Canterbury Tales*. Since he is defined as an "ensaumple" of moral behavior in the *General Prologue* (I.496–97), his actions should exemplify the moral concepts he illustrates.[69] By featuring a male cleric who observes a male sartorial subject, the *Parson's Tale* calls into question the morality of its tale-teller because, as Boethius articulates in his *Consolation of Philosophy*, a text that Chaucer translated, "for al that evere is iknowe, it is rather comprehendid and knowen, nat aftir his strengthe and his nature, but aftir the faculte (that is to seyn, the power and the nature) of hem that knowen" (*Boece,* lines 137–41).[70] In this way, to understand an object means to consider the nature of the person who perceives it. The Parson's linguistic maneuvers, which focus on repetition and desire in his diatribe on prideful dress, suggest a struggle with sin because, as he outlines rhetorically the contours of the male body, he participates in the pleasure created by the narrative. This is not a case where a "confessor's diffidence wavers slightly," as one scholar has noted,[71] but one in which the confessor is not diffident at all.

While the rhetoric of the vernacular penitential manual exhibits bliss in the varied repetition of the very acts it condemns, and, as a result, each titillating new portrayal threatens to subvert the genre's moral end, the Parson's brutal description of corrupted male genitalia suggests something other than pure delight. The Parson links desire with disgust when he considers *mi-parti* hose, which renders "shameful privee membres" flayed, charred, or diseased. Such a description invites revulsion and triggers a rejection of pleasure-in-dress through an enunciation of shame. Yet the *Tale* illustrates a complexity in its demarcation of deviance by blurring the distinction between revulsion and arousal. The Parson's shame should restrain the desire to look. It should enforce appropriate behavior because shame reorients the self toward morally sound conduct after experiencing pleasure or joy.[72]

If the Parson does, in fact, experience illicit joy from his engagement with the prideful man and subsequently registers shame, then his subsequent turn to the fashionable female may be understood as an appropriate response to his humiliation. In shifting focus to a woman's "outrageous array," the Parson neutralizes any deviant tendency by resolving what would have been an unnatural coupling between male spectator and male spectacle. After those nine lines of prose that describe the scanty nature of men's clothing and that channel both the Parson's and the spectator's gaze to men's "private members," the focus, as we know, shifts to women's faces: "Now, as of the outrageous array of wommen, God woot that though the visages of somme of hem seme ful chaast and debonaire, yet notifie they in hire array of atyr likerousnesse and pride" (X.430). This description of the prideful woman appears anticlimactic for two reasons. First, after the Parson's tirade against the immorality of men's clothing, the ensuing turn to a woman's face and her nondescript "atyr" falls quite flat in comparison to the vivid nature of the preceding lines. Second, the clerical tradition articulates vehement opposition against women and their finery, especially in texts such as the French sermon of MS Bodley 90 and the *Memoriale Credencium*, which consistently treat women's garments in more comprehensive ways than they do men's. By moving from fashionable male to fashionable female in the *Parson's Tale*, Chaucer corrects the fleeting homoerotic moment unwittingly created by situating the male body as spectacle. While it has been suggested that "overabundant detail is the norm" in the *Parson's Tale*, this shift is precisely calculated and quite telling.[73] In replacing the man's body-spectacle with a woman's, the Parson draws on clerical antifeminism as a means to temper an unorthodox desire that appears both in the section on pride and in the *Prologue* to the *Tale*.

The *Parson's Prologue* establishes both innkeeper Harry Bailly's desire to explore further the male body and the Parson's commitment to conveying only "lawful pleasure" in the *Tale* when the host invites the Parson to "Unbokele and shewe us what is in [his] male" (X.26) in order to "knytte up wel" the tale-telling game (X.28). Though the common understanding of this request is that the Parson should "open the bag" or "tell a story"—the medieval equivalent to the modern adage, "let's see what's in his bag of tricks"—Harry's inquiry may be read as a pun on male sexuality in the sense that "unbokelen the male" denotes the medieval colloquialism to "display one's wares."[74] In the second half of the fourteenth century, "male" acquired alternate definitions from the usual sense of "bag" or "pouch," popular since the early thirteenth century, and came to mean the male sexual organ in addition to the male human being.[75] One of the first writers to capitalize on this linguistic development, Chaucer makes use of both novel definitions at a few select places across his text: the Wife of Bath employs it to mean "man" in her *Prologue* (III.122), while Chaucer's *Boece* (4 pr. 6.167) utilizes it as a referent to male sexuality. Given Harry's interest in questions of sexuality as they pertain to narrative in the *Canterbury Tales*, it is not surprising that he prompts the Parson with a sexually charged appeal to tell a tale that includes the unbuckling and revealing of the male body.[76] After all, Harry has already demonstrated an abiding interest in male clerics. In denouncing the perversions of the Pardoner's false relics, he imagines enshrining the Pardoner's genitals in a hog's turd (VI.951–55); he suggests that the monk could copulate as prolifically as a barnyard rooster if given permission (VII.1945–47); and he begins the *Epilogue* to the *Nun's Priest's Tale* with a comical blessing of the said priest's buttocks and testicles (VII.3447–48). The Parson fulfills Harry's wish to "shewe us what is in [his] male" by delivering an erotic vision of masculine desire within an orthodox tale that outlines sinfulness in the excessive nature of contemporary fashion. Indeed, the method by which he delivers this moral counsel serves as a didactic lesson on the very dangers posed to clergy and laity when considering pleasures in dress.

The Parson's strategy of using pleasures in dress at key moments in his exposition of the tripartite structure of penance adds another dimension to the educational endeavors undertaken by local English priests to instruct their parishioners through church wall paintings.[77] Given the widespread drive to teach the populace the arts of penance following the Christian reforms of Lateran IV, there was a surge in the creation of fourteenth-century murals in England's churches that were intended to invite self-examination and thereby encourage improved conduct in everyday life. Known to the art historian as "moralities," these paintings illustrated the seven deadly sins, the seven corporeal works of mercy, the doom, and the three living and the three dead (a scene of three corpses confronting three living kings to remind them, "As you are, so once were we; as we are, so you will be").

Murals in general, and moralities in particular, were didactic in nature in that they impressed moral teachings through visual images upon the lesser-educated and illiterate church-going public. They became, as E. W. Tristram notes, "the pictorial equivalents of medieval sermons and treatises, and served to some as illustrations of them."[78] In this way, the visual image complements the oral lesson of the sermon and the literary goal of the moral treatise to educate viewers, listeners, and readers on the constitution of sin. The popularity of this visual strategy became evident in the later Middle Ages with the proliferation of church murals depicting the cardinal sins. After 1300,

murals illustrating the sins were second in popularity only to portrayals of the three living and the three dead; and by 1350, renditions of
the sins were produced more often than any other iconographical
theme, except perhaps for images of saints.[79] Today, more than fifty
churches in England include medieval paintings of the seven deadly
sins.[80] Such popularity, it has been argued, has resulted from the influence of written moral treatises on English church painters.[81]

If moral treatises implicitly influenced the ways in which painters
rendered their subject, then explicit connections may be found between church murals at Hoxne (Suffolk), Brooke (Norfolk), Bardwell
(Suffolk), and Hessett (Suffolk) and the spiritual guides that person-
ify Pride as a man wearing fashionable aristocratic attire. At Hoxne
and Brooke, Pride either appears or once appeared as a courtier clad
in garments, styled much like those described in fourteenth-century
moral treatises. As if to give image to the *Memoriale Credencium*'s critique
of men wearing "streyt cloþus" [fitted clothes] that are "schort"
[short] in length, the very faded painting at Hoxne (ca. 1390–1400)
figures Pride as a young courtier wearing a jacket fitted through the
torso with large gaping sleeves, his lower torso and legs missing due
to fallen plaster.[82] Following suit, the now-lost paintings at Brooke
(late fourteenth century) show Pride dressed in a striped cotehardie
(see fig. 4), whose fitted shape resembles closely Charles du Blois's
pourpoint.[83] A similar rendition of aristocratic fashion once appeared
at Bardwell (fourteenth century) on Pride's three trumpeters, who
were clad in red and blue gypons.[84] However, the best-preserved image
of Pride as a nobleman that approximates the garb described by
Chaucer's *Parson* appears in the north aisle of St. Ethelbert's Church
at Hessett (see fig. 5, facing p. 123).

Hessett's tree of vices, with Pride as a fashionable male at the
apex, becomes particularly important with respect to Chaucer's arboreal taxonomy of penance and the figurations of dress in the *Parson's
Tale*. Just as the Parson describes vice as a tree with branches of each
cardinal sin, so does the mural at Hessett render the sins as men and
women who erupt from demonic heads at the end of six branches,
with the central trunk belonging to the greatest of all sins, Pride. And,
just as the Parson renders Pride as a scantily clad man in "kutted

Mural Painting from Brooke Church · Norfolk ·

Figure 4 Pride (at left) with comb and mirror. Sketch, ca. 1849, of the now lost wall paintings at St. Peter's Church, Brooke, Norfolk, England. © Norfolk and Norwich Archaeological Society.

sloppes" [loose outer jacket cut short] (X.422) with hose of "whit and blew" (X.426), so does the prideful man at Hessett appear in a short jacket with blue and light-colored hose as he emerges from the mouth of a demon at the end of the tree's central branch.

Although the didactic value of medieval wall paintings has recently been questioned by one scholar, medieval theologians found visual imagery in trees of vices and the corresponding virtues an effective method of conveying religious teachings.[85] As Conrad of Hirsau's twelfth-century treatise, *De fructibus carnis et spiritus,* argues,

> It is good to represent the fruits of humility and pride as a kind of visual image so that anyone studying to improve himself can clearly see what things will result from them. Therefore we show the novices and untutored men two little trees, differing in fruits and in size, each displaying the characteristics of the virtues and the vices, so that people may understand the products of each and choose which of the trees they would establish in themselves.[86]

Written two centuries before visual and textual compositions of trees of vices in England's churches and Chaucer's *Parson's Tale,* Conrad's treatise encourages depicting the sins, especially pride, as fruits from a tree so that observers may understand the effects of transgressive behavior. Muralists and writers alike seem to have taken Conrad's advice to heart. Coupled with the suggestion in the Lambeth Constitutions of 1281 that priests employ the metaphor of a tree to describe the sins, arboreal figuration becomes the most popular schema for depicting the sins in English wall painting by the mid-fourteenth century.[87] What the murals at Hoxne, Brooke, Bardwell, and Hessett add to Conrad's articulation of how to render virtue and vice are individuals dressed in contemporary garments. In particular, the branch of pride yields a fruit in the image of the gallant nobleman.

In the case of the *Parson's Tale*, as shown above, aristocratic attire also appears as the fruit of sin. However, the Parson's consideration of the third component of penance, satisfaction, includes a significant shift in his sartorial strategy of depicting pleasure-in-dress as sinful. While the Parson's interest in the erotic dangers of the male sartorial subject first evinces seemingly unorthodox pleasures in his treatment of pride as a subsection of confession, at the end of the penitential guide he situates sartorial delights as a licit means by which sinners can experience spiritual bliss.[88] His move is unusual and innovative in comparison to contemporary spiritual guides, which adopt the conventional motif of penitential garments as those that inflict pain in order to correct aberrant thoughts or behaviors. In this way, the Parson extends his sartorial strategy of pleasure-in-dress more broadly across the *Tale* as a method to teach the vicious and virtuous delights that dress evokes.

Bliss in Sartorial Satisfaction

Penitential manuals were designed to transmit codes of morally acceptable sexual behavior, but the presentation of prideful clothing in the *Parson's Tale*'s section on confession momentarily obscures the very opposition between morality and immorality. The *Tale* does not offer merely two options for action, as critical scholarship claims (it has a "double perspective,"[89] and the Parson himself is a "split" figure),[90]

or even as medieval clerics postulate (either a person is moral and behaves accordingly by feeling contrite, confessing, and satisfying one's
penance, or he is not). The *Tale* instead explores the complicated nuances in stipulating moral behavior through narrative and visual pleasures based on a sartorial subject. In the section on confession, which
enumerates the seven deadly sins, the Parson's pleasure serves as an example of the illicit enjoyment that should be avoided when watching
the fashionably dressed male. In the concluding section on satisfaction, the Parson's "insistent and pervasive doctrinal emphasis," which
purportedly makes the *Tale* "uninteresting or even repugnant to
many,"[91] discloses instead an engagement with sartorial delights in the
Tale's most original chapters that are neither doctrinal nor uninteresting. Moreover, this pleasure is consistent with the joys invoked in the
Parson's Prologue and ultimately embraced at the end of the *Tale* as
morally sound spiritual bliss.

The transition from illicit pleasures in prideful attire to licit joys
in dress so satisfactory that the sinner is restored to the church community recalls the pleasure that the Parson promises in his *Prologue*. In
response to Harry's request to bring the tale-telling game to a close
with a fable (X.28), the Parson pulls out of his proverbial bag of
tricks a tale that offers "'moralitee and vertuous mateere'" [morality
and virtuous matter] (X.38) while providing the pilgrims with "'ple-
saunce leefful'" [lawful pleasure] (X.41). As central issues in a text intended to teach clerics and laity the arts of contrition, confession, and
satisfaction of sin, then morality, virtue, and lawful pleasure appear as
part of a rhetorical strategy that uses aristocratic attire to evoke narrative, visual, and sartorial pleasures. In the end, his rhetoric of dress
returns as a legitimate system that figures moderate sartorial pleasure
as the means by which individuals may experience spiritual harmony.

As the Parson outlines how penitents may reconcile themselves
with God through satisfaction of sin, he notes two important measures that they should take: their penance should be publicly evident so
that "men seen it" (X.1035), and it must in the end yield pleasure.
Drawing directly from Raymond of Pennafort's *Summa de paenitentia*,
the Parson reiterates the various penitential "tribulations" [flagellis]
that Raymond cites, the first of which "consists in penitential equip-

ment, namely in ashes, a hairshirt, and tears" [Prima consistunt in armis paenitentialibus, scilicet, in cinere, cilicio, et lacrimis].[92] Chaucer expands Raymond's directives, however, in two important ways. First, the Parson broadens Raymond's conception of penitential dress to include other garments in addition to hairshirts. Second, he emphasizes pleasure-in-dress as a means to spiritual delight: although the penitent may satisfy sin by "werynge of heyres, or of stamyn [coarse wollen cloth], or of haubergeons [coats of mail] on hire naked flessh" (X.1052), the Parson nevertheless advises the individual to cast penitential garments aside if they make the heart bitter, angry, or annoyed: "But war thee wel that swich manere penaunces on thy flessh ne make nat thyn herte bitter or angry or anoyed of thyself, for bettre is to caste awey thyne heyre, than for to caste awey the swetenesse of Jhesu Crist" (X.1053).

For the Parson, satisfaction should ultimately appeal to the senses in order to produce spiritual delight, a position that the tale-teller alludes to in the beginning of his narrative when explaining how men may recognize penance by the fruit of satisfaction that grows on the tree of penance (X.115). The *Compileison de Seinte Penance*, a source text for lines 112–16 of the *Parson's Tale*, extends Conrad of Hirsau's directive to depict virtue as a fruit by asserting that "fruits are the deeds of penance." In the same vein as Conrad, the *Compileison* instructs the penitent to "create fruits" precisely because they are sweet. The *Compileison's* tree of penance should be recognized for sensory delight, not disgust, "for a tree is not truly known by its root nor by its leaves, but it is known by its fruit, because often there is bitterness in the leaves and in the root while there is sweetness in the fruit."[93] In other words, the punitive action that the penitent undertakes as a means of satisfaction must yield a particular enjoyment.

The Parson affirms the delights outlined by the *Compileison* in conceiving of sartorial satisfaction as pleasurable during an original moment, which, like his diatribe on prideful dress, does not derive from another source text. Chaucer departs from translating the penitential guides by Raymond of Pennafort, William Peraldus, or the *Compileison* in order to render adequately a unique sartorial strategy that takes aristocratic dress and the system of pleasure it evokes as a way to explore the tripartite structure of penance. Clothing's penitential role should be that of satisfaction of sin. However, if hairshirts and coarse woolen garments distract the individual's attention from the "swetenesse of Jhesu Crist"—a sweetness that by its medieval definition appeals to the senses[94]—then the Parson advocates jettisoning exterior evidence of penance in favor of spiritual bliss.

The call to abandon penitential garb because of its discomfort is particular to the *Parson's Tale*. Other contemporary religious handbooks tend to deploy penitential dress as deliberately painful; it is valued for its ability to transform the suffering individual from a sinner to a devout Christian. For example, the *Ayenbite of Inwit, Memoriale Credencium, The Book of Vices and Virtues, Jacob's Well, Speculum Vitae,* and its fifteenth-century prose translation, *A Myrour to Lewde Men and Wymmen,* all present the biblical figure of Judith in a hairshirt so as to celebrate her chastity in widowhood and to rehabilitate herself from vain tendencies. As if to answer the repeated concern with respect to women's sinful, extravagant attire, these handbooks all feature Judith as an ideal woman who, to quote from one, rejects "riche robes and noble atire" in favor of "cloþinge of widowhode, meke & symple."[95] These texts note that the shift from aristocratic attire to penitential garments expresses a move from "goye and ydele blisse" (as in the *Ayenbite of Inwit*) and "ioye and veyne glorie" (in *The Book of Vices and Virtues, Speculum Vitae,* and *A Myrour to Lewde Men and Wymmen*) to the satisfactory behavior of tears, sorrow, and "hardnes of clothyng . . . to hele þi wounde of synne" (the case in *Jacob's Well*).[96] The spiritual guides thus posit a direct relationship between humanity's physical discomfort and spiritual bliss: greater physical pain results in more spiritual pleasure. Or, according to *Speculum Vitae,* "For thinge þat bitter to þe body es / To þe saul es grete swetenes" (lines 7801–2). In terms of Judith, she "eschewe[s] veynglorie for þe loue of God," which is emblematized by the "grete penaunce of fastyng and wer[ing] þe heyre nexte [to] hir body."[97] Satisfying sin by means of a hairshirt allows for an experience of God's magnificence because pain, as stipulated by these particular guides, diverts the individual from fleshly temptations in order to concentrate on the spiritual delights of the afterlife.

Three analogues to the *Parson's Tale*— the *Boke of Penance*, the *Clensyng of Mannes Sowle*, and the French version of the *Weye of Paradys*, the *Voie de paradis*—likewise promote painful bodily penance as a response to the sensual delights of worldly excess and thereby distance themselves from the way in which the *Parson's Tale* depicts sartorial bliss in satisfactory attire.[98] The *Boke* affirms that castigation of the flesh, notably in the "wering of haire or oþer thing" (line 29,090), is the means to "win . . . heuen blisse" (line 28,997) because such physical suffering forces individuals to turn within so they may "kindly knaw [their] plight / And mendes mak with all [their] might" (lines 29,232–33). So, too, does the *Voie de paradis* mention the hairshirt as a means "tourmenter [la] char" [to torment the flesh] (chapter 287) in satisfying sin, but ultimately it broadens the sartorial options for penance to include coarse woolen cloth and hauberks, just as the *Parson's Tale* does. However, where the Parson maintains that penitents should relinquish discomfort in dress for bliss in Jesus, the *Voie* remains steadfast in its sartorial strategy: it continually advocates painful physical penance by reminding readers that holy men and women—both of Paradise and of this world—have endured similar trials and should thus be viewed as ideal examples to follow.[99] In anticipation of the resistance that penitents may feel against experiencing displeasure, the *Clensyng of Mannes Sowle* offers a sample confessional narrative for those who reject bodily penance:

> "Also I haue not done bodily penance as I might haue done, ne vsed bodily afflicciouns in hard goyng & liggynge or oþer hardnesse or scharpnesse. . . ; but in contrarie, I haue norisched my body wiþ soft lyenge & weryng. . . . Also I haue ben lothe . . . to haue eny scharp penaunce for my synne & my defautes."

> ———

> ["Also I have not completed bodily penance as I might have, nor have I used bodily afflictions such as walking about or lying down in discomfort or other self-mortification or hardship. On the contrary, I have nourished my body by lying down in and wearing soft things. Also, I have been loath to have any painful penance for my sin and faults."][100]

Designed for the individual who suffers from sloth, this excerpt views the refusal of corporal affliction as problematic. Here, the imagined speaker of this confession chooses comfort over discomfort, but he has misunderstood the benefits that physical pain may bring to an errant soul.

Indeed, the satisfactory behaviors that the *Clensyng of Mannes Sowle* promotes to render the soul "clerely purified to þe pleasaunce of þe sight" are not at all pleasurable to the body. In order to "make lowe þe flesch wiþ a desire to þe euerlastinge fulfillinge in blisse," the guide suggests engaging in the opposite of bliss while living in the present. In so doing, penitents follow the *Clensyng*'s directives not "principaly for drede of peyn," but rather "oonly for God" so they may reconcile themselves with Him.[101] The *Clensyng* notes a particular concern with feeling bodily pain and recognizes that penitents may not readily embrace a less than pleasant experience for reconciliation. Despite such an acknowledgment, the guide does not provide an option other than physical discomfort for sinners of the flesh. Any figuration of sensory pleasure appears in the *Clensyng* as sinful delight in earthly objects—a delight that needs to be remedied by tactile discomfort as felt by penitential garments worn on the body. Those who wish to cleanse their souls endure "scharp bodily penaunce" [painful bodily penance] and such "hard goyng & liggynge, as wiþ schertes of heere and such oþere weringe" [hard walking and lying down, as with hairshirts and other such garments], both to satisfy sin and to overcome any dread of discomfort.[102] In noting the difference between performing penance for God and completing the sacrament because of "dread of pain," the *Clensyng* expands the notion of "clothynge of penaunce" in another penitential, which describes satisfactory dress as a means to overcome temptation, rather than a way to rise above physical pain.[103] By broadening the sartorial hermeneutic, the *Clensyng* benefits the sinner in two ways: it most obviously provides an option for the completion of satisfaction; and it also ensures that the sinner performs penance with contrition (commonly understood as a desire to reconcile the self with God) rather than attrition (the desire to perform penance for fear of the anguish that the sinner would suffer in hell for not confessing).

At the conclusion of the section which outlines appropriate behaviors for satisfaction, the *Clensyng* reminds readers that regardless of any other instruction concerning bodily penance found in different spiritual guides, the penitent still must engage in bodily discomfort so as to assuage concupiscence of flesh:

> Of þis fastinge & bodily penaunce hit nedith not to write ȝow no more here, ffor ȝe haue in oþere bokes of Englisch and Frenche moche more & bettir þan I kan tell ȝow. Natheles somme þer ben þat sett but litell of such fastinge or be eny bodily penaunce. But what-euer sugestioun thei make, hit is due satisfaccion ordeigned aȝeins fleschly synnes; & ȝif thei excuse hem & put from hem in confessioun all maner bodily affliccioun, ȝif they ben in bodily hele, sikerly I kan not se þat they desire to do plenere and iust satisfaccion for here synnes. Therefore I counsell ȝow, how-euere hit be, þat ȝe excuse ȝow not aȝeins ȝoure conscience, ne put no such bodily peynes from ȝow þat is discretely enioyned ȝow in confessioun, and specially when ȝe haue demed ȝour-self þat ȝe haue offende God in eny fleschly steringes or lustes, & moche more in eny bodily vnclennes. For þis bodily affliccioun, as I haue schewed ȝow, is oo party of satsifaccioun aȝeins þe concupiscence of þe flesch of fleschly steringes.

———

[Concerning this fasting and bodily penance, (the text) does not need to communicate any more here for you, for you have (plenty of examples) in other French and English books in greater detail than I can tell you. Nonetheless, some make but little of such fasting or any bodily penance. But whatever suggestion they make, it is due satisfaction ordained against fleshly sins. And if they excuse them and put all kinds of bodily affliction away from them in confession, if they are in bodily health, surely I cannot say that they desire to do complete and just satisfaction for their sins. Therefore I counsel you, however it may be, that you excuse yourself not against your conscience, nor refuse any bodily pains that are judiciously imposed upon you in confession, and especially when you have judged yourself that you have offended God in any fleshly stirrings of lusts and much more in any bodily impurity. For this bodily affliction, as I have showed you, is one part of satisfaction against the concupiscence of the flesh and of fleshly stirrings.][104]

While the *Clensyng* notes that other books on bodily penance in fuller detail exist in French and English, the text nevertheless counsels the reader to reject other advice if it de-emphasizes physical affliction. "Bodily health," maintains the writer, is no indication of "complete and just satisfaction." Readers should therefore not reject "any bodily pains" if they are commanded in confession, because the physical pain that accompanies satisfaction of sin corrects fleshly stirrings of lust and uncleanness.

Satisfaction, in the *Parson's Tale*, could not be more different from that in the *Clensyng of Mannes Sowle*. Whereas the *Clensyng* maintains that bodily affliction is a necessary part of satisfying one's sin, the *Parson's Tale* argues the opposite. In replacing uncomfortable penitential clothing with metaphoric garments of "misericorde, debonairetee, suffraunce, and swich manere of clothynge" (X.1054) so as to experience the "swetenesse of Jhesu Crist" (X.1053), the Parson endorses enjoyment connected to the exteriorization of penance.

The Parson's attention to what appears on and off the body plays an important role in underscoring the value of attire to generate bliss. Despite the apparent originality of Chaucer's rejection of hairshirts, the suggestion to cover the body in metaphorical clothing of virtue accords with the ways in which other spiritual guides—in particular the fourteenth-century *Lay Folks' Catechism*—promote feelings of spiritual bliss in pastoral care.[105] Like the *Parson's Tale*, John Thoresby's *Lay Folks' Catechism* figures a positive relationship between literal dress, symbolic clothing, and delights registered by the five senses, though not in relation to satisfaction of sin. As an extension of John Pecham's important emendations made to the stipulations of Lateran IV, the *Catechism* argues that one will experience God's love and "reward of heuyn blysse" (line 1108) upon performing any of the seven works of mercy. For instance, if the individual dresses the poor in literal garments, then Jesus will return the favor in dress that symbolizes pleasure in salvation: "And ȝif we do þis wel he wyle cloþe oure sowlys /

with vertues and grace in body and sowle / with þe stole of vndedly-nesse and blysse of heuyn" (lines 1113–15).[106]

Here the reward that Christ confers to merciful individuals reso-nates with the pleasures that the Parson advocates. While the *Catechism* presents metaphorical clothing as a gift to be bestowed from God to his people, the *Parson's Tale* suggests that the ability to change dress, whether literal or metaphoric, resides with the individual through ex-piatory behavior. Part of this difference derives from the context in which the invitation to bliss appears. Satisfaction of sin demands ac-tion from the penitent in order to complete the sacrament of penance. For the *Parson's Tale*, bliss remains within the province of the individual who controls his reconciliation with God through satisfaction. If wearing penitential dress in any way interferes with the individual's experience of the goodness of Christ that should be found in satis-factory behavior, then the Parson advises the penitent to shed uncom-fortable physical garments for pleasurable metaphorical ones so as to fix his eye on the prize of salvation.

The Parson's nuanced sartorial strategy positions aristocratic attire as a metaphorical vehicle that conveys pleasure during his expo-sition of the tripartite structure of penance. Appearing as worldly goods that provide no protection from hell's miseries and thus en-courage contrition, and existing as the standard example of pride in the Parson's discourse on confession, dress emerges as a figural means to experience pleasure in satisfaction at select moments in the text. While the mere twenty-eight lines (lines 196–97, 412–35, 1052–54) describing clothing may appear paltry in a religious manual of 1080 lines, Chaucer nonetheless carefully employs a rhetoric of dress in the *Parson's Tale* that is innovative and important. Of these twenty-eight lines, nearly all are original Chaucerian additions. Furthermore, the disproportionate attention to men's dress may be better appreci-ated when considering that of the *Tale's* 1080 lines, Chaucer devotes over one-half (570 lines) to an exposition of the cardinal sins and, of that half, he dedicates nearly one-fifth (93 lines) to the sin of pride. It may not be surprising that the "roote of thise sevene synnes" (X.388) should command more attention than the six others. What is perplexing is that over a quarter of the prose on pride deals with clothing (23 lines: X.412–35). Such attention bespeaks an interest in attire that, in fact, begins in the *General Prologue*, resurfaces in the collection, and ends in the *Parson's Tale* with the rejection of penitential garb in favor of the figurative clothing of virtue.[107]

The literal and figurative prominence of dress accords with the attention Chaucer gives in the *General Prologue* to "the condicioun" (I.38), "degree" (I.40), and "array" (I.41) of each pilgrim. In naming condition, degree, and array as components that warrant attention, Chaucer first recalls priestly obligation during penance to "inquire about the [penitent's] status (religious, clerical, lay), condition (beneficed, married, widowed, single) and office (merchant, merce-nary, judge, prostitute, etc.)" and ultimately replaces an interest in of-fice with that of attire.[108] A pilgrim's "array" not only complements her social status and rank but also bespeaks a concern with the mate-riality and value of dress.[109] The *General Prologue* thus establishes a po-etic interest in aristocratic sartorial significations that contributes to social commentary on the ways in which individual pilgrims either conform to their degree, as the Squire does in his status-appropriate "short . . . gowne, with sleves longe and wyde" (I.93), or not, as sug-gested by the Monk's expensive fur-lined sleeves (I.193–94). Such an interest persists more broadly across the *Tales* when garments usually reserved for the upper echelon of society express the comedy of social climbing, as in the case of Alison in the *Miller's Tale*, whose expensive silken belt and gored skirt make her attractive enough to become ei-ther a lord's mistress or a yeoman's wife (I.3235–37); or the frivolity of sartorial value, as the strapping young knight Thopas is portrayed wearing hose from Bruges and a "robe . . . of syklatoun" [dress of costly silken material] (VII.734) that costs a mere half-penny. These moments validate Chaucer's sustained interest in aristocratic attire that appears most prominently in the *Parson's Tale*, where dress exists as the vehicle for conveying a crucial paradigmatic shift.

Moving from pleasure-in-dress as sinful to pleasure-in-dress as salvific, Chaucer teaches that penitents must reject not only the fourteenth-century clothing that marks prideful excess but also the penitential garb that occasions bitterness, anger, and irritation in favor of the figurative clothing of virtue that Paul promotes in Colossians 3:12. Had Chaucer included only the Parson's condemnation of prideful attire, the text would have remained like other contemporary religious guides that systematically decry fashion as sinful. While the moral directive of his *Tale* initially seems compromised by a variety of pleasures ranging from the visual and linguistic to the sexual and sartorial, the Parson shows that pleasure-in-dress is available to penitents who clothe themselves appropriately with virtue. As such, Chaucer's constellation of sartorial images through the *Parson's Tale* allows for an examination of interiority, which is the goal of penance, by way of considering splendor in attire.

Conclusion

When a plan has sorted out the subject in the secret places of the mind, then

let poetry come to clothe the material with words.

—Geoffrey of Vinsauf, *Poetria nova*

I close this study with a return to Geoffrey of Vinsauf's *Poetria nova*, in which he reveals the importance of dress in the rhetorical enter-prise: figurative garments dress plain verse with poetic figures of speech so as to beautify the body of poetry. The "skillful art" of po-etic adornment, he writes, "so inverts the material that it does not pervert it; art transposes, in order that it may make the arrangement of material better."[1] For Geoffrey, poetic garments refine the crude nature of plain verse. Far from perverting the subject matter, they transform unadorned language into something "better."

While Geoffrey focuses on the symbolic implications of clothing and the transformative possibilities of figurative garments, the me-dieval poets studied here, like many of their contemporaries, take a more literal engagement with dress. Just as figurative garments of po-etry ameliorate unrefined verse, so do literary representations of dress alter the bodies of chivalric knights and elegant ladies into figures of beauty, status, and virtue. These transformations were not always unproblematic. Although Geoffrey assumes that the transformative effects of figurative adornment propel narrative away from perversion and toward near-perfection, poets who literalize dress in their writings elicit strikingly negative responses from churchmen who often understand the opposite: the perfect *bliaut*, or short, fitted jacket, changes the plain aristocrat into a person of transgressive worldly excess. Sartorial displays thus become performances marked by vainglory that run counter to pious living in the Middle Ages. There were, however, notable exceptions to correlating the nobility's fine garments with moral decrepitude. This study has sought to elucidate the strategies of these four writers deeply interested in advancing a pedagogical curriculum that posits sumptuous aristocratic attire as indicators of right and honorable behavior.

My chapters have treated the sartorial intersections among romances and ecclesiastical texts as productive spaces for examining codes of aristocratic behavior that depend on sartorial luxuries as teaching tools for desirable conduct. Garments are capable of speaking volumes, and medieval writers capitalize on this potential by using dress as a means to explore a chivalric ethos that can have different meanings in dissimilar contexts. Chaucer's *Parson's Tale*, in particular, demonstrates the destabilizing effect of the fashionable body within the context of the penitential genre. As a figure of pride, the stylish aristocrat demarcates deviant dress and consequently encourages readers to reject such behavior. To read this isolated moment only as an example of pride, however, is to misunderstand Chaucer's broader engagement with dress that underpins his penitential guide. In appropriating the fashionable aristocrat from romance, Chaucer promotes more extensively a sartorial strategy that conceives of clothing as integral to understanding key moments at each of the three required ele - ments of penance: contrition, confession, and satisfaction of sin.

While Chaucer ultimately moves to clothe the body figuratively with virtues of mercy, suffering, and kindness during his explanation of penitential reconciliation, the *Gawain*-poet never espouses the tactic of exchanging literal with figural garments. Instead, he employs the sartorial trappings so important to medieval aristocrats to stage a scenario in which an expensive bejeweled belt, which often appears as a sign of sin in contemporary chivalric or ecclesiastical texts, reorients Gawain toward morally sound conduct. Gawain's change in comportment entails a rejection of the physical life-saving properties of the belt in favor of accepting its surprising, spiritual significance.

In similar fashion, romanciers Marie de France and Heldris de Cornuälle position their representations of attire in romance so as to bespeak ethically upright countenance in contrast to other contemporary poets and churchmen. Writers such as the *Enéas*-poet and Benoît de Sainte-Maure spoke a language common to clerics when they embellished the verse in their *romans antiques* with representations of dress that symbolized sexual licentiousness or personal failure. Marie de France, however, rejects that tactic and instead promotes tight garments as signifiers of restrained, virtuous love. Like Geoffrey Chaucer and the *Gawain*-poet, Marie reveals a language of clothing that does not malign, as in ecclesiastical histories or chronicles, but rather produces faith and courtesy. That dress communicates in unexpected ways is perhaps best illustrated in the *Roman de Silence*, when Heldris de Cornuälle depicts a transvestite knight as a paragon of virtue at a time when the poet found the political and religious climates to be marred by avarice. Long understood as a romance that deploys dress to investigate the complexities of gender construction in medieval literary texts, *Silence* reveals that aristocratic attire objectifies similar complexities with respect to conduct regardless of a person's gender or disguise.

The sartorial strategies evident in *Guigemar*, *Silence*, and *Sir Gawain and the Green Knight* encapsulate a directive advanced by the late fourteenth-century penitential manual, *Speculum Vitae*, which suggests that "fayre tales"—those, by definition, that are "courteous," "civil," and "morally good or proper"—can draw readers to a frame of mind that promotes heart-felt virtuous character through morally edifying lessons:

> Men suld þam comfort in alle þair bales
> Thurgh gode ensaumples and fayre tales

To brynge þam out of wrange thoght
So þat þair hertes faylle þam noght.

(lines 7691–94)

—

[Men should comfort themselves in all their misdeeds through good examples and fair tales, which bring them out of sinful thought so that their hearts do not mislead them.]

These "fayre tales" mirror the thematic concerns of romance. So for all of the criticism that vernacular penitentials have inveighed against romance, this excerpt suggests a valuable shift in one guide's understanding of the work that romances perform. With their tremendous architectural spaces, passionate love adventures, and expensive attire, romances may be read as texts that employ fashion as a vehicle to examine worthy conduct in chivalric and spiritual contexts.

For today's reader, understanding the sartorial strategies in this study means undoing modernity's conception of fashion's voice as one of change. Coco Chanel famously defined fashion as that which goes out of fashion—*la mode, c'est ce qui se démode*—yet the clothing I have addressed here is not solely predicated on variability. While I frame this book with two crucial changes in dress that would rightly be understood as "fashion" according to the term's current definition, my interest has been in examining it in the medieval sense of the word: as that which makes, builds, or shapes appearances and behaviors. My chapters argue that clothing not only delineates the body but also communicates constructive moral comportment, contrary to a widespread clerical understanding of fashion as transgressive. A unifying tendency between the chapters is that each deploys garments in a way that revises mainstream medieval understanding of clothing, whether it be the religious position articulated in Deuteronomy 22:5, that transvestism bespeaks unnatural and therefore punishable behavior, or the clerical assertion that excessive dress invites the late medieval sartorial subject into sin.

In redirecting the prominent position, articulated by churchmen, of luxury garments as superfluous, I have sought to reveal a wider hermeneutic agenda for the four medieval poets under consideration here. Gawain's ornamented girdle could be dangerous if read outside its spiritual context, yet the poem forces a consideration of Gawain's confession and girdle as penitential dress worn by all the king's men and women. The Parson's fashionable male signifies prideful behavior that should be avoided, but Chaucer's inclusion of sartorial imagery for each component of penance indicates a broader interest in the recuperative properties of attire. Even though *Guigemar's* tight garments may indicate a natural deficiency in his capability to love, Marie de France's premise to protect readers from vice encourages a recasting of fitted attire as that which fortifies virtuous restraint. *Silence's* transvestism should convey unnatural and condemnable conduct, but instead it conveys both filial loyalty and a commitment to largess that opposes the cardinal sin of avarice. These differing sartorial strategies reveal a rich conversation between romances and religious documents in the high and later Middle Ages that in turn engages broader cultural debates over morality at a time when changes in fashion and ecclesiastical practices shaped the literary landscape.

Geoffrey of Vinsauf conceives of a poet's ideas as a "body" of material and figures of speech as "clothing." Like many medieval clerics and poets, he suggests an opposition between the body and the dress that it wears figuratively or literally. Yet the intra- and extratextual interpretations presented over the course of this project find that the opposition between dress and body may not be quite so straightforward. Indeed, dress speaks social practices from the chivalric to the penitential in surprising and unexpected ways. In her late twentieth-century study of *Sex and Suits*, Anne Hollander asserts that "the language of clothes is essentially wordless—that is what it was created to be, so that it can operate freely below the level of conscious thought and utterance."[2] Yet medieval fashions rarely escaped "conscious thought" by poets or moralists who considered the ramifications of clothing by assigning a vocabulary to them. These writers acknowledge that the relationship between literary renditions of aristocratic attire and medieval moral conduct can be questioned, complicated, and revised by the imaginative process inherent in their sartorial strategies.

Notes

Introduction

1. Geoffrey of Vinsauf, *Poetria nova*, in Edmond Faral, *Les Arts poétiques du XIIe et du XIIIe siècle* (Paris: Librairie Honoré Champion, 1962), lines 756–58, 767–69: "Ut res ergo sibi pretiosum sumat amictum, / Si vetus est verbum, sis physicus et veteranum / Redde novum. / . . . quae sit sua propria vestis / In simili casu cum videro, mutuor illam / Et mihi de veste veteri transformo novellam." Geoffrey of Vinsauf, *The New Poetics*, trans. Jane Baltzell Kopp, in *Three Medieval Rhetorical Arts*, ed. James J. Murphy (Berkeley: University of California Press, 1971), 61. I have modified Kopp's translation.

2. *The Letters of Abelard and Heloise*, trans. Betty Radice, rev. M. T. Clanchy (London: Penguin, 2003), 51.

3. For social and economic shifts in the twelfth century as they pertain to dress, see Monica L. Wright, *Weaving Narrative: Clothing in Twelfth-Century French Romance* (University Park: Pennsylvania State University Press, 2009), 8–14; and Georges Duby, *Guerriers et paysans, VIIe–XIIe siècle: Premier essor de l'économie européenne* (Paris: Gallimard, 1973), 269–77. The social, political, and economic concerns are registered by several sumptuary statutes in England from 1337 through 1483. While the earliest entry in 1337 is protectionist in nature, stipu - lating that only the royal family may wear imported cloth and furs, the follow- ing Acts of Apparel in 1363, 1463, and 1483 bespeak social and political concerns in addition to that of economics, as the statutes attempted to control conspicuous consumption by rank and income. See *Statutes of the Realm*, 1810– 28, vol. 2 (reprint, London: Dawsons, 1963); Frances Baldwin, *Sumptuary*

Legislation and Personal Regulation in England (Baltimore: Johns Hopkins University Press, 1926); N. B. Harte, "State Control of Dress and Social Change in Pre-Industrial England," in *Trade, Government, and Economy in Pre-Industrial England*, ed. F. J. Fisher et al. (London: Weidenfeld and Nicolson, 1976), 132–65; Alan Hunt, *Governance of the Consuming Passions: A History of Sumptuary Law* (New York: St. Martin's Press, 1996); and Claire Sponsler, "Narrating the Social Order: Medieval Clothing Laws," *CLIO: A Journal of Literature, History, and the Philosophy of History* 21, no. 3 (1992): 265–83.

4.   For twelfth-century fashion, see Jennifer Harris, "'Estroit vestu et menu cosu': Evidence for the Construction of Twelfth-Century Dress," in *Medieval Art: Recent Perspectives*, ed. Gale Owen-Crocker and Timothy Graham (Manchester: Manchester University Press, 1998), 89–103, at 89; Françoise Piponnier and Perrine Mane, *Dress in the Middle Ages*, trans. Caroline Beamish (New Haven: Yale University Press, 1997), 57; Margaret Scott, *Medieval Dress and Fashion* (London: British Library, 2007); and Christina Frieder Waugh, "'Well-Cut Through the Body': Fitted Clothing in Twelfth-Century Europe," *Dress* 26 (1999): 3–16. Stella Mary Newton's *Fashion in the Age of the Black Prince* (Woodbridge: Boydell Press, 1980) is a seminal text on the development and reception of fashion in the fourteenth century; see also Anne H. Van Buren, *Illuminating Fashion: Dress in the Art of Medieval France and the Netherlands, 1325–1515* (New York: The Morgan Library and Museum, 2011), and Millia Davenport, *The Book of Costume* (New York: Crown, 1948), 1:190–91. In *Sex and Suits* (New York: Alfred A. Knopf, 1994), 42–44, Anne Hollander notes that plate armor first appeared in Europe at the end of the twelfth century, but men's fashions of the fourteenth through seventeenth centuries tended to emulate the "stiff abstract shapes around the body" characteristic of armor (44).

5.   *The Riverside Chaucer*, 3rd ed., ed. Larry D. Benson (Boston: Houghton Mifflin, 1987).

6.   Fashion historians generally locate the birth of fashion, in the technical sense, in the mid-fourteenth century when garments were tailored. These new styles required that fabric be cut from patterns with curved lines so as to achieve a fitted silhouette; see Piponnier and Mane, *Dress in the Middle Ages*, 63–65; Hollander, *Sex and Suits*, 42–47; and Newton, *Fashion in the Age of the Black Prince*, 1–6. Scott acknowledges that while many find fashion beginning in the fourteenth century, "there are clear signs two hundred years before that novelty was a driving force in many aspects of dress," *Medieval Dress and Fashion*, 35.

7.   *Middle English Dictionary*, ed. Hans Kurath (Ann Arbor: University of Michigan Press, 1954), includes "facioun," entry 1: "physical make-up or composition"; entry 3: (a) "style, fashion, manner (of make, dress, embellishment),"

(b) "way or mode (of behavior)"; entry 4: (a) "the act of making, fashioning, or manufacturing," (b) "the manner of fashioning or constructing; construction"; available at http://quod.lib.umich.edu/ (last accessed 15 April 2011). *The Oxford English Dictionary Online* notes that "fashion" as a "particular make, shape, style, or pattern," "especially with reference to attire," appears in the second quarter of the sixteenth century; see "fashion," entry 3 (b); available at http://www.oed.com/ (last accessed 15 April 2011).

8. See *Middle English Dictionary*, "conduyt," entry 5: "direction, management, and control," with clear ethical implications in the *Paston Letters*. Chaucer uses "port" to describe the highest-ranking aristocratic pilgrim, the Knight (I.69), and the aristocratically-minded Prioress (I.137 and I.138).

9. J. A. Watt, "The Papacy," in *The New Cambridge Medieval History*, vol. 5, *c. 1198–c. 1300*, ed. David Abulafia (Cambridge: Cambridge University Press, 1999), 119–20; Leonard E. Boyle, "The Fourth Lateran Council and Manuals of Popular Theology," in *The Popular Literature of Medieval England*, ed. Thomas Heffernan (Knoxville: University of Tennessee Press, 1985), 30–43, at 31; and Norman Tanner, "Pastoral Care: The Fourth Lateran Council of 1215," in *A History of Pastoral Care*, ed. G. R. Evans (London: Cassel, 2000), 112–25.

10. *Decrees of the Ecumenical Councils*, vol. 1, *Nicaea I to Lateran V*, ed. Norman P. Tanner (London: Sheed and Ward, 1990), 227–71, at 227.

11. *Decrees of the Ecumenical Councils*, 243. Canon 68 is another instance of sartorial regulation, which stipulates that Jews and Saracens should be distinguished from Christians in attire so as to avoid "damnable mixing," 266. See Helen Birkett, "The Pastoral Application of the Lateran IV Reforms in the Northern Province, 1215–1348," *Northern History* 43, no. 2 (2006): 199–219, at 201; and Thomas Izbicki, "Forbidden Colors in the Regulation of Clerical Dress from the Fourth Lateran Council (1215) to the Time of Nicholas of Cusa (d. 1464)," in *Medieval Clothing and Textiles*, ed. Robin Netherton and Gale Owen-Crocker, vol. 1 (Woodbridge: Boydell, 2005), 105–14.

12. Boyle, "The Fourth Lateran Council," 32.

13. *Decrees of the Ecumenical Councils*, 245.

14. Boyle, "The Fourth Lateran Council," 32.

15. Of the Latin texts, Raymond of Pennafort's *Summa de paenitentia* and William Peraldus's *Summa de vitiis et virtutibus* stand as seminal works that provide the foundation for the exposition of sin in the vernacular treatises. There have been several attempts to classify the numerous texts on penance and confession. Most notable are Joseph Goering, "The Internal Forum and the Literature of Penance and Confession," in *The History of Medieval Canon Law in the Classical Period, 1140–1234: From Gratian to the Decretals of Pope Gregory IX*, ed. Wilfried Hartmann

and Kenneth Pennington (Washington, DC: Catholic University of America Press, 2008), 379–428, at 410–27; Leonard E. Boyle, "Summa Confessorum," in *Les Genres littéraires dans les sources théologiques et philosophiques médiévales: Définition, critique, et exploitation* (Louvain-la-Neuve: Universite Catholique de Louvain, 1982), 227–37; Robert R. Raymo, "Works of Religious and Philosophical Instruction," in *A Manual of the Writings in Middle English, 1050–1500*, ed. Albert E. Hartung, vol. 7 (New Haven: Connecticut Academy of Arts and Sciences, 1986), 2255–2378, 2467–2582; and W. A. Pantin, *The English Church in the Four-teenth Century* (Cambridge: Cambridge University Press, 1955), 220–43. See also Vincent Gillespie, "Vernacular Books of Religion," in *Book Production and Publishing in Britain, 1375–1475*, ed. Jeremy Griffiths and Derek Pearsall (Cambridge: Cambridge University Press, 1989), 317–44; and P. S. Jolliffe, *A Check-list of Middle English Prose Writings of Spiritual Guidance* (Toronto: Pontifical Institute of Medieval Studies, 1974). For students in secular and religious schools as part of the intended audience for *pastoralia*, see Joseph Goering, *William de Mon-tibus (c. 1140–1213): The Schools and the Literature of Pastoral Care* (Toronto: Pontifi - cal Institute of Medieval Studies, 1992), 58–65.

16. Tertullian, "The Apparel of Women," in *Disciplinary, Moral and Ascetical Works*, trans. Rudolph Arbesmann, Sister Emily Joseph Daly, and Edwin A. Quain (New York: Fathers of the Church, 1959), 109–50.

17. John W. Baldwin, *Aristocratic Life in Medieval France: The Romances of Jean Re-nart and Gerbert de Montreuil, 1190–1230* (Baltimore: Johns Hopkins University Press, 2000), 192–93. See also Baldwin, *Masters, Princes, and Merchants: The Social Views of Peter the Chanter and His Circle*, 2 vols. (Princeton: Princeton University Press, 1970).

18. Orderic Vitalis, *The Ecclesiastical History of Orderic Vitalis*, ed. and trans. Marjorie Chibnall, 6 vols. (Oxford: Clarendon Press, 1969–80); and *Eulogium (historiarum sive temporis)*, ed. Frank Scott Haydon, Rolls Series 9, vol. 3 (London: Longman, Green, Longman, Roberts, and Green, 1863). These condemnations were not reserved to discourses produced in the Middle Ages; see Roze Hentschell, "Moralizing Apparel in Early Modern London: Popular Literature, Sermons, and Sartorial Display," *Journal of Medieval and Early Modern Studies* 39, no. 3 (2009): 571–95.

19. For a discussion of the historiography of dress from the classic work of Jules Quicherat to the modern study by Roland Barthes, see Odile Blanc, "Historiographie du vêtement: Un bilan," in *Le Vêtement: Histoire, archéologie, et sym-bolique vestimentaires au Moyen Age*, ed. Michel Pastoureau (Paris: Léopard d'Or, 1989), 7–33; Piponnier and Mane's *Dress in the Middle Ages* provides a broad ac-count of the production and acquisition of garments, their diffusion and regu -

lation, and their use within and beyond society. Scott's *Medieval Dress and Fashion*, as well as Joan Evans, *Dress in Mediaeval France* (Oxford: Clarendon Press, 1952), both offer perspectives from the art historian. Important anthropological studies include essays in *The Social Life of Things: Commodities in Cultural Perspective*, ed. Arjun Appadurai (Cambridge: Cambridge University Press, 1986); *The Socialness of Things: Essays on the Socio-semiotics of Objects*, ed. Stephen Harold Riggins (Berlin: Mouton de Gruyter, 1994); and *Clothing and Difference: Embodied Identities in Colonial and Post-Colonial Africa*, ed. Hildi Hendrickson (Durham, NC: Duke University Press, 1996). Hunt's *Governance of the Consuming Passions* investigates the economic and social implications of sumptuary legislation in the medieval and early modern periods. Scholarship on the role of garments in literary studies is vast, and specific works will be cited in each chapter of this book. See, for example, *Medieval Fabrications: Dress, Textiles, Cloth Work, and Other Cultural Imaginings*, ed. E. Jane Burns (New York: Palgrave, 2004); *Encountering Medieval Textiles and Dress*, ed. Désirée G. Koslin and Janet E. Snyder (New York: Palgrave, 2002); and the special issue, "Cultures of Clothing in Later Medieval and Early Modern Europe," ed. Margaret F. Rosenthal, *The Journal of Medieval and Early Modern Studies* 39, no. 3 (2009). Especially pertinent studies of dress with respect to courtly literature are E. Jane Burns, *Courtly Love Undressed* (Philadelphia: University of Pennsylvania Press, 2002); Susan Crane, *The Performance of Self: Ritual, Clothing, and Identity during the Hundred Years War* (Philadelphia: University of Pennsylvania Press, 2002); Sarah-Grace Heller, *Fashion in Medieval France* (Woodbridge: D. S. Brewer, 2007); and Wright, *Weaving Narrative*.

20. Some seminal titles on these issues include Fred Davis, *Fashion, Culture, and Identity* (Chicago: University of Chicago Press, 1992); J. C. Flugel, *The Psychology of Clothes* (London: Hogarth Press, 1930; reprint, New York: International Universities Press, 1969); Hollander, *Sex and Suits*; and Valerie Steele, *Fetish: Fashion, Sex, and Power* (New York: Oxford University Press, 1996). See also Piponnier and Mane, *Dress in the Middle Ages*; and Michèle Beaulieu, "Le Costume français: Miroir de la sensibilité (1350–1500)," in Pastoureau, ed., *Le Vêtement*, 255–77.

21. Some examples of knights moved to desire after witnessing ladies in expensive attire include Alexander in Thomas of Kent's late twelfth-century Anglo-Norman *Le Roman d'Alexandre ou le roman de toute chevalerie*, ed. Brian Foster and Ian Short (Paris: Honoré Champion, 2003), lines 7751–52, 7755–58; and Lanval in Marie de France's *Lanval*, in *Les Lais de Marie de France*, ed. Jean Rychner (Paris: Librairie Honoré Champion, 1983), lines 582–84.

22. For the treatment of attire by moralists, see, for example, G. R. Owst, *Literature and Pulpit in Medieval England* (Oxford: Blackwell, 1961); and Odile

Blanc, "Vêtement féminin, vêtement masculin à la fin du Moyen Age: Le Point de vue des moralistes," in Pastoureau, ed., *Le Vêtement*, 243–51. For sumptuary legislation on dress, see Sarah-Grace Heller, "Limiting Yardage and Changes of Clothes: Sumptuary Legislation in Thirteenth-Century France, Languedoc, and Italy," in Burns, ed., *Medieval Fabrications*, 121–36; Hunt, *Governance of the Consuming Passions*, 110–13, 132–36; Claire Sponsler, *Drama and Resistance: Bodies, Goods, and Theatricality in Late Medieval England* (Minneapolis: University of Minnesota Press, 1997), 1–23; and Sponsler, "Narrating the Social Order," 265–83.

23. Heller, *Fashion in Medieval France*, 8–9; Davis, *Fashion, Culture, and Identity*; and Hollander, *Sex and Suits*. For fashion as discipline, see Harold Koda, *Extreme Beauty: The Body Transformed* (New York: Metropolitan Museum of Art, 2001), 72.

24. Erich Auerbach, *Mimesis: The Representation of Reality in Western Literature*, trans. Willard R. Trask (Princeton: Princeton University Press, 1953), 123–42; and Wright, *Weaving Narrative*, 8–10.

25. Helen Cooper, *The English Romance in Time: Transforming Motifs from Geoffrey of Monmouth to the Death of Shakespeare* (Oxford: Oxford University Press, 2004), 3.

26. Neil Cartlidge, "Introduction," in *Boundaries in Medieval Romance*, ed. Neil Cartlidge (Woodbridge: D. S. Brewer, 2008), 1–11, at 9.

27. Helen Cooper, "When Romance Comes True," in *Boundaries in Medieval Romance*, ed. Cartlidge, 13–27, at 16.

28. See, for example, Dieter Mehl, *The Middle English Romances of the Thirteenth and Fourteenth Centuries* (New York: Barnes and Noble, 1969), 19; Paul Strohm, "The Origin and Meaning of Middle English *Romaunce*," *Genre* 10, no. 1 (1977): 1–28, at 18; C. Stephen Jaeger, *The Origins of Courtliness: Civilizing Trends and the Formation of Courtly Ideals, 939–1210* (Philadelphia: University of Pennsylvania Press, 1985), 234–42; Susan Crane, *Insular Romance: Politics, Faith, and Culture in Anglo-Norman and Middle English Literature* (Berkeley: University of California Press, 1986), 11; and Cooper, *The English Romance in Time*, 6 and 52, in particular.

29. Jaeger, *Origins of Courtliness*, 242.

30. The plays in which the gallant appears as demonic include the *Digby Mary Magdalene*, the *N-Town Passion Play I*, and the *Towneley Last Judgement*. See *The Late Medieval Religious Plays of Bodleian Mss. Digby 133 and E Museo 160*, ed. Donald C. Baker, John L. Murphy, and Louis B. Hall, Jr., EETS, o.s. 283 (Oxford: Oxford University Press, 1982), 40, lines 491–506; *The N-Town Play: Cotton MS Vespasian D.8*, ed. Stephen Spector, 2 vols., EETS, s.s. 11 and 12 (Oxford: Ox-

ford University Press, 1991), 248, lines 65–92; *The Towneley Plays,* ed. Martin Stevens and A. C. Cawley, 2 vols., EETS, s.s. 13 and 14 (Oxford: Oxford University Press, 1994), 414, lines 447–57. Tony Davenport's "'Lusty fresche galaunts,'" in *Aspects of Early English Drama,* ed. Paula Neuss (Cambridge: D. S. Brewer, 1983), 111–25, is useful here.

31. Crane, *Insular Romance,* 94.

32. Owst, *Literature and Pulpit,* 14, note 2, as cited in Crane, *Insular Romance,* 94. See also Ian Short, "Denis Piramus and the Truth of Marie's Lais," *Cultura Neolatina* 67, nos. 3–4 (2007): 319–40, at 330–31, for a similar citation from Ailred of Rievaulx in the 1140s about Arthurian fictions moving listeners to tears more easily than accounts of Christ's Passion.

33. Some critics who have cited the *Cursor Mundi* as a text that criticizes the content of romance are Derek Brewer, "The Popular English Metrical Romances," in *A Companion to Romance: From Classical to Contemporary,* ed. Corinne Saunders (Malden, MA: Blackwell, 2004), 45–64, at 50; Crane, *Insular Romance,* 96; and Larry Scanlon, "Introduction," in *The Cambridge Companion to Medieval English Literature, 1100–1500,* ed. Larry Scanlon (Cambridge: Cambridge University Press, 2009), 1–8, especially 1–3.

34. *Cursor Mundi,* ed. Richard Morris, EETS, o.s. 57 (London: Trübner and Co., 1874). Of those readers who like romance, the *Cursor* writer states that those "þat foly luue þat uanite, / þam likes now nan oþer gle" [who love folly and vanity now like no other entertainment] (lines 53–54).

35. Denis Piramus, *La Vie seint Edmund le rey,* ed. Ian Short, in Short, "Denis Piramus," 339–40, lines 60–68.

36. *Speculum Vitae: A Reading Edition,* ed. Ralph Hanna, EETS, o.s. 331 and 332 (Oxford: Oxford University Press, 2008), lines 35–48. Despite the fact that authorship of *Speculum Vitae* has long been attributed to William of Nassington, Hanna argues against this claim at lx–lxiii. For the nearly universal acceptance of William as author, see Ingrid J. Peterson, *William of Nassington* (New York: Peter Lang, 1986); and *The Cambridge History of Medieval English Literature,* ed. David Wallace (Cambridge: Cambridge University Press, 1999), 398, 548, and 694. See also Jonathan Hughes, "The Administration of Confession in the Diocese of York in the Fourteenth Century," in *Studies in Clergy and Ministry in Medieval England,* ed. David M. Smith (York: University of York, Borthwick Institute of Historical Research, 1991), 87–163, at 98.

37. *Speculum Vitae,* lines 55–56: "rewell here yhour lyf / And gouerne wele yhour wyttes fyue"; and line 60: "what way yhe sal to heuen take." Translations are mine.

38. Peter of Blois, quoted in Baldwin, *Aristocratic Life,* 224.

39.   Walter K. Everett dates *The Clensyng of Mannes Sowle* to between 1382 and 1419, concluding that it was most likely composed in the last quarter of the fourteenth century: "A Critical Edition of the Confession Section of *The Clensyng of Mannes Soule*" (Ph.D. diss., University of North Carolina-Chapel Hill, 1974), x–xii.

40.   Charles Lionel Regan, "*The Cleansing of Man's Soul:* Edited from MS Bodley 923" (Ph.D. diss., Harvard University, 1963), 127. Translation is mine.

41.   See, also, the late fourteenth-century Middle English *Of Shrifte and Penance* (a translation of the thirteenth-century *Manuel des péchés*, sometimes attributed to William of Wadington), which follows suit by warning its audience against reading romances on holy days: "Romaunces, fables, and songes, vpfyndinges, or oþer folies no man schulde do as many men doth," *Of Shrifte and Penance*, ed. Klaus Bitterling (Heidelberg: Universitätsverlag C. Winter, 1998), 51.

42.   Richard Newhauser, *The Treatise on Vices and Virtues in Latin and the Vernacular* (Turnhout: Brepols, 1993), 14.

43.   William of Malmesbury describes Ælfgifu, mother of King Edgar (ca. 973), and her expensive attire as signs of munificence: "The costly garments [in] which most women find a temptation to relax their chastity were to her the material of generosity, so that, however expensive a dress might be, she would give it at once to a beggar at the mere sight of him" [Pretiosus amictus, qui plerisque mulieribus est leno soluendi pudoris, illi erat suppellex munificentiae, ut quamlibet operosam uestem conspecto statim largiretur pauperi], in *Gesta regum Anglorum*, ed. and trans. R. A. B. Mynors, R. M. Thomson, and M. Winterbottom (Oxford: Clarendon Press, 1998), 253. Thomas Aquinas notably argues that women do not sin if they adorn themselves with costly apparel in order to please their husbands and thus discourage them from lustful behaviors, *Summa theologiae*, trans. Fathers of the English Dominican Province (New York: Benzinger Bros., 1938), IIaIIae, q. 69, art. 2.

44.   Lee Patterson, "Chaucer." Available at http://www.yale.edu/engl125 /text-only/lectures/lecture-1.html (last accessed 9 February 2011).

45.   David R. Carlson, *Chaucer's Jobs* (New York: Palgrave Macmillan, 2004), 4–5; *Chaucer Life-Records*, ed. Martin M. Crow and Clair C. Olson (Oxford: Clarendon Press, 1966), 94–105, 275.

46.   *Chaucer Life-Records*, 148–270.

47.   On the "French of England," see Jocelyn Wogan-Browne, "General Introduction: What's in a Name: The 'French' of 'England,'" in *Language and Culture in Medieval Britain: The French of England, c. 1100–c. 1500*, ed. Jocelyn Wogan-Browne (Woodbridge: York Medieval Press, 2009), 1–13; Susan Crane,

"Anglo-Norman Cultures in England, 1066–1460," in *The Cambridge History of Medieval English Literature*, ed. David Wallace (Cambridge: Cambridge University Press, 1999), 35–60; W. Rothwell, "The 'faus français d'Angleterre': Later Anglo-Norman," in *Anglo-Norman Anniversary Essays*, ed. Ian Short (London: Anglo-Norman Text Society, 1993), 309–26.

48. Larry Scanlon, *Narrative, Authority, and Power: The Medieval Exemplum and the Chaucerian Tradition* (Cambridge: Cambridge University Press, 1994), 14.

49. For "sourquydrye" as a branch of pride, see the *Parson's Tale*, X.403; *The Book of Vices and Virtues: A Fourteenth-Century English Translation of the* Somme le roi *of Lorens d'Orléans*, ed. W. Nelson Francis, EETS, o.s. 217 (London: Oxford University Press, 1942), 12, line 29; "The Mirror of St. Edmund," in *Religious Pieces in Prose and Verse*, ed. G. G. Perry, EETS, o.s. 26 (London: N. Trübner and Co., 1867; rev. 1914; reprint 1973), 24, line 10; and *A Myrour to Lewde Men and Wymmen*, ed. Venetia Nelson (Heidelberg: Carl Winter, 1981), 106, line 2.

50. These are two by Gautiers de Leus, *De Dieu et dou pescour* and *D[ou] prestre ki perdi les colles*, and two by anonymous authors, *Des iij commandemens* and *De l'arme ki guangna paradis par plait*. For a complete list of the codex's contents, see Lewis Thorpe's introduction to his edition, *Le Roman de Silence* (Cambridge: W. Heffer and Sons, 1972), 3–6. See also Keith Busby, *Codex and Context: Reading Old French Verse Narrative in Manuscript* (Amsterdam: Rodopi, 2002), 415–18.

51. Harley 978, with its 161 folia, is described by the British Library's on-line Catalogue of Illuminated Manuscripts as a "Musical, medical and literary miscellany, including 'Sumer is icumen in,' Fables and Lays of Marie de France (ff. 40–67v, 118–160), poems by Walter Map (ff. 68v–74v), goliardic satires and songs (ff. 75–107), and the 'Song of Lewes' (ff. 107–114)," an elegy for the baronial leader, Simon de Montfort. Available at http://www.bl .uk/catalogues/illuminatedmanuscripts/record.asp?MSID=8682&CollID=8 &NStart=978 (last accessed 16 February 2011). For an itemized list of Harley 978's contents, see British Museum, Robert Harley Oxford et al., *A Catalogue of the Harleian Manuscripts in the British Museum. With Indexes of Persons, Places, and Matters*, vol. 1 (London, 1808; rep., Hildesheim: Georg Olms, 1973), 488–89. Of particular interest are the Goliardic macaronic poem concerning clothing changes [*De transmutatione vestis*], a poem on worldly vanities [*De vanitate mundi*], and the additional eight works on sin and confession that appear at ff. 68v–107 (items 13 and 14 in the on-line catalogue, and items 77, 84–89, 90–91 in the print version cited above). For an extensive reading of the contents of Harley 978 and its possible owner, see Andrew Taylor, *Textual Situations: Three Medieval Manuscripts and Their Readers* (Philadelphia: University of Pennsylvania Press, 2002). The remaining two manuscripts that include *Guigemar* also situate

it with works that address morally sound comportment: Paris, Bibliothèque Nationale, nouv. acq. fr. 1104 follows its series of Breton *lais* with a Latin commentary on Job; and Paris, Bibliothèque Nationale, fr. 2168 does the same with a life of Charlemagne, *Le Vie Carlemaine*, which would have been read as a secular hagiography illustrating ideal Christian behavior. For the former, see Henri Omont, *Bibliothèque Nationale, Catalogue général des manuscrits français: nouvelles acquisitions françaises*, vol. 1, nos. 1–3060 (Paris: Ernest Leroux, 1899), 145–46. For the latter, see Jules-Antoine Taschereau et al., *Catalogue des manuscrits français*, vol. 1, *anciens fonds* (Paris: Firmin Didot, 1868), 366–68.

52. Rosamond McKitterick and Richard Beadle, *Catalogue of the Pepys Library at Magdalene College Cambridge*, vol. 5, part 1 (Cambridge: D. S. Brewer, 1992), 39–44, at 42. Another Chaucerian manuscript, London, British Library, MS Harley 7333, offers similar contextualization of romances and didactic literature. Called a "library of secular literature" with romances such as the *Brut*, *Guy of Warwick*, and an incomplete *Canterbury Tales* with the *Parson's Tale*, Harley 7333 nonetheless contains Burgh's Cato, a Latin collection of moral and wise proverbs, and excerpts of Guillaume de Guileville's *Pilgrimage*, which Eleanor Prescott Hammond does not specify as an English translation of *Le Pèlerinage de la vie humaine*, *Le Pèlerinage de l'Âme*, or *Le pèlerinage de Jhesucrist* in her *Chaucer: A Bibliographic Manual* (New York: Macmillan, 1908), 176–77. See John M. Manly and Edith Rickert, *The Text of the Canterbury Tales: Studied on the Basis of All Known Manuscripts*, vol. 1 (Chicago: University of Chicago Press, 1940), 207–18.

53. Mary C. Erler, "Fifteenth-Century Owners of Chaucer's Work: Cambridge, Magdalene College MS Pepys 2006," *The Chaucer Review* 38, no. 4 (2004): 401–14, at 402. See also Charles A. Owen, *The Manuscripts of the Canterbury Tales* (Cambridge: D. S. Brewer, 1991), 116.

54. The contents of British Library, MS Cotton Nero A.x, as they appeared in 1696 are found in Thomas Smith, *Catalogue of the Manuscripts in the Cottonian Library 1696 (Catalogus librorum manuscriptorum bibliothecae Cottonianae)*, ed. C. G. C. Tite (Cambridge: D. S. Brewer, 1984), 49–50. A. S. G. Edwards notes, "unrelated materials, with which [the manuscript] had been bound in the seventeenth century, were removed in 1964," in "The Manuscript: British Library MS Cotton Nero A.x," in *A Companion to the* Gawain-*Poet*, ed. Derek Brewer and Jonathan Gibson (Cambridge: D. S. Brewer, 1997), 197–220, yet the seemingly "unrelated materials" included a prayer dedicated to a religious man who demonstrates the inseparability of spiritual office with aristocratic pomp. Upon his appointment as rector of two Jurist Universities in Padua, Archdeacon John Chelworth staged a celebration with feasting, tournaments, games,

and display that exceeded the usual magnificence and invited spectators to come clad in their best attire. During the following year, Chelworth was expected to maintain his rich appearance by wearing silk robes in summer and purple velvet and furs in winter, according to R. J. Mitchell, "English Students at Padua, 1460–75," *Transactions of the Royal Historical Society* (Fourth Series) 19, no. 1 (1936): 101–17, at 109–10.

55. Ralph Hanna, "Producing Manuscripts and Editions," in *Textual Editing and Criticism: An Introduction*, ed. Erick Kelemen (New York: W. W. Norton, 2009), 333–62, versions of which appeared initially in *Crux and Controversy in Middle English Textual Criticism*, ed. Charlotte Brewer and Alastair Minnis (Cambridge: D. S. Brewer, 1992), 109–30; and subsequently in Hanna's monograph, *Pursuing History: Middle English Manuscripts and Their Texts* (Stanford: Stanford University Press, 1996), 63–82. See also Busby, *Codex and Context*, 368 and 415.

56. Viscount Dillon and W. H. St. John Hope, "Inventory of the Goods and Chattels Belonging to Thomas, Duke of Gloucester, and Seized in his Castle at Pleshy, Co. Essex, 21 Richard II (1397)," *Archaeological Review* 54 (1897): 275–308, at 300–303. See also V. J. Scattergood, "Literary Culture at the Court of Richard II," in *English Court Culture in the Later Middle Ages*, ed. V. J. Scattergood and J. W. Sherborne (London: Duckworth, 1983), 29–43.

57. Scattergood, "Literary Culture," 35.

58. Orderic Vitalis, *Ecclesiastical History*, 188–89.

59. Guillaume de Nangis, *Chronique latine de Guillaume de Nangis de 1113 à 1300*, ed. H. Géraud, 2 vols. (Paris: Jules Renouard, 1843), 2:185; John of Reading, *Chronica Johannis de Reading et anonymi Cantuariensis, 1346–1367*, ed. James Tait (Manchester: Manchester University Press, 1914), 167. See also *The Brut, or the Chronicles of England*, ed. Friedrich W. D. Brie, EETS, o.s. 136 (London: Kegan Paul, Trench, Trübner and Co., 1908), 296–97, for the folly of the strangers who change dress every year since the arrival of the Hainaulters.

60. Marjorie Garber, *Vested Interests: Cross-Dressing and Cultural Anxiety* (New York: Routledge, 1997), 16.

CHAPTER ONE   **Marie de France**

1. Harris, "'Estroit vestu et menu cosu,'" 89. See also Piponnier and Mane, *Dress in the Middle Ages*, 57; Scott, *Medieval Dress and Fashion*; Waugh, "'Well-Cut Through the Body,'" 3–16.

2. Harris, "'Estroit vestu et menu cosu,'" 90–94; and Millia Davenport, *The Book of Costume*, 1:104. See also François Boucher, *Histoire du costume en Occident*

de l'antiquité à nos jours (Paris: Flammarion, 1965), 172; and Eunice Rathbone Goddard, *Women's Costume in French Texts of the Eleventh and Twelfth Centuries* (Baltimore: Johns Hopkins University Press, 1927), 10–21.

3. Doreen Yarwood, *English Costume from the Second Century B.C. to 1967,* 3rd ed. (London: B. T. Batsford, 1967), 44; Francis M. Kelly and Randolph Schwabe, *A Short History of Costume and Armour: 1066–1485* (New York: Arco, 1972), 1:10–12.

4. Scott, *Medieval Dress and Costume,* 41–77. For the two competing notions of dress in illuminations, Scott points to images in Gregory the Great's *Moralia in Job,* Cîteaux, ca. 1111–15: Dijon, Bibliothèque Municipale, MS 168, f. 4v; and *Psalter of Henry of Blois,* Winchester, ca. 1145–55, London, British Library, Cotton Nero C. IV, f. 18r. Like Scott, Millia Davenport notes that aristocratic men as well as women wore the *bliaut,* 104.

5. Recent scholarship suggests that Marie authored *La vie seinte Audree*: see June Hall McCash, "*La vie seinte Audree*: A Fourth Text by Marie de France?," *Speculum* 77, no. 3 (2002): 744–77; and Virginia Blanton, "Chaste Marriage, Sexual Desire, and Christian Martyrdom in *La vie seinte Audrée*," *Journal of the History of Sexuality* 19, no. 1 (2010): 94–114.

6. Marie's *lais* survive in five manuscripts known to date: London, British Library, MS Harley 978 (all *lais*); Paris, Bibliothèque Nationale, MS nouvelles acquisitions françaises 1104 (*Guigemar, Lanval, Yonec, Chevrefoil, Deus Amanz, Bisclavret, Milun, Fresne,* and *Equitan*); Paris, Bibliothèque Nationale, MS anciens fonds français 2168 (the end of *Yonec, Guigemar,* and *Lanval*); London, British Library, MS Cotton Vespasian B.xiv (*Lanval*); and Bibliothèque Nationale, anciens petits fonds français 24432 (*Yonec*). For a complete description of these manuscripts as they pertain to Marie's *lais,* see Jean Rychner's "Introduction" to his edition, *Les lais de Marie de France,* xix–xx. "Web of interlocution" is Charles Taylor's phrase, *Sources of the Self: The Making of Modern Identity* (Cambridge, MA: Harvard University Press, 1989), 36.

7. For a detailed reading of BL Harley 978, see Andrew Taylor, *Textual Situations.*

8. A general list of the contents of BL Harley 978 is available at http://www.bl.uk/catalogues/illuminatedmanuscripts/record.asp?MSID=8682&ColIID=8&NStart=978 (last accessed 28 February 2011). For an itemized list, see British Museum, Robert Harley Oxford et al., *A Catalogue of the Harleian Manuscripts,* 1:488–89. BnF nouv. acq. fr. 1104 follows its series of Breton *lais* with a Latin commentary on Job; BnF fr. 2168 positions *Yonec, Guigemar,* and *Lanval* in context with a secular hagiography of Charlemagne; BL Cotton Vespasian B.xiv includes *Lanval* with the life and martyrdom of Saint Thomas à Becket;

and BnF fr. 24432 lists *Yonec* along with the *Pater noster, Ave Maria,* and other religious verses. For more detailed descriptions of these manuscripts and their contents, see Omont, *Bibliothèque Nationale, Catalogue, nouvelles acquisitions françaises,* vol. 1, nos. 1–3060, 145–46; Taschereau, *Catalogue des manuscrits français,* 1: 366–68; Omont, *Bibliothèque Nationale, Catalogue, anciens petits fonds français,* vol. 2, nos. 22885–25696, 361–68; and the British Library's on-line manuscript catalogue for Cotton Vespasian B.xiv, available at http://www.bl.uk/catalogues/manuscripts/HITS0001.ASP?VPath=html/65614.htm&Search=vespasian+b+xiv&Highlight=F (last accessed 28 February 2011). For discrete genres arriving at similar ends, see Newhauser, *Treatise on Vices and Virtues,* 14.

9. Gervase of Tilbury, *Otia Imperialia: Recreation for an Emperor,* ed. and trans. S. E. Banks and J. W. Binns (Oxford: Clarendon Press, 2002), Book II, ch. 10, 299: "Quamuis tempore mores hominum mutante, . . . uiri ac mulieres . . . artius uestiuntur, ita quod insuta potius quam induta corpora iudicantur."

10. For the notion that Henry II and Eleanor of Aquitaine helped to disseminate ideals of courtliness, though not specifically those pertaining to dress, see Peter Dronke, "Peter of Blois and Poetry at the Court of Henry II," *Mediaeval Studies* 38 (1976): 185–235; Jaeger, *Origins of Courtliness,* 205–6; and Roberta Krueger, "Marie de France," in *The Cambridge Companion to Medieval Women's Writing,* ed. Carolyn Dinshaw and David Wallace (Cambridge: Cambridge University Press, 2003), 172.

11. Quotations from the *lais* in this chapter are from Rychner's edition, *Les Lais de Marie de France.* Translations are from *The Lais of Marie de France,* ed. Robert Hanning and Joan Ferrante (Durham, NC: Labyrinth Press, 1978); I note where I have modified translations in some cases. For Marie writing at Henry II's court, see Krueger, "Marie de France," 172; and Michelle A. Freeman, "Marie de France's Poetics of Silence: The Implications for a Feminine 'Translatio,'" *PMLA* 99, no. 5 (1984): 860–83. R. Howard Bloch, however, notes that there is no concrete evidence identifying for whom Marie wrote in his *The Anonymous Marie de France* (Chicago: University of Chicago Press, 2003), 1.

12. Of the five manuscripts that contain one or more *lais, Guigemar* appears in three: BL Harley 978, BnF nouv. acq. fr. 1104, and BnF fr. 2168.

13. Steele, *Fetish,* 83.

14. Wright, *Weaving Narrative,* 9. Wright provides an account of the social changes and cultural fields within which aristocratic fashions operate.

15. See Leo Spitzer, "The Prologue to the 'Lais' of Marie de France and Medieval Poets," *Modern Philology* 41, no. 2 (1943): 96–102; D. W. Robertson,

"Marie de France, Lais, Prologue, 13–16," *Modern Language Notes* 64, no. 5 (1949): 336–38; Alexandre Leupin, "The Impossible Task of Manifesting 'Literature': On Marie de France's Obscurity," *Exemplaria* 3, no. 1 (1991): 221–42; and Andrew Cowell, "Deadly Letters: 'Deus Amanz,' Marie's Prologue to the Lais and the Dangerous Nature of the Gloss," *Romanic Review* 88, no. 3 (1997): 337–56. For glossing as a twelfth-century secular poetic practice, see Tony Hunt, "Glossing Marie de France," *Romanische Forschungen* 86 (1974): 396–418.

16. Matilda Tomaryn Bruckner, *Shaping Romance* (Philadelphia: University of Pennsylvania Press, 1993), 159; Spitzer, "Prologue to the 'Lais,'" 96–97; and Cowell, "Deadly Letters."

17. Jaeger, *Origins of Courtliness*, 242.

18. Crane, *Insular Romance*, 102.

19. I quote from Ian Short's re-edited prologue to Denis Piramus's vernacular life of Saint Edmund (London, British Library, MS Cotton Domitian A.XI, ff. 3a–3c) in the appendix to his "Denis Piramus and the Truth of Marie's Lais," 339–40. For a complete edition of the saint's life, see Denis Piramus, *La Vie Seint Edmund le Rei*, ed. Hilding Kjellman (Göteborg, 1935). Translation is Crane's, *Insular Romance*, 95.

20. See Short, "Denis Piramus," 321–22, for the condemnation by cleric Denis Piramus, the anonymous chaplain who wrote the *Passion of St. Andrew*, and Guillaume le Clerc de Normandie; Crane, *Insular Romance*, 94–96; and *Speculum Vitae*, ed. Hanna, lines 35–48, for a condemnation of romances *Octavian, Isumbras, Bevis of Hampton,* and *Guy of Warwick*.

21. Jaeger, *Origins of Courtliness*, 197.

22. Leonard E. Boyle cites Augustine's *De fide, spe et caritate* and *De doctrina christiana* along with Gregory the Great's *Liber regulae pastoralis* in "The Inter-Conciliar Period, 1179–1215, and the Beginnings of Pastoral Manuals," in *Miscellanea Rolando Bandinelli Papa Alessandro III*, ed. F. Liotta (Siena: Accademia Senesi degli Intronati 1986), 45–56, at 46. John T. McNeill and Helena M. Gamer provide an overview of the Celtic and Anglo-Saxon penitential guides in their *Medieval Handbooks of Penance*, rev. ed. (New York: Columbia University Press, 1990).

23. Goering, "The Internal Forum," 411–14; and Boyle, "The Inter-Conciliar Period," 46–48.

24. Boyle, "The Inter-Conciliar Period," 47.

25. For positions on dress in the early church, see Clement of Alexandria, *Christ the Educator*, trans. Simon P. Wood (New York: Fathers of the Church, 1954), 181; and Tertullian, "The Apparel of Women," 140.

26. Orderic Vitalis, *Ecclesiastical History*, 4:188. See also Antonia Gransden, *Historical Writing in England*, vol. 1 (London: Routledge, 1974).

27. Joseph Stevenson, ed., *The Church Historians of England*, vol. 4, part 2 (London: Seeleys, 1854), 547–48; for the Latin, see William of Newburgh, *Historia rerum Anglicarum*, ed. Hans Claude Hamilton (London: Sumptibus Societatis, 1856), 276. For the importance of William's chronicle, see Gransden, *Historical Writing in England*, 1:263–68; and Nancy F. Partner, *Serious Entertainments: The Writing of History in Twelfth-Century England* (Chicago: University of Chicago Press, 1977), 51–113.

28. Michel Zink, *La Prédication en langue romane avant 1300* (Paris: Editions Honoré Champion, 1976), 373. The translation is by E. Jane Burns, *Courtly Love Undressed*, 39–40.

29. Burns, *Courtly Love Undressed*, 40–41.

30. Albert Lecoy de la Marche, *La Chaire française au Moyen Age* (Paris: Didier et Cie. Librairies, 1868), 405. Translation is mine. Etienne de Bourbon (ca. 1190–1261) also notes that belts may communicate the physical and spiritual state of the wearer; see Albert Lecoy de la Marche, *Le Rire du prédicateur* (1888; reprint, with introduction and notes by Jacques Berlioz; Paris: Brepols, 1999), 140.

31. Thomas Wright and James Orchard Halliwell, eds., *Reliquae Antiquae: Scraps from Ancient Manuscripts Illustrating Chiefly Early English Literature and the English Language*, vol. 1 (London: William Pickering, 1841), 41–42.

32. Freeman, "Marie de France's Poetics of Silence," 879, note 3. See also Philippe Ménard, *Les Lais de Marie de France: Contes d'amour et d'aventure du Moyen Age* (Paris: Presses Universitaires de France, 1979), 32; Ernest Hœpffner, "Pour la chronologie des *Lais* de Marie de France," *Romania* 60 (1934): 36–66, and "Marie de France et l'*Enéas*," *Studi Medievali*, n.s. 5 (1932): 272–308, at 283–85; Rychner, "Introduction," *Les Lais*, vii–xlv; Earl Jeffrey Richards, "Les Rapports entre le *Lai de Guigemar* et le *Roman d'Enéas*: Considérations génériques," in *Le Récit bref au Moyen Age*, ed. Danielle Buschinger (Paris: Librairie Honoré Champion, 1980), 45–56; Glyn S. Burgess, *The Lais of Marie de France: Text and Context* (Athens: University of Georgia Press, 1987), 4–6 and 24; Simon Gaunt, *Gender and Genre in Medieval French Literature* (Cambridge: Cambridge University Press, 1995), 71–121; Gaunt, "From Epic to Romance: Gender and Sexuality in the *Roman d'Enéas*," *Romanic Review* 83, no. 1 (1992): 1–27, at 8; and Jean-Charles Huchet, *Le Roman médiéval* (Paris: Presses Universitaires de France, 1984), 60.

33. *Enéas*, ed. J. J. Salverda de Grave (Paris: Librairie Ancienne Edouard Champion, 1929). Translations are from John A. Yunck, ed. and trans., *Enéas* (New York: Columbia University Press, 1974). Christopher Baswell reads this

moment as an example of Dido's eroticism in *Virgil in Medieval England: Figuring the* Aeneid *from the Twelfth Century to Chaucer* (Cambridge: Cambridge University Press, 1995), 194.

34. *Roman de Thèbes*, ed. Francine Mora-Lebrun (Paris: Librairie Générale Française, 1995), lines 4123–30: "D'une porpre inde fu vestue / tot senglement a sa char nue: / la blanche char desoz pareit. / Li bliauz detrenchiez esteit / par menue detrencheüre / entresqu'a val vers la ceinture. / Vestue fu estreitement, / d'un baudré ceinte laschement" [She was dressed in a dark, precious Indian silk, all simply in naked flesh: her white flesh appeared underneath; the tunic was cut in pieces, with small incisions; between and across (the cuts) she had a belt. She was dressed tightly, with a belt tied loosely].

35. Benoît de Sainte-Maure, *Roman de Troie*, ed. Emmanuèle Baumgartner and Françoise Vielliard (Paris: Librairie Générale Française, 1998): "D'un drap de seie a or brosdé, / O riches huevres bien ovré, / Ot un bliaut forré d'ermine, / Lonc que par terre li traïne, / Qui fu riches e avenanz / E a son cors se bien estanz / Qu'el mont n'a rien, que le vestist, / Qui plus de ce li avenist" [She wore a *bliaut* lined with ermine, made of silk fabric woven with gold, marvelously embroidered, and which fell to the ground. The *bliaut* was so rich and elegant that it would have enhanced the beauty of any woman who would have worn it] (lines 13,333–40).

36. Jean Renart, *Le Roman de la Rose ou de Guillaume de Dole*, ed. G. Servois (Paris: Firmin Didot, 1893), lines 195–97, 208: "Ne verrai gent a tel solaz / Ne tante dame estroite a laz, / En chainses ridez lor biauz cors . . . De corroietes, de blans ganz" [I really don't expect ever again to see people have such a wonderful time, nor so many ladies with pleated tunics laced tightly about their beautiful bodies. . . . They wore fine slender belts and white gloves]. For the English translation, see *The Romance of the Rose or Guillaume de Dole*, trans. Patricia Terry and Nancy Vine Durling (Philadelphia: University of Pennsylvania Press, 1993).

37. Mireille Madou, *Le Costume civil* (Turnhout: Brepols, 1986), 16: "L'étranglement de la taille, par exemple, y attire l'attention, ce qui n'est pas sans conséquences dans la relation homme-femme." English translation is mine.

38. Among many moments when Antigone's garments may elicit sexual desire is the following: "Partonopex vit la pucele: / soz ciel n'en ot un tant bele; / s'il la covit, ne m'en merveil, / soz ciel n'eüst tant gent pareil" [Parthenopex saw the girl; there was none other so beautiful under the sky. If he desires her, I am not surprised; there was no person similar to her under the heavens] (lines 4208–11); see also lines 4238–39, 4274, and 4276, respectively.

39. *Jean Renart and the Art of Romance: Essays on Guillaume de Dole*, ed. Nancy Vine Durling (Gainesville: University Press of Florida, 1997), 1–3.

40. "Candace fu bele, blanche cum flur d'espine, / Estroit estoit lacee en un[e] purprine . . . / E vont desur le lit parler d'amur fine; / Recordent la lesçon qu'afiert a tel doctrine. / Quant a lur voleir ont fete la medecine, / Montent les degrez de la sale marbrine" [Candace was beautiful, white like a May blossom; she was tightly laced in a purple dress. . . . They go on to the bed to speak of courtly love, they remember the lesson, which asserts such doctrine. When they have satisfied their desire, they climb the steps to the marble room] (lines 7751–52, 7755–58), Thomas of Kent, *Roman d'Alexandre*. English translation is mine.

41. "La sist Orable, la dame o le cler vis / Ele est vestue d'un peliçon hermin, / Et par desoz d'un bliaut de samit; / Estroit a laz par le cors qui bien sist. / Voit la Guillelmes, tot le cors li fremist" [There sits Orable, the lady with the fair face. She is wearing an ermine tunic covered by a bliaut of figured silk tightened with laces over her torso, which is well shaped. When Guillaume sees her, his whole body trembles] (lines 683–87). *La Prise d'Orange*, ed. Claude Régnier (Paris: Editions Klincksieck, 1986). The translation is Waugh's, 7.

42. Hans Robert Jauss, *Toward an Aesthetic of Reception* (Minneapolis: University of Minnesota Press, 1982).

43. Gaunt, "From Epic to Romance," 8; Gaunt, *Gender and Genre*, 71–121; and Huchet, *Le Roman médiéval*, 60.

44. Virgil writes, "Tandem corripuit sese atque inimica refugit / in nemus umbriferum, coniunx ubi pristinus illi / respondet curis aequatque Sychaeus amorem" [At length she flung herself away and, still his foe, fled back to the shady grove, where Sychaeus, her lord of former days, responds to her sorrows and gives her love for love] (VI.472–74) in *Aeneid*, trans. H. Rushton Fairclough, Loeb Classical Library, no. 63 (Cambridge, MA: Harvard University Press, 1999). Alternatively, the *Enéas*-poet describes the situation in this way at 2657–62: "Por ce qu'el li avoit mentie / la foi qu'el li avoit plevie, / ne s'osoit pas vers lui torner, / ne ne l'osot mie esgarder, / ne pres de lui ne s'aprismot: / por son forfet se vergondot" [Because she had belied the faith she had pledged to Sychaeus, she did not dare turn toward him, nor even look at him at all, nor approach near him. By her misdeed she was dishonored].

45. Camille "dresses herself very tightly in a precious black fabric over her naked flesh" [bien fu la dame estroit vestue / de porpre noire a sa char nue] (lines 4011–12), and "places a sash embroidered in gold over her fitted clothing" [Vestue an fu estroitement; / dessus fu ceinte cointement / d'une sozceinte

a or broudee] (lines 4021–23). For readings of gender and sexuality in depictions of Camille, see Gaunt, "From Epic to Romance," 13; and Huchet, *Le
Roman médiéval*, 63–64.

46. All but two of her twelve *lais*—*Equitan* and *Chevrefoil*—position expensive clothing as indicators of courtliness. *Laüstic* is also an exception in that it
uses luxurious fabric instead of a garment as an expression of love: the lady
wraps a dead nightingale in the fabric and sends it to her lover as a reminder of
their affair: "En une piece de samit / A or brusdé e tut escrit / Ad l'oiselet en-
volupé; / Un suen vaslet ad apelé, / Sun message li ad chargié, / A sun ami l'ad
enveié" [In a piece of samite, embroidered in gold and written upon, she
wrapped the little bird. She called one of her servants, charged him with her
message, and sent him to her lover] (lines 135–40).

47. See especially Burns, *Courtly Love Undressed*; E. Jane Burns, "Why Tex-
tiles Make a Difference," in *Medieval Fabrications: Dress, Textiles, Cloth Work, and Other
Cultural Imaginings*, ed. E. Jane Burns (New York: Palgrave, 2004), 1–18; Crane,
The Performance of Self; Koslin and Snyder, eds., *Encountering Medieval Textiles*; and
Heller, *Fashion in Medieval France*. An exception is Wright's *Weaving Narrative*.

48. For critical interpretations of the knot and belt unrelated to fashion,
see Tracy Adams, "'Arte regendus amor': Suffering and Sexuality in Marie de
France's *Lai de Guigemar*," *Exemplaria* 17, no. 2 (2005): 285–315, at 307–10;
Bloch, *The Anonymous Marie de France*, 48–50; Bruckner, *Shaping Romance*, 165–66;
Joan Brumlik, "The Lyric Malmariée: Marie's Subtext in *Guigemar*," *Romance
Quarterly* 43, no. 2 (1996): 67–71; Nancy Vine Durling, "The Knot, the Belt,
and the Making of *Guigemar*," *Assays*, vol. 6, ed. Peggy Knapp (Pittsburgh:
Carnegie Mellon University Press, 1991), 29–53; Susanne Klerks, "The Pain
of Reading Female Bodies in Marie de France's *Guigemar*," *Dalhousie French Studies*
33 (1995): 1–14; Thomas L. Reed, Jr., "Marie de France's *Guigemar* as Art of
Interpretation (and Ambiguity)," in *Speaking Images: Essays in Honor of V. A. Kolve*,
ed. Robert F. Yeager, Charlotte Morse, and V. A. Kolve (Asheville, NC: Pegasus
Press, 2001), 1–26; Robert M. Stein, "Desire, Social Reproduction, and
Marie's *Guigemar*," in *In Quest of Marie de France*, ed. Chantal A. Maréchal (Lewis-
ton, Queenstown, Lampeter: Edwin Mellon Press, 1992), 283–86; Monica L.
Wright, "Chemise and Ceinture: Marie de France's *Guigemar* and the Use of
Textiles," in *Courtly Arts and the Arts of Courtliness*, ed. Keith Busby and Christo-
pher Kleinhenz (Cambridge: D. S. Brewer, 2006), 771–77; and Wright, *Weaving
Narrative*, 147–55.

49. For example, Amelia E. Van Vleck argues that Marie "use[s] textiles
as documents of feminine testimony in questions of sexual contracts" in *Laüstic*,
Fresne, and Lanval in "Textiles as Testimony in Marie de France and *Philomena*,"

Medievalia et Humanistica 22 (1995): 31–60, at 33. Gloria Thomas Gilmore understands clothing as a means "to comment on the theme of subject formation" in *Bisclavret;* see her "Marie de France's *Bisclavret:* What the Werewolf Will
and Will Not Wear," in *Encountering Medieval Textiles,* ed. Désirée G. Koslin and
Janet E. Snyder (New York: Palgrave, 2002), 67–84, at 67. E. Jane Burns asserts that garments "disrupt stereotypes of femininity" by providing the female
protagonist in *Lanval* with newfound agency in *Courtly Love Undressed,* 73.

50. Scholars have convincingly argued that Guigemar's lady does not wear
a chastity belt. See Shira Schwam-Baird, "Would a Gentleman Belt a Lady?
Chastity Belts (and Knots) in Marie de France's *Guigemar,*" *Mediaevalia* 22, no. 2
(1999): 323–42, 329; and, more recently, Albrecht Classen, *The Medieval Chastity
Belt: A Myth-Making Process* (New York: Palgrave, 2007), 108–10. Reed notes that
the belt "signals fidelity and physical restraint" (20), but he does not make this
connection in relation to twelfth-century fashion or Marie's poetics of restraint
in the *lai.*

51. "De sun bliaut trenche les laz: / La ceinture voelt ovrir, / Mes n'en
poeit a chief venir" [He cut the laces of her tunic, and tried to open the belt.
But he didn't succeed] (lines 738–40).

52. Adams, "'Arte regendus amor,'" 301 and 305.

53. "Me duce damnosas, homines, conpescite curas" [under my guidance,
ye men, control your ruinous passions] (*Remedia Amoris,* line 69); "Publicus as-
sertor dominis suppressa levabo / Pectora: vindictae quisque favete suae" [A
public champion, I shall relieve hearts that groan beneath their lords: welcome
each of you the rod that liberates] (lines 73–74). Quotations are from Ovid's
The Art of Love and Other Poems, ed. and trans. J. H. Mozley, Loeb Classical Library
232 (Cambridge, MA: Harvard University Press, 1979).

54. Here my argument complements Antoinette Knapton's idea, that
there is a comparable relationship between the tower and the belt that Guigemar
later assigns to his lady, in *Mythe et psychologie chez Marie de France dans* Guigemar
(Chapel Hill: North Carolina Studies in the Romance Languages and Literatures, 1975), 107. See also Durling, "The Knot, the Belt," 38, who notes "various metaphoric representations of enclosure—belt, tower, and chamber" but
reads these enclosures as "the externalization and symbolic representation of
female experience."

55. Adams, "'Arte regendus amor,'" 289–93, 312; Bruckner, *Shaping Ro-
mance,* 164; Hanning and Ferrante, eds., *Lais of Marie de France,* 37, n. 5; Laurence
Harf-Lancner, trans., *The Lais of Marie de France,* ed. Karl Warnke (Paris: Lettres
Gothiques, 1990), 39, n. 6; Klerks, "Pain of Reading Female Bodies," 3; and
Reed, "Marie de France's *Guigemar,*" 17, all conclude that the book is the *Remedia*

amoris. For the book as either *Remedia amoris* or *Ars amatoria*, see Robert W. Hanning, "The Talking Wounded: Desire, Truth Telling, and Pain in the *Lais* of Marie de France," in *Desiring Discourse: The Literature of Love, Ovid through Chaucer,* ed. James J. Paxson and Cynthia A. Gravlee (Selinsgrove: Susquehanna University Press, 1998), 140–61; and Roberta L. Krueger, "Beyond Debate: Gender in Play in Old French Courtly Fiction," in *Gender in Debate from the Early Middle Ages to the Renaissance,* ed. Thelma S. Fenster and Clare A. Lees (New York: Palgrave, 2002), 79–95, at 83.

56. Quoted in Adams, "'Arte regendus amor,'" 299.

57. "Moderate debet taxillorum deservire ministeriis. Magna debet antiquorum libenter gesta recolere atque asserere. Animosus debet esse in proelio et contra inimicos arditus, sapiens, cautus et ingeniosus. Plurium non debet simul mulierum esse amator, sed pro una omnium debet feminarum servitor existere atque devotus" [He should be moderate about indulging in games of dice. He should gladly call to mind and take to heart the great deeds of the men of old. He ought to be courageous in battle and hardy against his enemies, wise, cautious, and clever. He should not be a lover of several women at the same time, but for the sake of one he should be a devoted servant of all]. The Latin is from *Andreas Capellanus on Love,* ed. P. G. Walsh (London: Duckworth, 1982), 82–84; for the English translation, see Andreas Capellanus, *The Art of Courtly Love,* ed. and trans. John Jay Parry (New York: Columbia University Press, 1960). Although scholars disagree as to whether Andreas's text should be understood as either a product of the late twelfth-century French courtly milieu of Marie de Champagne or a clerical reaction to and subsequent condemnation of courtly love motifs evident in secular poetry, I am inclined to accept Don A. Monson's suggestion that Andreas's audience comprised both clerics and courtiers in his "Andreas Capellanus and the Problem of Irony," *Speculum* 63, no. 3 (1988): 539–72.

58. Guigemar's wound has garnered much critical attention. See, in particular, Adams, "'Arte regendus amor,'" 301–10; R. Howard Bloch, "The Medieval Text—'Guigemar'—as a Provocation to the Discipline of Medieval Studies," *Romanic Review* 79 (1988): 63–73, at 70; Durling, "The Knot, the Belt"; Hanning, "Talking Wounded"; Klerks, "Pain of Reading Female Bodies," Sarah Spence, "Double Vision: Love and Envy in the *Lais,*" in *In Quest of Marie de France: A Twelfth-Century Poet,* ed. Chantal A. Maréchal (Lewiston: Edwin Mellon Press, 1992), 262–79; Stephen G. Nichols, "Deflections of the Body in the Old French Lay," *Stanford French Review* 14 (1990): 27–50; and Wright, "Chemise and Ceinture," 771–77.

59. For gift-giving as a means of recognition in Marie's *lais*, see the following examples: *Fresne*, lines 413–50, in which a mother recognizes her daughter by an embroidered silk coverlet and a ring that she had given her before abandoning her as an infant; and *Milun*, in which the eponymous protagonist recognizes his son, who wears a ring that Milun gave to the boy's mother, lines 429–72. For gift-giving as a sign of love, see *Chaitivel*, lines 57–58; *Eliduc*, lines 379–81; *Equitan*, lines 181–82; *Lanval*, lines 135–42; *Milun*, lines 39–46; and *Yonec*, lines 415–20.

60. Sun Hee Kim Gertz, "Echoes and Reflections of Enigmatic Beauty in Ovid and Marie de France," *Speculum* 73, no. 2 (1998): 372–96, at 385. See also her *Echoes and Reflections: Memory and Memorials in Ovid and Marie de France* (Amsterdam: Rodopi, 2003); and Hanning, "Talking Wounded," 140–61.

61. For belts and knots in medieval sorcery, see J. G. Frazer, *Taboo and the Perils of the Soul* (London: Macmillan and Co., 1914), 299–314; Vincent Foster Hooper, "Greyon and the Knotted Cord," *Modern Language Notes* 51, no. 7 (November 1936): 445–49; Richard Kieckhefer, "Erotic Magic in Medieval Europe," in *Sex in the Middle Ages*, ed. Joyce E. Salisbury (New York: Garland, 1991), 30–55; and John R. Reinhard, *The Old French Romance of Amadas and Ydoine* (Durham, NC: Duke University Press, 1927), 72–97.

62. Frazer, *Taboo*, 304, cites Virgil's *Eclogues*, viii.78–80: "The lovesick maid in Virgil seeks to draw Daphnis to her from the city by spells and by tying three knots on each of three strings of different colors." Kieckhefer writes that Albert the Great "says that if a knot is tied around the phallus of a wolf in the name of a man or woman (the wolf being presumably dead, and the phallus removed), that the person will be incapable of copulation until the knot is untied" (43). See Albert the Great, *Man and the Beasts: De animalibus, Books 22–26*, trans. James J. Scanlan (Binghamton, NY: Medieval and Renaissance Texts and Studies, 1987), 158.

63. For the belt and knot as magical elements in *Guigemar*, see Francis Dubost, "Les motifs merveilleux dans les lais de Marie de France," in *Amour et merveille: Les Lais de Marie de France*, ed. Jean Dufournet (Paris: Honoré Champion, 1995), 41–80, at 61–62; Pierre Jonin, "Merveilleux celtique et symbolisme universel dans 'Guigemar' de Marie de France," in *Mélanges de philologie et de littératures romanes offerts à Jeanne Wathelet-Willem*, ed. Jacques DeCaluwé (Liège: Marche Romane, 1978), 239–55, at 246; Ana Pairet, "Magie et pureté dans *Tristan*, *Cligès*, et *Raoul de Cambrai*," in *Souillure et pureté: le corps et son environnement culturel*, ed. Jean-Jacques Vincensini (Paris: Maisonneuve et Larose, 2003), 258–66, at 265; and Schwam-Baird, "Would a Gentleman Belt a Lady?" 31.

64. Quotations of *Sir Gawain and the Green Knight* are from *The Complete Works of the* Pearl-*Poet*, ed. Malcolm Andrew, Ronald Waldron, and Clifford Peterson (Berkeley: University of California Press, 1993).

65. Helen Cooper, *The English Romance in Time*, 4.

66. Helen Cooper, "The Supernatural," in *A Companion to the Gawain-Poet*, ed. Derek Brewer and Jonathan Gibson (Woodbridge: D. S. Brewer, 1997), 277–91, at 290. See also Kieckhefer, "Erotic Magic," who notes that erotic magic is at odds with appropriate courtly behavior in romance, 46.

67. Andreas Capellanus, *The Art of Courtly Love*, 68; *Andreas Capellanus on Love*, ed. Walsh, 96.

68. William of Malmesbury, *Gesta regum Anglorum*, 494: Describing a speech by Maurilius, a monk of Fécamp with many virtues, William of Malmesbury writes: "Ductores spiritus mei uultibus et uestibus ad omnem elegantiam erant compositi; concordabat uerborum lenitas cum nitore uestium, ut nichil desiderarem preter talium uirorum obsequium" [Those who guided my spirit matched the highest standard of elegance in countenance and in raiment; the courtesy of their language was equal to the brilliance of their apparel, so that I felt no lack of anything as long as I enjoyed the services of men like them]. John of Salisbury, *Policraticus*, ed. Clement C. J. Webb, 2 vols. (1909; reprint, New York: Arno, 1979), Book VI, chapter 13: "Non enim restituebantur qui meruerant priuari cingulo, antequam eos prae ceteris uirtutum merita insignirent" [Those who had thus deserved to be deprived of their belts were not restored before they had signalized themselves by the merit of virtues excelling others]. The English translation is from *The Statesman's Book of John of Salisbury: Being the Fourth, Fifth, and Sixth Books and Selections from the Seventh and Eighth Books, of the* Policraticus, ed. and trans. John Dickenson (New York: Russell and Russell, 1963), 217.

69. Brian Golding describes a "famous passage" in Gerald's auto-biography that recounts his presentation of six books to Innocent III: "the pope kept all the volumes at his bedside for about a month before distributing five of them to five of his cardinals who requested them, but he would not allow himself to be parted from the *Gemma*, which he loved above all the rest," "Gerald of Wales, the *Gemma Ecclesiastica* and Pastoral Care," in *Texts and Traditions of Medieval Pastoral Care: Essays in Honour of Bella Millett*, ed. Cate Gunn and Catherine Innes-Parker (Woodbridge: York Medieval Press, 2009), 47–61, at 47.

70. Giraldus Cambrensis, *Opera*, vol. 2, ed. J. S. Brewer (London, 1882; reprint, Kraus, 1964), 173. For the English translation, see Gerald of

Wales, *Jewel of the Church*, ed. and trans. John J. Hagen (Leiden: E. J. Brill, 1979), 311.

71. Brian Golding, in "Gerald of Wales," 61, argues against scholars who believe the *Gemma* to be destined for a clerical audience, proposing rather that the work was "for the approbation and use of scholars like himself, rather than an ill-educated parish clergy." For the *Gemma* directed toward Welsh clergy, see Goering, "The Internal Forum," 416.

72. Golding, "Gerald of Wales," 61.

73. John of Salisbury, *Policraticus*, 2:314: ". . . uir utique alloquio ex professo mollis et in praecinctu ponens omnem decorem suum. Fuit enim uestitu ad immunditiem curioso et, ut bene amictus iret, faciem quaerebat in speculo. Vbi se intuens, togam corpori sic applicabat ut rugas ne forte sed industria locatas artifex nodus astringeret et sinus ex composito defluens modum lateris ambiret" [(the statesman Hortensius) displayed great elegance in dress. He clothed himself with a care that verged upon indecency. To be sure that he made a good appearance when he went out, he paraded before a mirror. Gazing at himself, he would so drape the toga upon his person that the ingenious knot would hold the pleats, which had been formed with care, and the drapery flowing as intended would mold itself into his shape]. The English translation is from John of Salisbury, *Frivolities of Courtiers and Footprints of Philosophers: Being a Translation of the First, Second, and Third Books and Selections from the Seventh and Eighth Books of the* Policraticus *of John of Salisbury*, ed. Joseph B. Pike (Minneapolis: University of Minnesota Press, 1938), 372.

74. Lecoy de la Marche, *La Chaire française*, 441, n. 1, quoted in and translated by Burns, *Courtly Love Undressed*, 41.

75. Scott, *Medieval Dress and Fashion*, 52–53.

76. Klerks, "Pain of Reading Female Bodies," 8.

77. Reed, "Marie de France's *Guigemar*," 20.

78. Orderic Vitalis, *Ecclesiastical History*, IV.188.

79. For the English, see *Chronicle of the Third Crusade: A Translation of the* Itinerarium Peregrinorum et Gesta Regis Ricardi, ed. Helen J. Nicholson (Aldershot: Ashgate, 1997), Bk. 5, ch. 22, 299–300; for the Latin, see *Chronicles and Memorials of the Reign of Richard I*, ed. William Stubbs (London: Longman, Green, Longman, Roberts, and Green, 1864; reprint, Krause, 1964), 1:331.

80. Ibid.

81. John of Salisbury, *Policraticus*, Bk. VI, ch. 14: "necessaria est disciplina militaris," 37; and Bk. VI, ch. 3: "In eo namque militarem constare gloriam opinantur, si nitidiori splendeant habitu, ut lineas suas uestes uel sericas sic

perstringant et torqueant ut quasi cutem cerussatam aliisue fucis obnoxiam carni faciant coherere," 12; English translation, *Statesman's Book,* 220 and 184.

82. John of Salisbury, *Policraticus,* Bk. VI, ch. 19, 55; English translation, *Statesman's Book,* 239.

83. Ibid., "Hoc autem uolo ire persuasum nostratibus, si exerceantur, uirtutem non deesse, quae tamen frequenter intercidit, si non disciplina firmatur" [I wish that our countrymen would be persuaded that to train themselves properly is no sign of a want of valor, which so often comes to nought unless discipline is firmly established].

84. William of Malmesbury, *Gesta regum Anglorum,* 558–60: "Soluta militari disciplina. . . . Tunc fluxus crinium, tunc luxus uestium, tunc usus calceorum cum arcuatis aculeis inuentus; mollitie corporis certare cum feminis, gressum frangere, gestu soluto et latere nudo incedere adolescentium specimen erat. Enerues, emolliti, quod nati fuerant inuiti manebant, expugnatores alienae pudicitiae, prodigi suae" [The knightly code of conduct disappeared. . . . Long flowing hair, luxurious garments, shoes with curved and pointed tips became the fashion. Softness of body rivaling the weaker sex, a mincing gait, effeminate gestures and a liberal display of the person as they went along, such was the ideal fashion of the younger men. Spineless, unmanned, they were reluctant to remain as Nature had intended they should be; they were a menace to the virtue of others and promiscuous with their own].

85. Geoffrey of Monmouth, *The Historia Regum Britannie,* ed. and trans. Neil Wright (Cambridge: D. S. Brewer, 1985), 113: "When the use of arms is seen to be absent and replaced with inflamed pleasures of women, there is no doubt that laziness may defile manliness, honor, audacity, and fame" [Quippe ubi usus armorum uidetur abesse et alee et mulierum inflammationes ceteraque oblectamenta adesse, dubitandum non est ne id quod erat uirtutis, quod honoris, quod audacie, quod fame, ignauia commaculet]. Similarly, John of Salisbury warns that "the leader in war must also use the utmost care 'that women and wine do not make soft the soldier's heart'" in *Policraticus,* Bk. VI, ch. 14, 221 [Duci quoque in re militari diligentissime praecauendum est "ne Venus et uinum pugnantia pectoral frangant," 39].

86. John of Salisbury, *Policraticus,* Bk. VI, ch. 13, 35; 217 in *Statesman's Book.*

87. Guillaume de Lorris and Jean de Meun, *Le Roman de la rose,* ed. Armand Strubel (Paris: Librairie Générale Française, 1992). The English translation is Charles Dahlberg's, *The Romance of the Rose,* 3rd ed. (Princeton: Princeton University Press, 1995).

88. C. Stephen Jaeger, *The Envy of Angels* (Philadelphia: University of Pennsylvania Press, 1994), 317–22.

CHAPTER TWO   **Heldris de Cornuälle**

1. Jean Baudrillard, *The Ecstasy of Communication* (Brooklyn: Autonomedia, 1988), 81.

2. Tanner, ed., *Decrees of the Ecumenical Councils*, 1:227.

3. Marion Gibbs and Jane Lang, *Bishops and Reform, 1215–1272* (Oxford: Oxford University Press, 1934, reprint, London: Cass, 1962), 96.

4. Geoffrey of Vinsauf, *The New Poetics*, in *Three Medieval Rhetorical Arts*, ed. Murphy, 27–108, at 34–35: "In each section, let everything in its own way do honor to the poem; neither let anything in any section sink or in any way suffer eclipse." The Latin version of Geoffrey's *Poetria nova* appears in Faral, *Les Arts poétiques du XIIe et du XIIIe siècle*, 197–262, at 199: "Omni parte sui modus omnis carmen honoret, ne qua parte labet, ne quam patiatur eclipsim."

5. As stated earlier, "web of interlocution" is Charles Taylor's term, from *Sources of the Self*, 36.

6. Lewis Thorpe provides details about the manuscript, its contents, sources of *Silence*, and the poem's language in his introduction to *Le Roman de Silence*, 1–62. *Silence* is one of six romances and eleven fabliaux included in Nottingham, University Library, MS Mi.LM.6. Four of eleven fabliaux include religious figures and moral themes: two by Gautiers de Leus, *De Dieu et dou Pescour* and *D[ou] prestre ki perdi les colles*; and two by anonymous authors, *Des iij commandemens* and *De l'arme ki guangna paradis par plait*. See also Busby, *Codex and Context*, 415–18.

7. For some, dress expresses power: see Lorraine Kochanske Stock, "The Importance of Being Gender 'Stable': Masculinity and Feminine Empowerment in *Le Roman de Silence*," *Arthuriana* 7, no. 2 (1997): 7–34, at 24; Roberta L. Krueger, *Women Readers and the Ideology of Gender in the Old French Verse Romance* (Cambridge: Cambridge University Press, 1993), 101–27; and Loren Ringer, "Exchange, Identity, and Transvestism in *Le Roman de Silence*," *Dalhousie French Studies* 28 (1994): 3–13, at 12. Others associate masculinity with Silence's cross-dressing: Michèle Perret argues that transvestism allows women to benefit from masculine privilege, while Simon Gaunt shows that Silence's success in battle indicates the poet's anxiety over men's capacity to wage war effectively: Perret, "Travesties et transsexuelles: Yde, Silence, Grisandole, Blanchandine," *Romance Notes* 25, no. 3 (1985): 328–40; and Gaunt, "The Significance of Silence," *Paragraph* 13 (1990): 202–16, at 212. For cross-dressing fueling the performance of gender by either eliminating gender ambiguity or creating it, see Elizabeth A. Waters, "The Third Path: Alternative Sex, Alternative Gender in *Le Roman de Silence*," *Arthuriana* 7, no. 2 (1997): 35–46; Peggy McCracken, "'The

Boy Who Was a Girl': Reading Gender in the *Roman de Silence*," *Romance Review* 85, no. 4 (1994): 517–36; Kathleen M. Blumreich, "Lesbian Desire in the Old French *Roman de Silence*," *Arthuriana* 7, no. 2 (1997): 47–62, at 47; and Erika E. Hess, *Literary Hybrids: Cross-dressing, Shapeshifting, and Indeterminacy in Medieval and Modern French Narrative* (New York: Routledge, 2004), 56. For transvestism engaging with biological sexuality, see Valerie R. Hotchkiss, *Clothes Make the Man: Female Cross Dressing in Medieval Europe* (New York: Garland, 1996), 106–13; Florence Ramond Jurney, "Secret Identities: (Un)masking Gender in the *Roman de Silence* by Heldris de Cornouaille and *L'enfant de sable* by Tahar Ben Jelloun," *Dalhousie French Studies* 55 (2001): 3–10, at 5; Kate Mason Cooper, "Elle and L: Sexualized Textuality in *Le Roman de Silence*," *Romance Notes* 25, no. 3 (1985): 341–60; and Barbara Newman, *From Virile Woman to Woman Christ* (Philadelphia: University of Pennsylvania Press, 1995), 165. Susan Crane focuses on the materiality of men's dress, arguing that dress shapes individual identity, in *The Performance of Self*, 102. For dress as a sign of linguistic ambiguities and the poetic ramifications of dress, see R. Howard Bloch, "Silence and Holes: The *Roman de Silence* and the Art of the Trouvère," *Yale French Studies* 70 (1986): 81–99, at 95; and Peter L. Allen, "The Ambiguity of Silence: Gender, Writing, and *Le Roman de Silence*," in *Sign, Sentence, Discourse: Language in Medieval Thought and Literature*, ed. Julian N. Wasserman and Lois Roney (Syracuse: Syracuse University Press, 1989), 98–112. For garments as a poetic trope that creates subjectivity, see E. Jane Burns, *Bodytalk: When Women Speak in Old French Literature* (Philadelphia: University of Pennsylvania Press, 1993), 243–46, at 245.

8. Garber, *Vested Interests*, 16–17.

9. Critics have addressed romance as both a mode and a genre: see Helen Cooper, *The English Romance in Time;* and W. R. J. Barron, *English Medieval Romance* (London: Longman, 1987), 1–9, 25–27, and 57–59, in particular.

10. *Silence: A Thirteenth-Century French Romance*, ed. and trans. Sarah Roche-Mahdi (East Lansing: Michigan State University Press, 2007).

11. See Lewis Thorpe, "Raoul de Houdenc: A Possible New Poem," *Modern Language Review* 47 (1952): 512–15, in which he cites Raoul's *Le Songe d'Enfer* and *Le borjois Borjon,* a thirteenth-century Latin poem, *Peregrinus,* and John of Salisbury's *Entheticus* as articulating the minstrel's complaint.

12. Alexander Murray, *Reason and Society in the Middle Ages* (Oxford: Clarendon Press, 1978), 74; Richard Newhauser, *The Early History of Greed: The Sin of Avarice in Early Medieval Thought and Literature* (Cambridge: Cambridge University Press, 2000), 121–31.

13. Lester K. Little, *Religious Poverty and Profit Economy in Medieval Europe* (Ithaca: Cornell University Press, 1978), 19–41; and Little, "Pride Goes before

Avarice: Social Change and the Vices in Latin Christendom," *The American Historical Review* 76, no. 1 (1971): 16–49, at 29.

14. Richard Newhauser, "Avarice and Apocalypse," in *The Apocalyptic Year 1000: Religious Expectation and Social Change, 950–1050,* ed. Richard Allen Landes, Andrew Colin Gow, and David C. Van Meter (Oxford: Oxford University Press, 2003), 109–19, at 113. See also Phyllis A. Tickle, *Greed: The Seven Deadly Sins* (New York: Oxford University Press, 2004).

15. Canon 16 states, "Clerici officia vel commercia saecularia non exerceant, maxime inhonesta, mimis, ioculatoribus et histrionibus non intendant," *Decrees of the Ecumenical Councils,* 243. John W. Baldwin, "The Image of the Jongleur in Northern France around 1200," *Speculum* 72, no. 3 (1997): 635–63, at 640–41, notes that prohibitions for clergy against courtly entertainment began in the late twelfth century; see also Edmond Faral, *Les Jongleurs en France au Moyen Age* (Paris: Librairie Honoré Champion, 1910).

16. Jean-Charles Payen, "La Pénitence dans le contexte culturel des XIIe et XIIIe siècles," *Revue des sciences philosophiques et théologiques* 61 (1977): 399–428, at 420.

17. Rutebeuf's denunciation appears in his *Renard le Bestourne;* see *Rutebeuf, Œuvres complètes,* ed. Edmond Faral and Julia Bastin, 2 vols. (Paris: Picard, 1970), 1:532–44.

18. Faral and Bastin, eds., *Rutebeuf,* 420.

19. Ibid., 532–37; and Rutebeuf, *Œuvres complètes,* ed. Michel Zink (Paris: Classiques Garnier, 1989), 1:253.

20. *Trésor de la langue française informatisé,* Analyse et traitement informatique de la langue française—Centre National de la Recherche Scientifique, Nancy Université: "franc," definitions I.3 and II.3. Available at http://atilf.atilf.fr /dendien/scripts/tlfiv5/affart.exe?56;s=3609769800;?b=0 (last accessed 8 April 2011).

21. Tanner, ed., *Decrees of the Ecumenical Councils,* 1:245.

22. Mary C. Mansfield cites Caesarius of Heisterbach, who recounts an instance where a priest gathered together six to eight penitents, had them repeat a generic list of sins that he read aloud to them, and then assigned the same penance to them all, *The Humiliation of Sinners: Public Penance in Thirteenth-Century France* (Ithaca: Cornell University Press, 1995), 67. Studies on the history of penance in the Christian church are vast. Older seminal work includes Bernhard Poschmann, *Penance and the Anointing of the Sick,* trans. Francis Courtney (London: Burns and Oates, 1964); John Baldwin, *Masters, Princes, and Merchants,* 47–59; Thomas N. Tentler, *Sin and Confession on the Eve of the Reformation* (Princeton: Princeton University Press, 1977), 21–23; Cyrille Vogel, *En rémission des péchés:*

Recherches sur les systèmes pénitentiels dans l'Eglise latine, ed. Alexandre Faivre (Aldershot: Variorum, 1994), for essays written by Vogel between 1952 and 1983. More recent contributions are *A New History of Penance*, ed. Abigail Firey (Boston: Brill, 2008); Goering, "The Internal Forum," 379–428; *Handling Sin: Confession in the Middle Ages*, ed. Peter Biller and A. J. Minnis (Woodbridge: York Medieval Press, 1998); Goering, *William de Montibus*; Mansfield, *Humiliation of Sinners*; and *Texts and Traditions of Medieval Pastoral Care*, ed. Gunn and Innes-Parker.

23. For the intended audience of the guides, see Goering, *William de Montibus*, 58–67; and Joseph Goering, "The Scholastic Turn (1100–1500): Penitential Theology and Law in the Schools," in *A New History of Penance*, ed. Abigail Firey, 219–37. For the penitential guides produced between Lateran III and Lateran IV as foundations for those created in the thirteenth, fourteenth, and fifteenth centuries, see Boyle, "The Inter-Conciliar Period," 45–56; and Goering, "The Internal Forum," 379–428. Pierre Payer notes a clear trajectory in penitential theories both pre- and post-Lateran IV in "The Humanism of the Penitentials and the Continuity of the Penitential Tradition," *Mediaeval Studies* 46 (1984): 340–54.

24. R. W. Southern, *The Making of the Middle Ages* (New Haven: Yale University Press, 1959), 227.

25. Ibid., 230–45.

26. For the *effictio* describing Hera, see *The Iliad*, XIV.161–88; "Lanval," in *Les Lais de Marie de France*, ed. Rychner, lines 559–72. The *effictio* of Alison is in the *Miller's Tale*, in *The Riverside Chaucer*, ed. Benson, I.3233–70.

27. See James J. Murphy, *Rhetoric in the Middle Ages: A History of Rhetorical Theory from Saint Augustine to the Renaissance* (Berkeley: University of California Press, 1974), 135–93; and Douglas Kelly, *Medieval Imagination: Rhetoric and Poetry of Courtly Love* (Madison: University of Wisconsin Press, 1978).

28. See the introduction to Geoffrey of Vinsauf, *The New Poetics*, ed. Murphy, 28–31.

29. Ibid., 30.

30. Alice M. Colby, *The Portrait in Twelfth-Century French Literature* (Geneva: Librairie Droz, 1965), 92.

31. *Poetria nova*, ed. Faral, 220: "Dives honoretur sententia divite verbo, / Ne rubeat matrona potens in paupere panno," lines 754–55. The English translation is Kopp's in *Three Medieval Rhetorical Arts*, ed. Murphy, 60.

32. Geoffrey of Vinsauf, *The New Poetics*, 55. *Poetria nova*, ed. Faral, 215–16, lines 600–611: "Formae tam pictae si vis appingere cultum, / Nexilis a tergo coma compta recomplicet aurum; / Irradiet frontis candori circulus auri; / Se nudet facies proprium vestita colorem; / Lactea stelliferum praecingat colla

monile; / Instita candescat bysso, chlamis ardeat auro; / Zona tegat medium, radiantibus undique gemmis; / Brachia luxurient armillis; circinet aurum / Subtiles digitos et gemma superbior auro / Diffundat radios; certent in veste serena / Ars cum materia. Nihil addere cultibus illis / Aut manus aut animus posit."

33. The English translation is Kopp's, 54. For the Latin, see Faral, 214–15, lines 562–97.

34. Derek Pearsall, "Rhetorical 'Descriptio' in 'Sir Gawain and the Green Knight,'" *Modern Language Review* 50 (1955): 129–34, at 130.

35. "Ele iert vestue en itel guise / De chainse blanc e de chemise / Que tuit li costé li pareient, / Ki de deus parz lacié esteient. / Le cors ot gent, basse la hanche, / Le col plus blanc que neif sur branche; / Les oilz ot vairs e blanc le vis, / Bele buche, neis bien asis, / Les surcilz bruns e bel le frunt, / E le chief cresp e aukes blunt: / Fils d'or ne gette tel luur / Cum si chevel cuntre le jur! / Sis manteus fu de purpre bis; / Les pans en ot entur li mis" (lines 559–72) [She was dressed in this fashion: in a white linen shift that revealed both her sides since the lacing was along the side. Her body was elegant, her hips slim, her neck whiter than snow on a branch, her eyes bright, her face white, a beautiful mouth, a well-set nose, dark eyebrows and an elegant forehead, her hair curly and rather blond; golden thread does not shine like her hair in the light. Her cloak, which she had wrapped around her, was dark purple]. I have slightly modified the English translation by Hanning and Ferrante, ed. and trans., *The Lais of Marie de France*. For Alison in the *Miller's Tale:* "Fair was this yonge wyf, and therwithal / As any wezele hir body gent and smal. / A ceynt [belt] she werede, barred al of silk, / A barmclooth [apron] as whit as morne milk / Upon her lendes [loins], ful of many a goore. / Whit was hir smok, and broyden [embroidered] al bifoore / And eek bihynde, on hir coler aboute, / Of col-blak silk, withinne and eek withoute. / The tapes of hir white voluper [cap] / Were of the same suyte of hir coler; / Hir filet [headband] brood of silk, and set ful hye. / And sikerly she hadde a likerous ye; / Ful smale ypulled were hire browes two, / And tho were bent and blake as any sloo [a plum-like fruit]. / She was ful moore blisful on to see / Than is the newe pere-jonette tree, / And softer than the wolle is of a wether. / And by hir girdel heeng a purs of lether, / Tasseled with silk and perled with latoun [a brass-like alloy]. / In al this world, to seken up and doun, / There nys no man so wys that koude thenche [imagine] / So gay a popelote or swiche a wenche. / Ful brighter was the shynyng of hir hewe / Than in the Tour the noble yforged newe. / But of hir song, it was as loude and yerne [lively] / As any swalwe sittynge on a berne. / Therto she koude skippe and make game, / As any kyde or calf fowlynge his dame. / Hir

mouth was sweete as bragot [country drink] or the meeth, / Or hoord of apples leyd in hey or heeth. / Wynsynge she was, as is a joly colt, / Long as a mast, and upright as a bolt. / A brooch she baar upon hir lowe coler, / As brood as is the boos of a bokeler [raised center of a shield]. / Hir shoes were laced on hir legges hye. / She was a prymerole [primrose], a piggesnye ["pig's-eye" flower], / For any lord to leggen in his bedde, / Or yet for any good yeman to wedde" (I.3233–70).

36. I have modified the last line of Roche-Mahdi's translation, and I thank Christophe Chaguinian and Samuel N. Rosenberg for their assistance.

37. Geoffrey of Vinsauf, *The New Poetics*, 34; *Poetria nova*, ed. Faral, 198, lines 44–47.

38. *Augustine: Confessions*, 3 vols., ed. James J. O'Donnell (Oxford: Clarendon Press, 1992); and Augustine, *Confessions*, trans. Henry Chadwick (Oxford: Oxford University Press, 1991).

39. Taylor, *Sources of the Self*, 139. Taylor's reading of Augustine has been met with some resistance by those who find that he does not take into consideration adequately Augustine's *City of God* and the role of the community in conversion. See Stanley Hauerwas and David Matzko, "The Sources of Charles Taylor," *Religious Studies Review* 18 (1992): 286–89, at 289; and chapter 1 in David Aers, *Salvation and Sin: Augustine, Langland and the Fourteenth Century* (Notre Dame: University of Notre Dame Press, 2009). I thank David Aers for sharing his work with me before its publication.

40. For some examples of Augustine's profound influence on medieval writers, see Tracy Adams, "'Pur vostre cor su jo em paine': The Augustinian Subtext of Thomas's Tristan," *Medium Ævum* 68, no. 2 (1999): 278–91, at 279–81; Aers, *Sin and Salvation*; and Servais Pinckaers, *The Sources of Christian Ethics*, trans. Sr. Mary Thomas Noble (Washington, DC: Catholic University of America Press, 1995). Bonaventure argues that Augustine was in the thirteenth century "the most authentic doctor among all the expositors of Sacred Scripture," in Jaroslav Pelikan, *The Growth of Medieval Theology (600–1300)*, vol. 3 of *The Christian Tradition: A History of the Development of Doctrine* (Chicago: University of Chicago Press, 1978), 271.

41. Pinckaers, *Sources of Chirstian Ethics*, 154.

42. Alan of Lille, *The Plaint of Nature*, trans. James J. Sheridan (Toronto: Pontifical Institute of Mediaeval Studies, 1980), 98; William Langland, *Piers Plowman: The B Version*, ed. George Kane and E. Talbot Donaldson (London: Athlone Press, 1975), XIII.272–456; "Cleanness," in *The Complete Works of the Pearl-Poet*, ed. Andrew and Waldron, 103–81.

43. *Aucassin et Nicolette* dates from the twelfth century and is extant in one manuscript, Paris, Bibliothèque Nationale, fr. 2168, ff. 70r–80v. *Yde et Olive* ex-

ists in two versions: the first is part of the thirteenth-century continuations of the epic poem, *Huon de Bordeaux*, which appears in one manuscript from 1311, located in Turin; the second version is a dramatic adaptation, known as the *Miracle de la fille d'un roy*, dating from the late fourteenth century, also extant in one manuscript, known as Cangé, at the Bibliothèque Nationale de France. See Robert L. A. Clark, "A Heroine's Sexual Itinerary: Incest, Transvestism, and Same-Sex Marriage in *Yde et Olive*," in *Gender Transgressions: Crossing the Normative Barrier in Old French Literature*, ed. Karen J. Taylor (New York: Garland, 1998), 89–105; and Diane Watt, "Behaving Like a Man? Incest, Lesbian Desire, and Gender Play in *Yde et Olive* and Its Adaptations," *Comparative Literature* 50:4 (1998): 265–85. *Tristan de Nanteuil* dates from the mid-fourteenth century and appears in one manuscript dating from the fifteenth century: Paris, Bibliothèque Nationale, fr. 1478.

44. *Aucassin et Nicolette: Chantefable du XIIIe siècle*, ed. Mario Roques (Paris: Champion, 1982); *Aucassin et Nicolette*, ed. and trans. Jean Dufournet (Paris: Garnier-Flammarion, 1973); *Lestoire de Merlin, The Vulgate Version of the Arthurian Romances*, vol. 2, ed. H. Oskar Summer (Washington, DC: Carnegie Institution, 1908), 300–312; *Esclarmonde, Clarisse et Florent, Yde et Olive: Drei Fortsetzungen der Chanson von Huon de Bordeaux, nach der einzigen Turiner Handschrift zum erstenmal veröffenlicht*, ed. Max Schweigel, Ausgaben und Abhandlungen aus dem Gebiete der romanischen Philologie 83 (Marburg: Elwert'sche Verlagsbuchhandlung, 1889): 152–73; *Tristan de Nanteuil*, ed. Keith V. Sinclair (Assen: Van Gorcum, 1971), lines 15298–16423.

45. Garber, *Vested Interests*, 16.

46. Ibid., 17.

47. Working from Garber's premise, Robert S. Sturges and Robert L. A. Clark are two of the few critics to shift the conversation concerning transvestism in *Silence* from gender toward these alternate medieval social discourses. They respectively argue that Silence's transvestism represents a crisis pertaining to either economics or one's individual nature. For Sturges, the cross-dresser embodies the irresolvable financial predicament experienced by the emerging class of penniless noble younger sons who had been disenfranchised by England's system of primogeniture, while Clark reads the transvestite as exemplifying "an acute crisis in the way the category of nature is conceptualized." See Robert S. Sturges, "The Cross-Dresser and the *Juventus*: Category Crisis in *Silence*," *Arthuriana* 12, no. 1 (2002): 37–49; and Robert L. A. Clark, "Queering Gender and Naturalizing Class in the *Roman de Silence*," *Arthuriana* 12, no. 1 (2002): 50–63, at 59.

48. I follow the text's use of a masculine pronoun when Silence is cross-dressed as a man.

49. Chrétien de Troyes, *Erec et Enide*, ed. Jean-Marie Fritz (Paris: Lettres Gothiques, 1992), lines 89–104: "Mout estoit beax et prouz et genz, / Se n'avoit pas .xxv. anz. / Onques nuns hom de son aage / Ne fu de greignor vasselage. / Que diroie de ses bontez? / Sor un destrier estoit montez: / Afublez d'un mantel hermin, / Vient galopant par le chemin; / S'ot cote d'un dÿapre noble / Qui fi faiz en Constantenople. / Chauces ot de paile chaucies, / Mout bien faites et bien taillies, / Et fu es estriers esfichiez, / Uns esperons a or chauciez; / Ne n'ot arme o lui aportee / Fors que tant soulement s'espee" [He was very handsome, valiant and noble, and he was not yet twenty-five years old; never was any man of his youth so accomplished in knighthood. What should I say of his virtues? Mounted on a charger, he came galloping along the road; he was dressed in a fur-lined mantle and a tunic of noble, patterned silk that had been made in Constantinople. He had put on silken stockings, very finely made and tailored; he was well set in his stirrups and was wearing golden spurs; he was unarmed except for his sword]. For an instance that deals specifically with Erec's armaments and the crowd's perception of him as "hardis et fiers" (line 754) [brave and proud] and a "gentil vassal" (line 770) [valiant knight] in direct response to his battle garments, see lines 707–75. The English translation is from Chrétien de Troyes, *Arthurian Romances*, ed. and trans. William W. Kibler (London: Penguin, 1991), 38. For the *effictio* and its communication of virtue in *Sir Gawain and the Green Knight*, see lines 631–65.

50. Lorraine Kochanske Stock, "'Arms and the (Wo)man' in Medieval Romance: The Gendered Arming of Female Warriors in the *Roman d'Enéas* and Heldris's *Roman de Silence*," *Arthuriana* 5, no. 4 (1995): 56–83. Colby's work on *effictio* shows that the trope may articulate character and nature, *Portrait in Twelfth-Century French Literature*, 6. Derek Brewer's "The Arming of the Warrior in European Literature and Chaucer," in *Chaucerian Problems and Perspectives: Essays Presented to Paul E. Beichner*, ed. Edward Vasta and Zacharias P. Thundy (Notre Dame: University of Notre Dame Press, 1979), 221–43, is an often-cited text on the issue.

51. *Enéas*, ed. Salverda de Grave. Translations are from Yunck, ed. and trans., *Enéas*.

52. Stock, "'Arms and the (Wo)man,'" 72–73.

53. Frédérique Lachaud, "Liveries of Robes in England, c. 1200–c. 1330," *The English Historical Review*, 111. 441 (1996): 279–98, at 281–82. Lachaud quotes the *Histoire des ducs de Normandie et des rois d'Angleterre*, ed. Francisque Michel (Paris: J. Renouard, 1840), 105.

54. "Et montent o lor avoé, / Dont ont soshaidié et voé / Que ja ne puist entrer en glize / Uns d'als, s'il i fait coärdize" (lines 5371–74) [They mounted

together with their chosen leader, for whose sake they had sworn a vow that not one of them might ever enter a church again if he showed any signs of cowardice.]

55. Poschmann, *Penance*, is pertinent here.

56. Ad Putter, "Transvestite Knights in Medieval Life and Literature," in *Becoming Male in the Middle Ages*, ed. Jeffrey Jerome Cohen and Bonnie Wheeler (New York: Routledge, 1999), 279–302, at 281–82.

57. Ibid., 281.

58. I have modified Roche-Mahdi's translation.

59. I have modified Roche-Mahdi's translation.

60. I have modified Roche-Mahdi's translation.

61. Tertullian, "The Apparel of Women," 132 and 136.

62. "Auferimur cultu; gemmis auroque teguntur / Omnia; pars minima est ipsa puella sui," *Ovid*, ed. and trans. Mozley, 201. John Baldwin, *Aristocratic Life in Medieval France*, xiii, 192–93, describes Peter the Chanter's engagement with Ovid in *Verbum abbreviatum*, *PL*, 205: 26. Baldwin does not include Tertullian in his reading of sartorial superfluity.

63. Hotchkiss, *Clothes Make the Man*, 145.

64. Sturges, "The Cross-Dresser and the *Juventus*," 42–45; and Garber, *Vested Interests*, 16–17.

65. John Baldwin, *Aristocratic Life*, 69–70.

66. Translation is mine.

67. I have slightly modified Roche-Mahdi's translation.

68. Vern L. Bullough, "Transvestites in the Middle Ages," *The American Journal of Sociology*, 79, no. 6 (1974): 1381–94, at 1392. Though not addressing the *Roman de Silence* in particular here, Bullough's assertion that "the church did not seem to be too concerned about cross-dressing, providing it took certain socially desirable forms and was rigidly circumscribed" is appropriate.

69. Steele, *Fetish*, 46.

70. Charlotte Suthrell, *Unzipping Gender: Sex, Cross-Dressing, and Culture* (Oxford: Berg, 2004), 24.

71. Bullough, "Transvestites in the Middle Ages," 1382.

72. Suthrell, *Unzipping Gender*, 16.

73. A notable exception is Blanchandine, in *Tristan de Nanteuil*, who cross-dresses at the request of her lover, Tristan.

74. I have modified Roche-Mahdi's translation here.

75. For confession to laity, see Amédée Teetaert, *La Confession aux laïques dans l'Église latine depuis le 8e jusqu'au 14e siècle* (Wetteren: J. de Meester et fils, 1926), especially 51, 61, 74, and 477–85; R. Emmet McLaughlin, "Truth,

Tradition and History: The Historiography of High/Late Medieval and Early Modern Penance," in *A New History of Penance*, ed. Abigail Firey (Boston: Brill, 2008), 19–71, at 46; and Poschmann, *Penance*, 176. For psychological discomfort associated with confession, see Paul Anciaux, *La Théologie du sacrament de pénitence au XIIe siècle* (Louvain: E. Nauwelaerts, 1949), 258.

76.   Kathleen J. Brahney, "When Silence Was Golden: Female Personae in the *Roman de Silence*," in *The Spirit of the Court: Selected Proceedings of the Fourth Congress of the International Courtly Literature Society* (Dover, NH: Brewer, 1985), 52–61, at 60.

77.   Gaunt, "The Significance of Silence," 213; and Sarah Roche-Mahdi, "A Reappraisal of the Role of Merlin in the *Roman de Silence*," *Arthuriana* 12, no. 1 (2002): 6–21, at 15. See also Stock, "The Importance of Being Gender 'Stable.'"

78.   Krueger, *Women Readers*, 103.

79.   Anciaux, *Théologie du sacrament*, 262.

80.   Tentler, *Sin and Confession*, 67.

81.   Kathy M. Krause, "'Li Mireor du Monde': Specularity in the *Roman de Silence*," *Arthuriana* 12, no. 1 (2002): 85–91. Krause does not address the role of clothing or transvestism in her article.

82.   My claim is influenced by Tickle, who writes about greed and the cultivation of ethical behavior, *Greed*, 8.

CHAPTER THREE   **The *Gawain*-Poet**

1.   *The Book of Vices and Virtues*, ed. Francis, 20: "Þe goodes of fortune are hiʒenesses, honoures, richesses, delices, prosperites; and in þes men synneþ in many maneres bi vayn glorie. For whan a man is brouʒt so hiʒe in prosperite, he þenkeþ first in his herte on his grete dignite, and after on his prosperite, after on his richesse, after in delices of his body, after of his grete felaschip þat foleweþ hym, after on al þe faire mayne þat serueþ hym, after on his faire maners and castelles, after on his faire hors and hors-men þat beþ wiþ hym, and after on his faire roobes and riche cloþynge in dyuerse wise & manye, after in aray of his hous, in vessel, in beddynge and in oþere manere harneys þat is fair and good, and after in grete presentz & ʒiftes & in grete festes þat men makeþ hym ouer-al, & after of his good loos & and preisynges þat spreden and flen ouer-al of hym. Of al þis he gladeþ him & glorifieþ hym as a wrecche in his herte, so þat he wot not were he is. Þes beþ þe twelue wyndes of veyn glorie; þat is to seie, twelue manere of temptacions and moo, of veyn glorie þat þei

haue þat beþ in grete staat in þis world, be it religious or clerke or lewed man." Translation is mine.

2. Wendy Clein, *Concepts of Chivalry in* Sir Gawain and the Green Knight (Norman, OK: Pilgrim Books, 1987), 30. See also David Aers, "Christianity for Courtly Subjects: Reflections on the *Gawain*-Poet," in *A Companion to the* Gawain-*Poet*, ed. Derek Brewer and Jonathan Gibson (Cambridge: D. S. Brewer, 1997), 91–101; Aers, *Community, Gender, and Individual Identity: English Writing, 1360–1430* (London: Routledge, 1988), 153–78; John A. Burrow, *A Reading of* Sir Gawain and the Green Knight (London: Routledge and Kegan Paul, 1965), 105; Lynn Staley Johnson, *The Voice of the* Gawain-*Poet* (Madison: University of Wisconsin Press, 1984), 75–81; Derek Pearsall, "Courtesy and Chivalry in *Sir Gawain and the Green Knight:* The Order of Shame and the Invention of Embarrassment," in *A Companion to the* Gawain-*Poet*, 351–62; A. C. Spearing, *The* Gawain-*Poet* (Cambridge: Cambridge University Press, 1970), 174–80; and Nicholas Watson, "The *Gawain*-Poet as a Vernacular Theologian," in *A Companion to the* Gawain-*Poet*, 293–313.

3. Hollander, *Sex and Suits*, 42–44.

4. *Sir Gawain and the Green Knight* in *The Complete Works of the* Pearl-*Poet*, ed. Andrew et al. Translation is mine.

5. Newton, *Fashion in the Age of the Black Prince*, 35.

6. Stephanie Trigg provides an extensive survey of the various interpretations of the belt in "The Romance of Exchange: Sir Gawain and the Green Knight," *Viator* 22 (1991): 251–66. For the girdle's supernatural value, see Helen Cooper, "The Supernatural," 277–91.

7. Lynn Staley Johnson argues that the girdle "could signify . . . penance" because it is "a memorial token of [Gawain's] failure," *Voice of the* Gawain-*Poet*, 92; similarly, Geraldine Heng reads "Gawain's gloomy projection of the girdle as a penitential sign" in her "Feminine Knots and the Other *Sir Gawain and the Green Knight*," *PMLA* 106 (1991): 500–514, at 508. See also Burrow, *A Reading of* Sir Gawain, 150–53; W. R. J. Barron, *Trawthe and Treason: The Sin of Gawain Reconsidered* (Manchester: Manchester University Press, 1980), 135–37; and Gregory W. Gross, "Secret Rules: Sex, Confession, and Truth in *Sir Gawain and the Green Knight*," *Arthuriana* 4, no. 2 (1994): 146–74, at 167. In reading the girdle as an article that engages with fourteenth-century social concerns and practices, I complement Helen Barr's work on *Pearl* in "Pearl—or 'The Jeweller's Tale,'" *Medium Aevum* 69, no. 1 (2000): 59–70.

8. John A. Burrow, "The Two Confession Scenes in *Sir Gawain and the Green Knight*," *Modern Philology* 57, no. 2 (1959): 73–79, at 79.

9. Burrow, *A Reading of* Sir Gawain, 151.

10. Jill Mann, "Courtly Aesthetics and Courtly Ethics in *Sir Gawain and the Green Knight*," *Studies in the Age of Chaucer* 31 (2009): 231–65, at 231–35. See also *English Court Culture*, ed. Scattergood and Sherborne; Michael J. Bennett, "The Court of Richard II and the Promotion of Literature," in *Chaucer's England*, ed. Barbara Hanawalt (Minneapolis: University of Minnesota Press, 1992), 3–20; Nigel Saul, *Richard II* (New Haven: Yale University Press, 1997); Kay Staniland, "Medieval Courtly Splendour," *Costume* 14 (1980): 7–23; and Staniland, "Extravagance or Regal Necessity? The Clothing of Richard II," in *The Regal Image of Richard II and the Wilton Diptych*, ed. Dillian Gordon, Lisa Monnas, and Caroline Elam (London: Harvey Miller, 1997), 85–93.

11. Malcolm Vale, *The Princely Court: Medieval Courts and Culture in North-West Europe, 1270–1380* (Oxford: Oxford University Press, 2001), 300.

12. Watson, "The *Gawain*-Poet," 294 and 312.

13. Lawrence Besserman, "Gawain's Green Girdle," *Annuale Mediævale* 22 (1982): 84–101, at 86.

14. *The Statutes of the Realm*, 1810–28, 2:380–81. Similarly, on the Continent, Charles V of France restricts the use of precious gems to decorate belts in a letter dating from 1367; see *Histoire générale de Languedoc*, ed. Claude Devic and Jean Joseph Vaissete, vol. 10 (Toulouse: Edouard Privat, 1885), col. 1375, no. 532. For general studies on the sumptuary statutes, see Frances Baldwin, *Sumptuary Legislation*; Etienne Giraudias, *Etude historique sur les lois somptuaires* (Poitiers: Société Française d'Imprimerie et de Librairie, 1910); Harte, "State Control of Dress," 132–65; and Hunt, *Governance of the Consuming Passions*.

15. *The St. Alban's Chronicle: The Chronica maiora of Thomas Walsingham, 1376–1394*, ed. and trans. John Taylor, Wendy R. Childs, and Leslie Watkiss (Oxford: Clarendon Press, 2003), 576.

16. *John of Gaunt's Register, 1379–1383*, ed. Eleanor C. Lodge and Robert Somerville, 2 vols. (London: Camden Society, 1937), 1:178–79; and W. Paley Baildon, "A Wardrobe Account of 16–17 Richard II, 1393–4," *Archaeologia* 62 (1911): 497–514, at 500. For "goldsmith's work," understood in regard to clothing and accessories, and a variety of literary examples, including an anecdote of Henry of Lancaster's costume for a joust during the time of Richard II, see Staniland, "Medieval Courtly Splendour," 18. For the prevalence of sumptuous excess at the Ricardian court, see Mann, "Courtly Aesthetics"; Scattergood and Sherborne, eds., *English Court Culture*; Bennett, "The Court of Richard II"; and Staniland, "Extravagance or Regal Necessity?"

17. See *Middle English Dictionary Online* (hereafter cited as *MED*), "jeuel," n. 1(a) and (c), available at http://quod.lib.umich.edu/cgi/m/mec/med-idx?type=id&id=MED23849 (last accessed 25 March 2011). Also pertinent is Fe -

licity Riddy, "Jewels in *Pearl*," in *A Companion to the* Gawain-*Poet*, ed. Derek Brewer and Jonathan Gibson (Cambridge: D. S. Brewer, 1997), 143–55, at 147.

18. *Speculum Christiani*, ed. Gustaf Holmstedt (London: Oxford University Press, 1933), 58. Translation is mine.

19. *Memoriale Credencium: A Late Middle English Manual of Theology for Lay People: Edited from Bodley MS Tanner 201*, ed. J. H. L. Kengen (Nijmegen: Katholieke Universiteit, 1979), 52–53. Translation and italics are mine.

20. Regan, "*The Cleansing of Man's Soul*," 116. For an introductory study of the text, see Walter Everett, "*The Clensyng of Mannes Soule*: An Introductory Study," *Southern Quarterly: A Journal of the Arts in the South* 13, no. 4 (1975): 265–79.

21. St. John's College, Cambridge, MS S 35, fol. 1r, by permission of the Master and Fellows of St. John's College, Cambridge. For an additional reading of St. John's S 35, see Eamon Duffy, *The Stripping of the Altars* (New Haven: Yale University Press, 1992), 58–60.

22. Owst, *Literature and Pulpit*, 337: "and the leste page in his house, hire clothynge also axeth so hie cost, bothe in cloth, peerlis and pelure, that oo garnemente passeth in coste half moneie of hire lifelodes in a ʒeer."

23. Ibid., 404.

24. Siegfried Wenzel, ed. and trans., *Preaching in the Age of Chaucer: Selected Sermons in Translation* (Washington, DC: Catholic University of America Press, 2008), 84.

25. *The Riverside Chaucer*, ed. Benson. Translation is mine.

26. Kay Staniland, "Court Style, Painters, and the Great Wardrobe," in *England in the Fourteenth Century: Proceedings of the 1985 Harlaxton Symposium*, ed. W. M. Ormrod (Woodbridge: Boydell, 1986), 236–46, at 245. Staniland reproduces the king's motto as it appears in the Great Wardrobe.

27. Richard Lavynham, *A Litil Tretys on the Seven Deadly Sins*, ed. J. P. W. M. Van Zutphen (Rome: Institutum Carmelitanum, 1956), 1. Translation is mine.

28. *Memoriale Credencium*, 63. Translation is mine.

29. Charles de Beaurepaire, "Complainte de la bataille de Poitiers," *Bibliothèque de l'Ecole de Chartres* 12 (1851): 257–63. I thank Catherine Batt for her assistance with this translation.

30. *The Chronicle of Jean de Venette*, ed. Richard A. Newhall, trans. Jean Birdsall (New York: Columbia University Press, 1953), 63.

31. *Eulogium*, ed. Haydon, 230–31. Translation is mine.

32. The Book of Chivalry *of Geoffroi de Charny*, ed. and trans. Richard W. Kaeuper and Elspeth Kennedy (Philadelphia: University of Pennsylvania Press, 1996), 24–25.

33. *Oeuvres complètes de Froissart,* ed. Kervyn de Lettenhove (Brussels: Victor Devaux, 1867–77), 5:412.

34. See Kaeuper and Kennedy's introduction to Geoffroi's *Book of Chivalry,* especially 26 and 30.

35. Book of Chivalry *of Geoffroi de Charny,* 168.

36. Ibid., 188.

37. Ibid., 190.

38. Both Larry Benson, in *Art and Tradition in* Sir Gawain and the Green Knight (New Brunswick, NJ: Rutgers University Press, 1965), 83, and Burrow, in *A Reading of* Sir Gawain, 40, note the moral valence of "vylany," but neither reads the term in relation to jewels or expensive attire.

39. *MED,* "vileinie," defs. 1 and 2. Available at http://quod.lib.umich.edu /cgi/m/mec/med-idx?type=id&id=MED51141 (last accessed 25 March 2011).

40. Aers, *Community, Gender, and Individual Identity,* 158.

41. See *MED,* "pure," def. 4. Available at http://quod.lib.umich.edu/cgi /m/mec/med-idx?type=id&id=MED35235 (last accessed 25 March 2011).

42. My argument complements Mann's "Courtly Aesthetics," 249.

43. These confessions have garnered much critical attention. Some read the first as ecclesiastically sound because a priest administers the sacrament, while others find it invalidated because Gawain subsequently betrays Bertilak by not handing over the girdle that he has received from the lady. The second confession arguably depicts Gawain's introspection and contrition that several critics find lacking in the former, but some have suggested that the latter is "unsacramental" because of the role of the Green Knight who, as a fellow lay aristocrat, shrives, absolves, and administers penance to Gawain by way of a small neck wound. See Sir Israel Gollancz's note to line 1880, *Sir Gawain and the Green Knight,* EETS, o.s. 210 (London: Oxford University Press, 1940); Burrow, "The Two Confession Scenes," 73–79; Burrow, *A Reading of* Sir Gawain, 105–10, 132–33; Aers, *Community, Gender, and Individual Identity,* 169–70; Mary Braswell, *The Medieval Sinner: Characterization and Confession in the Literature of the English Middle Ages* (Rutherford, NJ: Fairleigh Dickinson University Press, 1983), 95–100; Michael Foley, "Gawain's Two Confessions Reconsidered," *The Chaucer Review* 9, no. 1 (1974): 73–79; Nicholas Jacobs, "Notes and News: Gawain's False Confession," *English Studies* 51, no. 5 (1970): 433–35; Anthony Low, "Privacy, Community, and Society: Confession as a Cultural Indicator in *Sir Gawain and the Green Knight,*" *Religion and Literature* 30, no. 2 (1998): 1–20, at 10; Low, *Aspects of Subjectivity: Society and Individuality from the Middle Ages to Shakespeare and Milton* (Pittsburgh: Duquesne University Press, 2003), 22–59, at 49;

Charles R. Sleeth, "Gawain's Judgment Day," *Arthuriana* 4, no. 2 (1994): 175–83; and Spearing, *The* Gawain-*Poet*, 224–31. For the second confession as unsacramental, see Burrow, *A Reading of* Sir Gawain, 132. David Aers refutes Burrow, asserting the orthodoxy of confessing to a layman when no priest is available in "Christianity for Courtly Subjects," 84.

44. Richard Newhauser, "The Meaning of Gawain's Greed," *Studies in Philology* 87, no. 4 (1990): 410–26, at 414.

45. Geoffroi de Charny succinctly insists: "while cowards have a great desire to live and a great fear of dying, it is quite contrary for the men of worth" [Et la ou li chaitis ont grant envie de vivre et grant paour de mourir, c'est tout au contraire des bons], in The Book of Chivalry *of Geoffroi de Charny*, 126. See also Aers, who argues that a "sleȝt" would not be considered noble in the chivalric world, in *Community, Gender, and Individual Identity*, 165.

46. Gawain's "sin" has been interpreted in several ways by many critics. See, as examples, Newhauser, "The Meaning of Gawain's Greed," 410–26; Robert L. Kindrick, "Gawain's Ethics: Shame and Guilt in *Sir Gawain and the Green Knight*," *Annuale Mediaevale* 20 (1981): 5–32, at 26; V. J. Scattergood, "'Sir Gawain and the Green Knight' and the Sins of the Flesh," *Traditio* 37 (1981): 347–71; A. Francis Soucy, "Gawain's Fault: 'Angardez Pryde,'" *The Chaucer Review* 13, no. 2 (1978): 166–76; and Foley, "Gawain's Two Confessions."

47. Newhauser, "The Meaning of Gawain's Greed," 421–25.

48. For the shift in emphasis on avarice as the deadliest of sins in the later Middle Ages, see Lester Little, "Pride Goes before Avarice," 16–49. For a reading of Augustine by the fifth-century rhetorician, Julianus Pomerius, who suggests "that greed and pride must actually be the same vice," see Richard Newhauser, *The Early History of Greed*, 99–100. Despite these assertions on the primacy of greed as the deadliest of sins, late medieval vernacular penitential manuals, such as Geoffrey Chaucer's *Parson's Tale* and *The Book of Vices and Virtues*, uphold pride (*superbia*) as the first and deadliest of the cardinal sins, and late medieval wall paintings in English churches consistently depict pride personified as the central figure among the six other sins. Alexander Murray questions Little's conclusions and, in referencing Morton Bloomfield's *Seven Deadly Sins*, asserts that "apparently all the penitential theologians of the thirteenth century upheld the hegemony of pride," *Reason and Society in the Middle Ages*, 436, n. 62. For English wall paintings that present the primacy of pride, see Ann Marshall's website, http://www.paintedchurch.org/index.htm (last accessed 23 March 2011).

49. Gregory the Great, *Homiliae in Evangelia*, 2.40.3, in *Patrologiae cursus completus, Series Latina*, ed. Jacques-Paul Migne (Paris: Apud Garnieri Fratres,

1844–64), vol. 76, col. 1305: "Nemo quippe vestimenta praecipua nisi ad inanem gloriam quaerit, videlicet, ut honorabilior caeteris esse videatur."

50. Thomas Aquinas, *Summa theologiae*, trans. Fathers of the English Dominican Province, IaIIae, q. 77, a. 5.

51. *The Book of Vices and Virtues*, 19. For the remedy to sartorial pride, see Gregory the Great, *Homiliae in Evangelia*, 2.40.3.

52. *Speculum Vitae*, ed. Hanna. Despite the fact that authorship of *Speculum Vitae* has long been attributed to William of Nassington, Hanna argues against this claim at lx–lxiii. For the nearly universal acceptance of William as author, see Ingrid Peterson, *William of Nassington*; and *The Cambridge History of Medieval English Literature*, ed. Wallace, 399, 548, and 694. See also Hughes, "Administration of Confession in the Diocese of York," 98.

53. "Astonished" and "angry with himself" [. . . al forwondered watz þe wyȝe and wroth with hymseluen] (line 1660), Gawain nevertheless ignores the difficulty he feels about colluding with his host's wife in ways that threaten to betray his courtly reputation, and instead he "deal[s] with her courteously, even if their dealings turn awry" [Bot he nolde not for his nurture nurne hir aȝaynez / Bot dalt with hir al in daynté, how-se-euer þe dede turned / Towrast] (lines 1661–63), quoted in Aers, *Community, Gender, and Individual Identity*, 164. See also Spearing, *The* Gawain-*Poet*, 174 and 202.

54. See *Sir Gawain and the Green Knight*, ed. and trans. James Winny (Toronto: Broadview, 2001); Marie Borroff, ed., *Sir Gawain and the Green Knight: A New Verse Translation* (New York: Norton, 1967); Andrew et al., eds., *The Complete Works of the* Pearl-*Poet*, trans. Casey Finch, 1993; and "Sir Gawain and the Green Knight," trans. Keith Harrison, in *Medieval English Literature*, 2nd ed., ed. J. B. Trapp, Douglas Gray, and Julia Boffey (New York: Oxford University Press, 2002), 360–416. Though not an editor of the poem, Jill Mann understands "apert" as "visible" in her "Sir Gawain and the Romance Hero," in *Heroes and Heroines in Medieval English Literature*, ed. Leo Carruthers (Cambridge: D. S. Brewer, 1994), 105–17; and in "Courtly Aesthetics," 257–58. J. J. Anderson, however, does translate "aperte" as "public" in his edition of *Sir Gawain and the Green Knight, Pearl, Cleanness, Patience* (London: J. M. Dent, 1996).

55. Tentler, *Sin and Confession*, 4–6; Mayke de Jong, "Transformations of Penance," in *Rituals of Power from Late Antiquity to the Early Middle Ages*, ed. Frans Theuws and Janet L. Nelson (Leiden: Brill, 2000), 185–224; Sarah Hamilton, "The Unique Flavor of Penance: The Church and the People, c. 800–c. 1100," in *The Medieval World*, ed. Peter Linehan and Janet L. Nelson (London: Routledge, 2001), 229–45.

56. De Jong, "Transformations of Penance," 185.

57. Mansfield, *The Humiliation of Sinners*, 127. See also Hamilton, "The Unique Flavor of Penance," 229; Braswell, *The Medieval Sinner*, 20.

58. Henry of Lancaster, *Le Livre de seyntz medicines*, ed. E. J. Arnould (Oxford: Basil Blackwell, 1940), 114–15.

59. Quoted in Clein, *Concepts of Chivalry*, 42. See Jean Froissart, *Les Chroniques de Sire Jean Froissart*, vol. 1, ed. J. A. C. Buchon (Paris: Société du Panthéon Littéraire, 1840), 14, 186, 194. Translations are Clein's.

60. Michael Haren notes Henry's "intensely self-critical character" when it comes to the social abuses of knights, "Confession, Social Ethics, and Social Discipline in the *Memoriale Presbiterorum*," in *Handling Sin: Confession in the Middle Ages*, ed. Peter Biller and A. J. Minnis (Woodbridge: York Medieval Press, 1998), 109–22, at 120.

61. Clein, *Concepts of Chivalry*, 45.

62. Richard Firth Green, "Sir Gawain and the *Sacra Cintola*," *English Studies in Canada* 11, no. 1 (March 1985): 1–11, at 2–4. For artistic renditions of the girdle in religious traditions, see Phillipa Hardman, "Gawain's Practice of Piety in *Sir Gawain and the Green Knight*," *Medium Aevum* 68, no. 2 (1999): 247–68, note 41.

63. Regan, "*Cleansing of Man's Soul*," 178. Translations are mine.

64. Mansfield, *The Humiliation of Sinners*, 16.

65. Mark C. Amodio, "Tradition, Modernity, and the Emergence of the Self in *Sir Gawain and the Green Knight*," *Assays* 8 (1995): 47–68, at 56.

66. Regan, "*Cleansing of Man's Soul*," 178.

67. Robert Mannyng, *Handlyng Synne*, ed. Idelle Sullens (Binghamton: Medieval and Renaissance Texts and Studies, 1983), 287.

68. On the *Manuel des pechiez*, see Burrow, "The Two Confession Scenes," 79, n. 14. *Ancrene Riwle*, trans. M. B. Salu (London: Burns and Oates, 1955), 143. Quoted in Burrow, *A Reading of* Sir Gawain, 151. Barron also considers this passage in *Trawthe and Treason*, 136.

69. Regan, "*Cleansing of Man's Soul*," 193.

70. *Ancrene Wisse: A Corrected Edition of the Text in Cambridge, Corpus Christi College, MS 402, with variants from other manuscripts*, ed. Bella Millett, EETS, o.s. 325 (Oxford: Oxford University Press, 2005), 149, [part 7, line 172].

71. Henry Lea, *History of Auricular Confession and Indulgences in the Latin Church*, vol. 2 (Philadelphia: Lea Brothers, 1896), 84.

72. For "therapy of distance," see Peter R. L. Brown, *The Cult of the Saints: Its Rise and Function in Latin Christianity* (Chicago: University of Chicago Press, 1982), 87, quoting Alphonse Dupront, "Pèlerinages et lieux sacrés," in *Mélanges en l'honneur de F. Braudel* (Toulouse: Privat, 1973), 2:190. For souvenirs, from

pilgrimages, hanging about the neck, see *From St. Francis to Dante: A Translation of All that is of Primary Interest in the Chronicle of the Franciscan Salimbene (1221–1288)*, ed. G. G. Coulton (London: David Nutt, 1906), 140.

73. *Speculum Sacerdotale*, ed. Edward H. Weatherly, EETS, o.s. 200 (London: Oxford University Press, 1936), 123–24.

74. *The Romance of the Sowdone of Babylone and of Ferumbras his sone who conquerede Rome*, ed. Emil Hausknecht, EETS, e.s. 38 (London: Trübner and Co., 1881), a late fourteenth-century Charlemagne romance, features a heroine who presents her magic girdle to knights so that they may not suffer from starvation (lines 2299–2318). In *Yvain*, Lunete gives the protagonist a ring that will protect him; Yvain later receives a ring as a sign of his lady's love; see Chrétien de Troyes, *Arthurian Romances*, 307 and 328. Similarly, the Middle English *Ywain* shows Alundyne conferring her ring on her lover both to protect him and to show her fidelity: *Ywain and Gawain*, ed. Albert B. Friedman and Norman T. Harrington, EETS, o.s. 254 (London: Oxford University Press, 1964), lines 1527 and 1737.

75. *The Letters of Abelard and Heloise*, trans. Radice, 51; and *The Historical Works of Master Ralph de Diceto*, vol. I, ed. William Stubbs, in *Rerum Britannicarum Medii Aevi Scriptores*, Rolls Series, no. 68, vol. I (London: Longman and Co., 1876), 307: "Postquam autem induit vestes summis sacerdotibus Domino disponente collates, habitum sic mutavit ut mutaret et animum" [However, after he put on the vestments that were bestowed by the Lord's will upon high priests, he changed his clothes in such a way that he also changed his heart].

76. Here I differ from David Aers's assertion that reading this scene in light of any *Summa theologiae*, penitential manual, or sermon is inappropriate because Gawain never thinks to turn inwardly during his confessions to evaluate his comportment in *Community, Gender, and Individual Identity*, 169. Rather than focus on introspection and self-reflexivity, which Aers sees lacking, I turn to the sartorial behaviors that run concurrently through the penitential guides and *SGGK*.

77. *Memoriale Credencium*, 166.

78. Aers, *Community, Gender, and Individual Identity*, 173. However shameful Gawain's conduct appears, it is still one that Aers finds rooted in the pride that any one of Arthur's knights would have felt as a member of his court.

79. *A Myrour to Lewde Men and Wymmen*, ed. Nelson, 230.

80. *MED*, "token," def. 3. Available at http://quod.lib.umich.edu/cgi /m/mec/med-idx?size=First+100&type=headword&q1=token&rgxp= constrained (last accessed 25 March 2011).

81. *MED*, "moten." See definition 2c, which defines "mote nedes" as "to do, be, suffer, or undergo something under compulsion; must necessarily." Available at http://quod.lib.umich.edu/cgi/m/mec/med-idx?type=id&id=MED28752 (last accessed 25 March 2011).

82. Karma Lochrie, *Covert Operations: The Medieval Uses of Secrecy* (Philadelphia: University of Pennsylvania Press, 1999), 52.

83. I differ from Burrow, who argues that Gawain remains in a state of sin at the end of the poem, *A Reading of* Sir Gawain, 156. For the orthodoxy of laymen administering the sacrament of penance in an emergency when a priest is unavailable, see *Fasciculus Morum: A Fourteenth-Century Preacher's Handbook*, ed. and trans. Siegfried Wenzel (University Park: Pennsylvania State University Press, 1989), 466–67, quoted in David Aers, *Faith, Ethics, and Church: Writing in England, 1360–1409* (Cambridge: D. S. Brewer, 2000), 84.

84. W. David Myers, *"Poor, Sinning Folk": Confession and Conscience in Counter-Reformation Germany* (Ithaca: Cornell University Press, 1996), 16. Myers notes that satisfaction as a requisite for absolution declines as a popular practice by the eleventh century and is replaced with an emphasis on contrition as the requirement to reconcile one's offenses.

85. *Memoriale Credencium*, 166. See also Mansfield, *The Humiliation of Sinners*, for an extended reading of the function of shame in penitential practices.

86. Alasdair MacIntyre, *After Virtue: A Study in Moral Theory*, 2nd ed. (Notre Dame: University of Notre Dame Press, 1984), 174.

87. Aers, *Community, Gender, and Individual Identity*, 162.

88. St. John's College, Cambridge, MS S 35, f. 25v. Translation is mine.

89. See *Memoriale Credencium*, 166; and *John Mirk's* Festial: *Edited from British Library MS Cotton Claudius A.II*, ed. Susan Powell, vol. 1, EETS, o.s. 334 (Oxford: Oxford University Press, 2009), 4: "For ryght as a knyght schowuet þe wondes þat he hadde in batel in moch comendyng to hym, ryght so alle þe synnes þat a mon hath scryuen hym of and taken hys penans fore schul ben þer schewet to moch honour and worschep to hym and moch confucyoun to þe fynd." [For just as a knight shows the injuries he sustained in battle, for which he is commended, so shall all the sins that a man has confessed, and for which he has taken his penance, be shown. They bring much honor to him and much confusion to the fiend.]

90. Crane, *The Performance of Self*, 134–35. Italics are Crane's.

91. Leo Carruthers, "The Duke of Clarence and the Earls of March: Garter Knights and *Sir Gawain and the Green Knight*," *Medium Ævum* 70, no. 1 (2001): 66–79, at 67.

92. My argument derives from Tickle, *Greed*, 8.

93. Ernest Dupreel, "Le problème sociologique du rire," *Revue philosophique de la France et de l'étranger* 106 (1928): 213–60, at 234. Translation is mine.

94. Philippe Ménard, *Le rire et le sourire dans le roman courtois en France au Moyen Age, 1150–1250* (Geneva: Librairie Droz, 1969), 32. Ménard argues that when laughter is sincere, it conveys joy.

95. Jacques Le Goff, "Laughter in the Middle Ages," in *A Cultural History of Humor from Antiquity to the Present*, ed. Jan Bremmer and Herman Roodenburg (Cambridge: Polity Press, 1997), 40–53, at 47.

96. John Haldon, "Humor and the Everyday in Byzantium," in *Humour, History and Politics in Late Antiquity and the Early Middle Ages*, ed. Guy Halsall (Cambridge: Cambridge University Press, 2002), 48–71, at 58. For an explanation of humor as a strategy for people to reconcile their conflicting experiences and perceptions, see George H. Mead, *Mind, Self and Society* (Chicago: University of Chicago Press, 1934), 206–8.

97. Carruthers, "The Duke of Clarence," 66, provides an outline of the scholarship that has considered Edward's Order of the Garter in relation to *SGGK*. See also Francis Ingledew, Sir Gawain and the Green Knight *and the Order of the Garter* (Notre Dame, IN: University of Notre Dame Press, 2006).

98. Book of Chivalry *of Geoffroi de Charny*, 190.

99. Besserman, "Gawain's Green Girdle," 89, and Johnson, *The Voice of the* Gawain-*Poet*, 89.

100. Spearing, *The* Gawain-*Poet*, 183, comments on Gawain's role at the onset of the beheading game: "Thus, when Gawain, with a formal gesture of submission, receives the Green Knight's axe from the king, he is becoming both his personal substitute and, in the most open and official way, the representative of the whole court who is to redeem their initial hesitance."

101. Aers, "Christianity for Courtly Subjects," 95.

102. Ann Astell, "*Sir Gawain and the Green Knight:* A Study in the Rhetoric of Romance," *Journal of English and Germanic Philology* 84 (1985): 188–202.

CHAPTER FOUR   **Geoffrey Chaucer**

1. Stella Mary Newton's *Fashion in the Age of the Black Prince* is the key text on the development and reception of fashion in the fourteenth century. See, too, Scott, *Medieval Dress and Fashion;* Boucher, *Histoire du Costume*, 191–97; Nancy Bradfield, *Historical Costumes of England*, 3rd ed. (New York: Barnes and Noble, 1971), 43–45; Millia Davenport, *The Book of Costume*, 1:190–91; Kelly and

Schwabe, *A Short History of Costume and Armour*, 1:17–25; and Yarwood, *English Costume*, 70.

2. In addition to *Sir Gawain and the Green Knight*, *Sir Launfal*, Thomas Chestre's late fourteenth-century revision of Marie de France's *Lanval*, incorporates significant sartorial additions to the Breton lay, especially in terms of men's noble dress. See "Sir Launfal" in *The Middle English Breton Lays*, ed. Anne Laskaya and Eve Salisbury (Kalamazoo, MI: TEAMS, 1995), 201–62.

3. For a more expansive justification of the *Parson's Tale* as the concluding chapter, see the Introduction to this volume.

4. Boyle, "The Inter-Conciliar Period," 47; and Goering, "The Internal Forum," 413.

5. Leonard E. Boyle, *Pastoral Care, Clerical Education, and Canon Law, 1200–1400* (London: Variorum Imprints, 1981), 82. See also Gibbs and Lang, *Bishops and Reform*, 94–179.

6. Goering, *William de Montibus*, 58–65; Goering, "The Internal Forum," 410–27; Pantin, *The English Church*, 220–43; Raymo, "Works of Religious and Philosophical Instruction," 2255–2378, 2467–2582; Gillespie, "Vernacular Books of Religion," 317–44; and Jolliffe, *A Checklist of Middle English Prose*. Pierre Payer maintains a clear trajectory in the theories of penance before and after 1215 in "The Humanism of the Penitentials," 340–54.

7. Scanlon, *Narrative, Authority, and Power*, 14. Lee Patterson's "The 'Parson's Tale' and the Quitting of the 'Canterbury Tales,'" *Traditio* 34 (1978): 331–80 establishes the genre of the *Tale* as a type of penitential manual. For the critical debate over the *Tale*'s genre prior to Patterson, see Coolidge O. Chapman, "The Parson's Tale: A Medieval Sermon," *Modern Language Notes* 43 (1928): 229–34; Homer G. Pfander, "Some Medieval Manuals of Religious Instruction in England and Observations on Chaucer's Parson's Tale," *Journal of English and Germanic Philology* 35 (1936): 243–58; and Siegfried Wenzel, "Notes on the *Parson's Tale*," *The Chaucer Review* 16, no. 3 (1982): 237–56, es - pecially 248–49. For a critical inquiry into the influence of meditative literature on the *Parson's Tale*, see Thomas H. Bestul, "Chaucer's *Parson's Tale* and the Late-Medieval Tradition of Religious Meditation," *Speculum* 64, no. 3 (1989): 600–619.

8. Patterson, "The 'Parson's Tale,'" 338–39. The *Clensyng of Mannes Sowle* exists completely in four manuscripts (Cambridge, University Library, MS Ii.1.2; London, British Library, MS Harley 4012; London, Lambeth Palace Library, MS 3597; Oxford, Bodleian Library, MS Bodley 923) and is excerpted in another three (Durham, Cathedral Library, MS Hunter 15; London, British Library, MS Sloane 774; Cambridge, Magdalene College, MS Pepys

2125). Regan edits the entire text based on Bodley 923 in his doctoral thesis. Everett uses all manuscripts except Hunter 15 and Pepys 2125 in his unpublished critical edition of the confession section. See also Everett, *"The Clensyng of Mannes Soule,"* 265–79. *The Weye to Paradys* survives in one manuscript, London, British Library, MS Harley 1671; see *The Middle English* Weye of Paradys *and the Middle French* Voie de Paradis, ed. F. N. M. Diekstra (Leiden: Brill, 1991). The *Boke of Penance* appears in six extant manuscripts and is reproduced as an addendum to *Cursor Mundi,* part 5, ed. Richard Morris (London: Trübner and Co., 1878), 1470–1586; see Guy Trudel, "The Middle English Book of Penance and the Readers of the Cursor Mundi," *Medium Ævum* 74, no. 1 (2005): 10–33.

9. See Glenn Burger, *Chaucer's Queer Nation* (Minneapolis: University of Minnesota Press, 2003), 194; Katherine Little, "Chaucer's Parson and the Specter of Wycliffism," *Studies in the Age of Chaucer* 23 (2001): 225–53; and Derrick G. Pitard, "Sowing Difficulty: *The Parson's Tale,* Vernacular Commentary, and the Nature of Chaucerian Dissent," *Studies in the Age of Chaucer* 26 (2004): 299–330.

10. Van Buren, *Illluminating Fashion,* 2, credits Paul Post for first suggesting that plate armor precipitated changes in civilian clothing in his "La Naissance du costume masculin moderne au XIVe siècle," in *Actes du premier Congrès international d'histoire du costume, Venise, 31 août–7 septembre 1952* (Venice: Centro Internazionale delle Arti e del Costume, 1955), 28–41. See also Odile Blanc, "From Battlefield to Court: The Invention of Fashion in the Fourteenth Century," in *Encountering Medieval Textiles and Dress: Objects, Texts, Images,* ed. Désirée G. Koslin and Janet E. Snyder (New York: Palgrave, 2002), 157–72, at 170; and Hollander, *Sex and Suits,* 42–47.

11. Madou, *Le Costume civil* (Twinhout: Brepols, 1986), 23; Elisabeth Crowfoot, Frances Pritchard, and Kay Staniland, *Textiles and Clothing, c. 1150–c. 1450,* 2nd ed. (Woodbridge: Boydell, 2001), 7.

12. Françoise Piponnier, "Une révolution dans le costume masculin au XIVe siècle," in *Le Vêtement: Histoire, archéologie et symbolique vestimentaires au Moyen Age,* ed. Michel Pastoureau (Paris: Léopard d'Or, 1989), 237; and Scott, *Medieval Dress and Fashion,* 113. For evidence of tight sleeves, see Crowfoot et al., *Textiles and Clothing,* 4; Newton, *Fashion in the Age of the Black Prince,* 1–13; Crane, *The Performance of Self,* 14; and Van Buren, *Illuminating Fashion,* 2.

13. Millia Davenport, *The Book of Costume,* 190; and Yarwood, *English Costume,* 70.

14. Yarwood, *English Costume,* 72–74. Van Buren, *Illluminating Fashion,* 291, cautions that names of medieval garments are notoriously difficult to learn:

glossaries were rarely illustrated, terms in medieval texts often were not explicitly defined, and a word could be used to mean more than one garment. As a result, it is not unusual to find scholars using a particular term differently. For instance, while Yarwood understands "paltock" as a tunic worn under a doublet and to which hose were attached, Van Buren reads "paltock" more generally as a "loose jacket with sleeves" (317).

15. Newton, *Fashion in the Age of the Black Prince*, 110. Crane notes that innovative weaves resulted in the production of woolen fabrics with increased elasticity; see *The Performance of Self*, 14.

16. See Wenzel's explanatory notes to the *Parson's Tale*, X.422–29, in Benson, ed., *The Riverside Chaucer*, 959; Mark Liddell, "A New Source of the Parson's Tale," in *An English Miscellany* (Oxford: Clarendon Press, 1901), 255–77; Liddell, "The Source of Chaucer's 'Person's Tale,'" *The Academy* 1259 (June 20, 1896): 509; D. Biggins, "*Canterbury Tales* X (I) 424: 'The Hyndre Part of a She-Ape in the Fulle of the Moone,'" *Medium Ævum* 33, no. 3 (1964): 200–203; Albert E. Hartung, "'The Parson's Tale' and Chaucer's Penance," in *Literature and Religion in the Later Middle Ages*, ed. Richard Neuhauser and John A. Alford (Binghamton: Medieval and Renaissance Texts and Studies, 1995), 61–80, at 71; Siegfried Wenzel, "The Source for Chaucer's Seven Deadly Sins," *Traditio* 30 (1974): 351–78, at 377; Wenzel's "The Source for the 'Remedia' of the Parson's Tale," *Traditio* 27 (1971): 433–53, at 453; and Patterson, "The 'Parson's Tale,'" 340, n. 29.

17. Kate Oelzner Petersen, *The Sources of the Parson's Tale* (Boston: Athenaeum Press, 1901); and Richard Newhauser, "The Parson's Tale," in *Sources and Analogues of the Canterbury Tales*, vol. 1, ed. Robert M. Correale and Mary Hamel (Cambridge: D. S. Brewer, 2002), 529–614.

18. Wenzel, "The Source for Chaucer's Seven Deadly Sins," 351–78, especially 377; and Newhauser, "The Parson's Tale," 531–36.

19. Newhauser, "The Parson's Tale," 534.

20. Patterson, "The 'Parson's Tale,'" 338–39.

21. None of the following twelve additional vernacular spiritual guides include the same vitriolic response to fashionable dress as Chaucer's Parson: Dan Michel, *Ayenbite of Inwit*, ed. Richard Morris (London: Trübner and Co., 1866); *The Book of Vices and Virtues*, ed. Francis; Mirk, *Festial*; *Jacob's Well*, ed. Arthur Brandeis (London: Kegan Paul, Trench, Trübner and Co., 1900); Lavynham, *A Litil Tretys*; *Memoriale Credencium*, ed. Kengen; *A Myrour to Lewde Men and Wymmen*, ed. Nelson; *Of Shrifte and Penance*, ed. Bitterling; Richard Rolle de Hampole, *The Pricke of Conscience*, ed. Richard Morris (1863; reprint, New York: AMS Press, 1973); *Lay Folks' Catechism*, ed. Thomas Frederick Simmons and Henry Edward

Nolloth (London: Kegan Paul, Trench, Trübner and Co., 1901); *Speculum Christiani*, ed. Holmstedt; *Speculum Sacerdotale*, ed. Weatherly.

22. *The Statutes of the Realm* include legislation for the years 1337, 1363, 1463, and 1483. The earliest entry is protectionist in nature, prohibiting individuals except members of the royal family from wearing imported fabric or furs. In 1363 the concern shifts from economics to social status with directives attempting to regulate conspicuous consumption, while the 1463 and 1483 Acts of Apparel mimic Chaucer's Parson's concern with the contours of the male body: "no knight under the estate of lord, esquire, gentleman, nor none other person" could wear a jacket "unless it be of such length that the same may cover his privy members and buttocks," *Statutes of the Realm*, 1810–28, 2:470. See also Frances Baldwin, *Sumptuary Legislation*; Harte, "State Control of Dress," 132–65; Hunt, *Governance of the Consuming Passions*; and Sponsler, "Narrating the Social Order," 265–83.

23. See Siegfried Wenzel's explanatory notes to the *Parson's Tale*, X.422–29, in *The Riverside Chaucer*, ed. Benson, 959; Liddell, "A New Source of the Parson's Tale," 255–77; Liddell, "The Source of Chaucer's 'Person's Tale,'" 509; Biggins, "'The Hyndre Part of a She-Ape,'" 200–203; Hartung, "'The Parson's Tale' and Chaucer's Penance," 71; Wenzel, "The Source for Chaucer's Seven Deadly Sins," 377; Wenzel's "The Source for the 'Remedia' of the Parson's Tale," 453; and Patterson, "The 'Parson's Tale,'" 340, n. 29.

24. Quotations are from *The Riverside Chaucer*, ed. Benson. Translation is mine.

25. Liddell, "The Source of Chaucer's 'Person's Tale,'" 509. Translation is mine.

26. Ibid.

27. Derek Pearsall, *The Canterbury Tales* (London: George Allen, 1985), 289.

28. John Finlayson, "The Satiric Mode and the *Parson's Tale*," *The Chaucer Review* 6 (1971): 94–116, at 116. For a reading that elides eroticism in the *Parson's Tale*, see Anne Laskaya, *Chaucer's Approach to Gender in the Canterbury Tales* (Cambridge: D. S. Brewer, 1995), 128–30.

29. Rolle de Hampole, *The Pricke of Conscience*, line 1542. Rolle notes the fickleness of change as it pertains to vanity at lines 1532–35. In a similar way, *The Book of Vices and Virtues* does not differentiate between men and women's apparel in its consideration of prideful attire at 20.

30. *Memoriale Credencium*, 62.

31. Ibid., 14. For William of Pagula, see Boyle, *Pastoral Care*, 81–110.

32. *Weye of Paradys*, 129.

33. Regan, *"Cleansing of Man's Soul,"* 124. For the variants of the *Memoriale Credencium*, see 245–46 in Kengen's edition: London, British Library, MS Harley 211, f. 72v; MS Harley 535; MS Harley 2398.

34. *Boke of Penance,* 1550. For the *Memoriale,* see Cambridge, University Library, MS Dd.I.1: "Oþere spices þer ben of pride whiche men and women ben founden jnne. and it encresiþ fro day to day of dyuers a tire a bout þe bodi. as ofte streyte clothes and schorte daggid hodis. chaunsemlees disgised and teyde vp streyt in .v. or .vj. stedis. women with schorte clothis vnneþe to þe hipes. booses and lokettes a bout þe heed. and vile stynkend hornes longe and brode. and oþere dyuers a tire þat I can nought witen ne discryen of swiche þinges. Eueri man and woman be his owne juge and loke weel if it be nought þus." Quoted in Kengen, ed., 245.

35. Suzanne Conklin Akbari surveys the correlation between vision and knowledge from Antiquity through the Middle Ages in her *Seeing through the Veil: Optical Theory and Medieval Allegory* (Toronto: University of Toronto Press, 2004), 3–6. See Dallas G. Denery II, *Seeing and Being Seen in the Later Medieval World: Optics, Theology and Religious Life* (Cambridge: Cambridge University Press, 2005), 5; and Richard Newhauser, "Peter of Limoges, Optics, and the Science of the Sense," *Senses & Society* 5, no. 1 (2010): 28–44.

36. Denery, *Seeing and Being Seen,* 5 and 77.

37. Newhauser, "Peter of Limoges," 31–32; Denery, *Seeing and Being Seen,* 78–81.

38. Hollander, *Sex and Suits,* 5.

39. Denery, *Seeing and Being Seen,* 14.

40. Augustine, *Concerning the City of God against the Pagans,* trans. Henry Bettenson (London: Penguin, 1984), Book XIV, ch. 18, at 579.

41. For confessional manuals promoting a heightened sense of self-awareness, see Denery, *Seeing and Being Seen,* 14.

42. Akbari, *Seeing through the Veil,* 24, is helpful here.

43. Michael Camille, "The Pose of the Queer: Dante's Gaze, Brunetto Latini's Body," in *Queering the Middle Ages,* ed. Glenn Burger and Steven F. Kruger (Minneapolis: University of Minnesota Press, 2001), 59. See, too, Richard Newhauser, "The Sin of Curiosity and the Cistercians," in *Erudition at God's Service,* ed. John R. Sommerfeldt (Kalamazoo, MI: Cistercian Publications, 1987), 71–95.

44. *Eulogium (historiarum sive temporis),* ed. Haydon, 231.

45. *The Late Medieval Religious Plays of Bodleian Mss. Digby 133 and E Museo 160,* ed. Baker, et al., 40, lines 491–506; *The N-Town Play Cotton MS Vespasian D.8,* ed. Spector, 248, lines 65–92; *The Towneley Plays,* ed. Stevens and Cawley, 414, lines

447–57. For a critical reception of the gallant in medieval drama, see Tony Davenport, "Lusty fresche galaunts," 111–25.

46. Quoted in Newton, *Fashion in the Age of the Black Prince*, 9. For the Latin, see John of Reading, *Chronica Johannis de Reading*, ed. Tait, 88–89.

47. Akbari, *Seeing through the Veil*, 24.

48. Michel, *Ayenbite of Inwit*, 176–77.

49. Regan, "*Cleansing of Man's Soul*," 123–24. I have corrected Regan's misprint of "cloing" to reflect the word as it appears in Oxford, Bodleian Library, MS Bodley 923, f. 80r. Translation is mine.

50. Ibid., 158.

51. *Speculum Vitae*, ed. Hanna, xiii.

52. *Weye of Paradys*, 265.

53. Ibid., 273: "By these fyve wittes synne entret in man oftetymes, as by foly heryng and by foly seyng and smellyng, and by the other wittes, and specyally by foly beholdyng; for by foly beholdyng entreth synne ofte in hym that beholdeth, and in hym that he beholdeth on."

54. Richard Firth Green, "'Allas, Allas! That evere love was synne!': John Bromyard v. Alice of Bath," *The Chaucer Review* 42, no. 3 (2008): 298–311, at 299.

55. Quoted in Owst, *Literature and Pulpit*, 397. See also Ruth Mazo Karras, "Misogyny and the Medieval Exemplum: Gendered Sin in John of Bromyard's *Summa Praedicantium*," *Traditio* 47 (1992): 233–57. Although Owst dates the *Summa* in the mid-1380s, which would make it concurrent with the composition of the *Canterbury Tales*, Leonard Boyle has argued for a more precise date of 1346–48 for the completion of the *Summa*, six to eight years after the onset of the revolutionary fashion changes in men's dress, in his "The Date of the *Summa Praedicatium* of John Bromyard," *Speculum* 48, no. 3 (1973): 533–37.

56. Owst, *Literature and Pulpit*, 404–5, italics are Owst's; translation is mine.

57. Morton Bloomfield, *Seven Deadly Sins* (East Lansing: Michigan State College Press, 1952), 75.

58. Augustine, *The Trinity*, trans. Stephen McKenna (Washington, DC: Catholic University of America Press, 1963), 318. "Quocirca ex uisibili et uidente gignitur uisio ita sane ut ex uidente sit sensus oculorum et aspicientis atque intuentis intentio; illa tamen informatio sensus quae uisio dicitur a solo imprimatur corpore quod uidetur, id est a re aliqua uisibili," *De Trinitate*, ed. W. J. Mountain and Fr. Glorie, *Corpus Christianorum, Series Latina*, vol. 50–50A (Turnhout: Brepols, 1968), XI.2.3. Quoted in Richard Zeikowitz, *Homoeroticism and Chivalry: Discourses of Male Same-Sex Desire in the Fourteenth Century* (New York:

Palgrave Macmillan, 2003), 87. For Augustine as an important interlocutor in fourteenth-century literature, see Aers, *Salvation and Sin*.

59. Denery, *Seeing and Being Seen*, 82; and Newhauser, "Peter of Limoges," 32. For Alhacen's impact on Western views of optics, see David C. Lindberg, *Theories of Vision from Al-Kindi to Kepler* (Chicago: University of Chicago Press, 1976), 58–86.

60. Katherine H. Tachau, *Vision and Certitude in the Age of Ockham: Optics, Epistemology and the Foundations of Semantics 1250–1345* (Leiden: E. J. Brill, 1988), 4, 16.

61. Quoted in Zeikowitz, *Homoeroticism and Chivalry*, 89. See Tachau for additional moments when Bacon shows the activity of the observer, *Vision and Certitude*, 16, n. 43.

62. Laura Mulvey, "Visual Pleasure and Narrative Cinema," *Screen* 16, no. 3 (1975): 6–18.

63. Beryl Rowland, "Chaucer's She-Ape (*The Parson's Tale*, 424)," *The Chaucer Review* 2 (1968): 159–65, at 163, 165.

64. *Eulogium*, 230–31.

65. Glenn Burger stands as a notable exception in that he argues for confession's "complex and sometimes contradictory relationship to pleasure," yet he finds perversities existing not in questions of sensuality, but in relationships of desire and authority between clerics and laity, *Chaucer's Queer Nation*, 191. See, too, Lochrie's *Covert Operations*, 40

66. Roland Barthes, *The Pleasure of the Text*, trans. Richard Miller (New York: Hill and Wang, 1975), 42.

67. Ibid., 41–42; and Carolyn Dinshaw, *Chaucer's Sexual Poetics* (Madison: University of Wisconsin Press, 1990), 41.

68. R. Howard Bloch, *The Scandal of the Fabliaux* (Chicago: University of Chicago Press, 1986), 89–90.

69. Scanlon, *Narrative, Authority, and Power*, 8.

70. Geoffrey Chaucer, "Boece," in *The Riverside Chaucer*, ed. Benson, Book V, pr. 4.

71. Allen J. Frantzen, "The Disclosure of Sodomy in the Middle English *Cleanness*," *PMLA* 111, no. 3 (1996): 451–64, at 455.

72. Eve Kosofsky Sedgwick, "Queer Performativity: Henry James's *The Art of the Novel*," *GLQ* 1 (1993): 1–16, at 5–7.

73. David Raybin, "'Manye been the weyes': The Flower, Its Roots, and the Ending of *The Canterbury Tales*," in *Closure in the Canterbury Tales: The Role of the Parson's Tale*, ed. David Raybin and Linda Tarte Holley (Kalamazoo, MI: Medieval Institute Publications, 2000), 11–43; see 30, n. 27.

74. *MED,* "male" (n. 2), I (a) and (c). Available at http://quod.lib.umich
.edu/cgi/m/mec/med-idx?type=id&id=MED26622 (last accessed 1 April
2011).

75. I thank Frank Grady, who alerted me to a 1382 Wycliffite Bible,
which seems to be the earliest citation for "male" as a male human being. For
"male" as a pun on male genitalia, see Eugene Vance, "Chaucer's Pardoner: Relics, Discourse, and Frames of Propriety," *New Literary History* 20 (1989):
723–45.

76. For a reading of Harry's interests in textuality and sexuality, see John
Plummer, "'Beth Fructuous and that in Litel Space': The Engendering of
Harry Bailly," in *New Readings of Chaucer's Poetry,* ed. Robert G. Benson and Susan
J. Ridyard (Cambridge: D. S. Brewer, 2003), 107–18. Though Plummer notes
that Harry often uses language that connects narrative with sexuality, he does
not cite this moment as an example.

77. For medieval wall paintings in England, see A. Caiger-Smith, *English
Medieval Mural Paintings* (Oxford: Clarendon Press, 1963); H. Munro Cautley,
Suffolk Churches and Their Treasures, 5th ed. (Woodbridge: Boydell, 1982); Roger
Rosewell, *Medieval Wall Paintings in English and Welsh Churches* (Woodbridge: Boydell,
2008); E. Clive Rouse, *Medieval Wall Paintings,* 4th ed. (Oxford: Shire Publications, 1991); and E. W. Tristram, *English Wall Painting of the Fourteenth Century* (London: Routledge, 1955).

78. Tristram, *English Wall Painting,* 95.

79. Caiger-Smith, *English Medieval Mural Paintings,* 44.

80. Rosewell, *Medieval Wall Paintings,* 86.

81. Tristram, *English Wall Painting,* 20 and 97.

82. *Memoriale Credencium,* 62. Images of the wall paintings at Hoxne and
other churches may be accessed at Anne Marshall's website, http://www.paint
edchurch.org.

83. The "Letter from the Rev. Wm. Beal, Vicar of Brooke, Norfolk, addressed to Dawson Turner, Esq., V.P., Descriptive of Certain Mural Paintings
Lately Discovered in his Church," *Norfolk Archaeology: Miscellaneous Tracts Relating to
the Antiquities of the County of Norfolk, Published by the Norfolk and Norwich Archæological
Society,* vol. 3 (Norwich: Charles Muskett, Old Haymarket, 1852), 62–70, appears to be the first publication that includes hand-drawn reproductions of the
paintings at Brooke Church that were discovered in either 1848 or 1849 and
subsequently lost through poor restoration techniques. M. R. James, "The Wall
Paintings in Brooke Church," in *A Supplement to Blomefield's Norfolk,* ed. Clement
Rolfe Ingleby (London: Clement Ingleby, 1929), 15–26, also reproduces draw-
ings of the lost murals.

84. Tristram, *English Wall Painting*, 103, 136–37, 143–44. Anne Marshall notes that when Bardwell's murals were revealed in 1853, they were copied and catalogued before being covered with whitewash. Later attempts to uncover the paintings failed due to the instability of the underlying plaster: http://www .paintedchurch.org (last accessed 18 January 2010).

85. Rosewell, *Medieval Wall Paintings*, 203, finds the idea of wall paintings as teaching aids "problematic and complex," though he concedes that murals of the seven deadly sins "may have had a self-teaching purpose" since Lateran IV required that laymen understand the tenets of Christian teaching.

86. Caiger-Smith, *English Medieval Mural Paintings*, 50, attributes the *De fructibus carnis et spiritus* to Hugh of Saint Victor, while Richard Newhauser states that Conrad of Hirsau has been accepted as the author of the work in *The Treatise on Vices and Virtues*, 160–61. For the questionable nature of Conrad's authorship, see Cheryl Gohdes Goggin, "Copying Manuscript Illuminations: The Trees of Vices and Virtues," *Visual Resources* 20, no. 2 (2004): 179–98, at 179.

87. H. L. Spencer, *English Preaching in the Late Middle Ages* (Oxford: Clarendon Press, 1993), 203. See also the work of Miriam Gill at the University of Leicester's Database of the Seven Deadly Sins and the Seven Corporeal Works of Mercy in British wall paintings available at http://www.le.ac.uk/ha /seedcorn/contents.html (last accessed 28 June 2011).

88. Although I have previously argued that the Parson's pleasures subvert the moral directive of the *Tale*, I now believe that dress functions more broadly across the text as a device to teach the tripartite structure of penance. For my initial argument, see Nicole D. Smith, "The Parson's Predilection for Pleasure," *Studies in the Age of Chaucer* 28 (2006): 117–40.

89. Carol V. Kaske, "Getting around the Parson's Tale: An Alternative to Allegory and Irony," in *Chaucer at Albany*, ed. Rossell Hope Robbins (New York: Burt Franklin, 1973), 147–77, at 168.

90. Scanlon, *Narrative, Authority, and Power*, 8–9; and Katherine Little, "Chaucer's Parson," 226.

91. Pearsall, *The Canterbury Tales*, 246.

92. I quote the excerpts of Raymond's *Summa* as they appear in Newhauser, "The Parson's Tale," 560.

93. Newhauser, "The Parson's Tale," 568–69: "'Fetes fruiz,' dit ele, e ne mie foilles, kar arbre ne est mie veraiement conu per la racine ne par les foilles, mes est par le fruit, pur ceo ke meintes fez est amertume en les foiz e en la racine e doucour est en la fruit."

94. The *MED* includes several definitions of "swetenesse" that pertain to the senses: (1) "the quality of being sweet or pleasant to the taste; also *fig.*

spiritual sweetness"; (2) "a sweet smell, a fragrance"; (3) "melodiousness, harmoniousness, sweetness of sound"; (4) "delight, pleasure, enjoyment, bliss"; (5) "tenderness, gentleness, loving-kindness."

95. *The Book of Vices and Virtues,* 251.

96. Michel, *Ayenbite of Inwit,* 226–27; *Book of Vices and Virtues,* 251; *Speculum Vitae,* line 11,422; *A Myrour to Lewde Men and Wymmen,* 189; *Jacob's Well,* 195.

97. *A Myrour to Lewde Men and Wymmen,* 189.

98. I quote the *Voie de paradis* in the parallel text that Diekstra prints because the chapters concerning bodily affliction are damaged in the Middle English *Weye.*

99. *Voie de paradis,* ch. 287: "Honme et fame peut tourmenter sa char et pener em pluseurs manieres. . . . En asprestés de vesteures, conme vestir lange, haires, haubres et autres aspres choses. Ainssi fesoient les sainz et les saintes de Paradis et font encore les saintes gens en cest monde." [A man and a woman can torment the flesh and pain themselves in many ways. . . . In coarseness of clothing, as in dressing in woolen cloth, hairshirts, hauberks, and other coarse things. Male and female saints in Paradise did it in this manner, and saints of this world continue to do so.] Translation is mine.

100. Regan, "*Cleansing of Man's Soul,*" 129; translation is mine.

101. Ibid., 176, 194, and 179, respectively.

102. Ibid., 193.

103. *Speculum Sacerdotale,* 139.

104. Regan, "*Cleansing of Man's Soul,*" 198. Translation is mine.

105. Bliss pervades *Speculum Vitae* and the *Boke of Penance,* respectively; see the *Speculum,* lines 8026 and 14,790–832 and the *Boke,* 1471, 1540, 1570, and 1577 for particularly pertinent examples. See also Michel, *Ayenbite of Inwit,* 75, 83, 88, 92–93, 243–44; Mirk's *Festial,* 268; *Weye of Paradise,* 301–3; *Memoriale Credencium,* 183–86; and *Of Shrifte and Penance,* 129.

106. *Lay Folks' Catechism,* 73.

107. In making this claim, I align myself with critics who read the *General Prologue* and the *Parson's Tale* as bookend texts to the collection. See, in particular, David Lawton, "Chaucer's Two Ways: The Pilgrimage Frame of the Canterbury Tales," *Studies in the Age of Chaucer* 9 (1987): 3–40; and Raybin, "'Manye been the weyes,'" 11–43.

108. Goering, "The Internal Forum," 396.

109. For a reading of dress in the *General Prologue,* see Laura F. Hodges, *Chaucer and Costume: The Secular Pilgrims in the General Prologue* (Woodbridge: D. S. Brewer, 2000); and her subsequent *Chaucer and Clothing: Clerical and Academic Cos-*

tume in the General Prologue to the Canterbury Tales (Woodbridge: D. S. Brewer, 2005).

Conclusion

1. "... ars callida res ita vertit, / Ut non pervertat; transponit ut hoc tamen ipso / Rem melius ponat" (lines 97–98), Geoffrey of Vinsauf, *Poetria nova*; Geoffrey of Vinsauf, *The New Poetics*, 35. The text for the epigraph is from *Patria nova*, lines 60–61: "Mentis in arcano cum rem digesserit ordo, / materiam verbis veniat vestire poesis."

2. Hollander, *Sex and Suits*, 13.

Bibliography

Primary Works

Alan of Lille. *The Plaint of Nature.* Translated by James J. Sheridan. Toronto: Pontifical Institute of Mediaeval Studies, 1980.

Albert the Great. *Man and the Beasts:* De animalibus, *Books 22–26.* Translated by James J. Scanlan. Binghamton, NY: Medieval and Renaissance Texts and Studies, 1987.

Anderson, J. J., ed. *Sir Gawain and the Green Knight, Pearl, Cleanness, Patience.* London: J. M. Dent, 1996.

Andreas Capellanus. *Andreas Capellanus on Love.* Edited by P. G. Walsh. London: Duckworth, 1982.

———. *The Art of Courtly Love.* Edited and translated by John Jay Parry. New York: Columbia University Press, 1960.

Andrew, Malcolm, Ronald Waldron, and Clifford Peterson, eds. *The Complete Works of the* Pearl-*Poet.* Translated by Casey Finch. Berkeley: University of California Press, 1993.

Aquinas, Thomas. *Summa theologiae.* Translated by Fathers of the English Dominican Province. New York: Benzinger Bros., 1938.

Augustine. *Concerning the City of God against the Pagans.* Translated by Henry Bettenson. London: Penguin, 1984.

———. *Confessions.* Translated by Henry Chadwick. Oxford: Oxford University Press, 1991.

———. *Confessions.* Edited by James J. O'Donnell. 3 vols. Oxford: Clarendon Press, 1992.

———. *De Trinitate*. Edited by W. J. Mountain and Fr. Glorie. *Corpus Christianorum Series Latina*, vol 50–50A. Turnhout: Brepols, 1968.

———. *The Trinity*. Translated by Stephen McKenna. Washington, DC: Catholic University of America Press, 1963.

Baker, Donald C., John L. Murphy, and Louis B. Hall, Jr., eds. *The Late Medieval Religious Plays of Bodleian Mss. Digby 133 and E Museo 160*. EETS, o.s. 283. Oxford: Oxford University Press, 1982.

Benoît de Sainte-Maure. *Roman de Troie*. Edited by Emmanuèle Baumgartner and Françoise Vielliard. Paris: Librairie Générale Française, 1998.

Bitterling, Klaus, ed. *Of Shrifte and Penance: The ME Prose Translation of* Le Manuel des péchés. Heidelberg: Universitätsverlag C. Winter, 1998.

Borroff, Marie, ed. *Sir Gawain and the Green Knight: A New Verse Translation*. New York: Norton, 1967.

Brandeis, Arthur, ed. *Jacob's Well*. EETS, o.s. 115. London: Kegan Paul, Trench, Trübner and Co., 1900.

Brie, Friedrich W. D., ed. *The Brut, or the Chronicles of England*. 2 vols. EETS, o.s. 131 and 136. London: Kegan Paul, Trench, Trübner and Co., 1908.

British Museum, Robert Harley Oxford et al. *A Catalogue of the Harleian Manuscripts in the British Museum. With Indexes of Persons, Places, and Matters*. Vol. 1. 1808. Reprint, Hildesheim: Georg Olms, 1973.

Chaucer, Geoffrey. *The Riverside Chaucer*. Edited by Larry D. Benson. 3rd ed. Boston: Houghton Mifflin, 1987.

Chaucer Life-Records. Edited by Martin M. Crow and Clair C. Olson. Oxford: Clarendon Press, 1966.

Chestre, Thomas. "Sir Launfal." In *The Middle English Breton Lays*. Edited by Anne Laskaya and Eve Salisbury, 201–62. Kalamazoo, MI: TEAMS, 1995.

Chrétien de Troyes. *Arthurian Romances*. Edited and translated by William W. Kibler. London: Penguin, 1991.

———. *Erec et Enide*. Edited by Jean-Marie Fritz. Paris: Lettres Gothiques, 1992.

Clement of Alexandria. *Christ the Educator*. Translated by Simon P. Wood. New York: Fathers of the Church, 1954.

Coulton, G. G., ed. *From St. Francis to Dante: A Translation of All that is of Primary Interest in the Chronicle of the Franciscan Salimbene (1221–1288)*. London: David Nutt, 1906.

Devic, Claude, and Jean Joseph Vaissete, eds. *Histoire générale de Languedoc*. Vol. 10. Toulouse: Edouard Privat, 1885.

Diceto, Ralph de. *Radulfi de Diceto decani Lundoniensis opera historica. The Historical Works of Master Ralph de Diceto, Dean of London*. Edited by William Stubbs.

Rerum Britannicarum Medii Aevi Scriptores, Rolls Series, no. 68. London: Longman and Co., 1876.

Diekstra, F. N. M., ed. *The Middle English* Weye of Paradys *and the Middle French* Voie de Paradis. Leiden: Brill, 1991.

Dufournet, Jean, ed. and trans. *Aucassin et Nicolette.* Paris: Garnier-Flammarion, 1973.

Everett, Walter K. "A Critical Edition of the Confession Section of *The Clensyng of Mannes Soule.*" Ph.D. dissertation, University of North Carolina-Chapel Hill, 1974.

Francis, W. Nelson, ed. *The Book of Vices and Virtues: A Fourteenth-Century English Translation of the* Somme le roi *of Lorens d'Orléans.* EETS, o.s. 217. London: Oxford University Press, 1942.

Friedman, Albert B., and Norman T. Harrington, eds. *Ywain and Gawain.* EETS, o.s. 254. London: Oxford University Press, 1964.

Froissart, Jean. *Les Chroniques de Sire Jean Froissart.* Edited by J. A. C. Buchon. Vol. 1. Paris: Société du Panthéon Littéraire, 1840.

———. *Oeuvres de Froissart.* Edited by Kervyn de Lettenhove. 25 vols. Brussels: Victor Devaux, 1867–77.

Geoffrey of Monmouth. *The* Historia Regum Britanniae *of Geoffrey of Monmouth.* Edited and translated by Neil Wright. Cambridge: D. S. Brewer, 1985.

Geoffrey of Vinsauf. *The New Poetics.* Translated by Jane Baltzell Kopp. In *Three Medieval Rhetorical Arts,* edited by James J. Murphy, 27–108. Berkeley: University of California Press, 1971.

———. *Poetria nova.* In *Les Arts poétiques du XIIe et du XIIIe siècle,* edited by Edmond Faral, 197–262. Paris: Librairie Honoré Champion, 1962.

Gerald of Wales. *Jewel of the Church.* Edited and translated by John J. Hagen. Leiden: E. J. Brill, 1979.

Gervase of Tilbury. *Otia Imperialia: Recreation for an Emperor.* Edited and translated by S. E. Banks and J. W. Binns. Oxford: Clarendon Press, 2002.

Giraldus Cambrensis. [Gerald of Wales]. *Opera.* 8 vols. Edited by J. S. Brewer. London, 1882. Reprint, Kraus, 1964.

Gollancz, Sir Israel, ed. *Sir Gawain and the Green Knight.* EETS, o.s. 210. London: Oxford University Press, 1940.

Gregory the Great. *Homiliae in Evangelia.* In *Patrologiae cursus completus, Series Latina,* vol. 76. Edited by Jacques-Paul Migne. Paris: Apud Garnieri Fratres, 1844–64.

Guillaume de Lorris and Jean de Meun. *Le Roman de la rose.* Edited by Armand Strubel. Paris: Librairie Générale Française, 1992.

———. *The Romance of the Rose*. Translated by Charles Dahlberg. 3rd ed. Princeton: Princeton University Press, 1995.

Guillaume de Nangis. *Chronique latine de Guillaume de Nangis de 1113 à 1300*. Edited by H. Géraud. 2 vols. Paris: Jules Renouard, 1843.

Hanna, Ralph, ed. *Speculum Vitae: A Reading Edition*. 2 vols. EETS, o.s. 331 and 332. Oxford: Oxford University Press, 2008.

Harrison, Keith, trans. "Sir Gawain and the Green Knight." In *Medieval English Literature*, 2nd ed. Edited by J. B. Trapp, Douglas Gray, and Julia Boffey, 360–416. New York: Oxford University Press, 2002.

Hausknecht, Emil, ed. *The Romaunce of the Sowdone of Babylone and of Ferumbras his sone who conquerede Rome*. EETS, e.s. 38. London: Trübner and Co., 1881.

Haydon, Frank Scott, ed. *Eulogium (historiarum sive temporis)*. Rolls Series 9, vol. 3. London: Longman, Green, Longman, Roberts, and Green, 1863.

Henry of Lancaster. *Le Livre de seyntz medicines*. Edited by E. J. Arnould. Oxford: Basil Blackwell, 1940.

Holmstedt, Gustaf, ed. *Speculum Christiani*. London: Oxford University Press, 1933.

Homer. *The Iliad*. Translated by Richmond Lattimore. Chicago: University of Chicago Press, 1951.

John of Reading. *Chronica Johannis de Reading et anonymi Cantuariensis, 1346–1367*. Edited by James Tait. Manchester: Manchester University Press, 1914.

John of Salisbury. *Frivolities of Courtiers and Footprints of Philosophers: Being a Translation of the First, Second, and Third Books and Selections from the Seventh and Eighth Books of the* Policraticus *of John of Salisbury*. Edited by Joseph B. Pike. Minneapolis: University of Minnesota Press, 1938.

———. *Policraticus*. Edited by Clement C. J. Webb. 2 vols. 1909. Reprint, New York: Arno, 1979.

———. *The Statesman's Book of John of Salisbury: Being the Fourth, Fifth, and Sixth Books and Selections from the Seventh and Eighth Books, of the* Policraticus. Edited and translated by John Dickenson. New York: Russell and Russell, 1963.

Kaeuper, Richard W., and Elspeth Kennedy, eds. and trans. The Book of Chivalry *of Geoffroi de Charny*. Philadelphia: University of Pennsylvania Press, 1996.

Kengen, J. H. L., ed. *Memoriale Credencium: A Late Middle English Manual of Theology for Lay People: Edited from Bodley MS Tanner 201*. Nijmegen: Katholieke Universiteit, 1979.

Langland, William. *Piers Plowman: The B Version*. Edited by George Kane and E. Talbot Donaldson. London: Athlone Press, 1975.

Lavynham, Richard. *A Litil Tretys on the Seven Deadly Sins*. Edited by J. P. W. M. Van Zutphen. Rome: Institutum Carmelitanum, 1956.

Lodge, Eleanor C., and Robert Somerville, eds. *John of Gaunt's Register, 1379–1383*. 2 vols. London: Camden Society, 1937.

Mannyng, Robert. *Handlyng Synne*. Edited by Idelle Sullens. Binghamton: Medieval and Renaissance Texts and Studies, 1983.

Marie de France. *Les Lais de Marie de France*. Edited by Jean Rychner. Paris: Librairie Honoré Champion, 1983.

———. *Lais de Marie de France*. Translated by Laurence Harf-Lancner. Edited by Karl Warnke. Paris: Lettres Gothiques, 1990.

———. *The Lais of Marie de France*. Edited and translated by Robert Hanning and Joan Ferrante. Durham, NC: Labyrinth Press, 1978.

McKitterick, Rosamond, and Richard Beadle. *Catalogue of the Pepys Library at Magdalene College Cambridge*. Vol. 5, part 1. Cambridge: D. S. Brewer, 1992.

McNeill, John T., and Helena M. Gamer. *Medieval Handbooks of Penance*. Rev. ed. New York: Columbia University Press, 1990.

Michel, Dan. *Ayenbite of Inwit*. Edited by Richard Morris. EETS, o.s. 23. London: Trübner and Co., 1866.

Michel, Francisque, ed. *Histoire des ducs de Normandie et des rois d'Angleterre*. Paris: J. Renouard, 1840.

Migne, Jacques-Paul, ed. *Patrologiae cursus completus, Series Latina*. 221 vols. Paris: Apud Garnieri Fratres, 1844–91.

Millett, Bella, ed. *Ancrene Wisse: A Corrected Edition of the Text in Cambridge, Corpus Christi College, MS 402, with variants from other manuscripts*. EETS, o.s. 325. Oxford: Oxford University Press, 2005.

Mirk, John. *Festial: Edited from British Library MS Cotton Claudius A.II*. Edited by Susan Powell. EETS, o.s. 334. Oxford: Oxford University Press, 2009.

Mora-Lebrun, Francine, ed. *Roman de Thèbes*. Paris: Librairie Générale Française, 1995.

Morris, Richard, ed. *Boke of Penance*. In *Cursor Mundi*, part 5. EETS, o.s. 68. London: Trübner and Co., 1878.

———. *Cursor Mundi*. EETS, o.s. 57. London: Trübner and Co., 1874.

Nelson, Venetia, ed. *A Myrour to Lewde Men and Wymmen*. Heidelberg: Carl Winter, 1981.

Nicholson, Helen J., ed. *Chronicle of the Third Crusade: A Translation of the* Itinerarium Peregrinorum et Gesta Regis Ricardi. Aldershot: Ashgate, 1997.

Omont, Henri. *Bibliothèque Nationale, Catalogue général des manuscrits français: anciens petits fonds français*. Paris: Ernest Leroux, 1902.

———. *Bibliothèque Nationale, Catalogue général des manuscrits français: nouvelles acquisitions françaises.* Paris: Ernest Leroux, 1899.

Orderic Vitalis. *The Ecclesiastical History of Orderic Vitalis.* Edited and translated by Marjorie Chibnall. 6 vols. Oxford: Clarendon Press, 1969–80.

Ovid. *The Art of Love and Other Poems.* Edited and translated by J. H. Mozley. Loeb Classical Library 232. Cambridge, MA: Harvard University Press, 1979.

Piramus, Denis. *La Vie Seint Edmund le Rei.* Edited by Hilding Kjellman. Göteborg, 1935.

———. *La Vie seint Edmund le rey.* Edited by Ian Short. In "Denis Piramus and the Truth of Marie's Lais." *Cultura neolatina* 67, nos. 3–4 (2007): 319–40, at 339–40.

Radice, Betty, trans. *The Letters of Abelard and Heloise.* Revised by M. T. Clanchy. London: Penguin, 2003.

Regan, Charles Lionel. *"The Cleansing of Man's Soul:* Edited from MS Bodley 923." Ph.D. dissertation, Harvard University, 1963.

Régnier, Claude, ed. *La Prise d'Orange.* 7th ed. Paris: Editions Klincksieck, 1986.

Renart, Jean. *Le Roman de la rose ou de Guillaume de Dole.* Edited by G. Servois. Paris: Firmin Didot, 1893.

———. *The Romance of the Rose or Guillaume de Dole.* Translated by Patricia Terry and Nancy Vine Durling. Philadelphia: University of Pennsylvania Press, 1993.

Roche-Mahdi, Sarah, ed. and trans. *Silence: A Thirteenth-Century French Romance.* East Lansing: Michigan State University Press, 2007.

Rolle de Hampole, Richard. *The Pricke of Conscience.* Edited by Richard Morris. 1863. Reprint, New York: AMS Press, 1973.

Roques, Mario, ed. *Aucassin et Nicolette: Chantefable du XIIIe siècle.* Paris: Champion, 1982.

Rutebeuf. *Œuvres complètes.* Edited by Michel Zink. Paris: Classiques Garnier, 1989.

———. *Œuvres complètes de Rutebeuf.* Edited by Edmond Faral and Julia Bastin. 2 vols. Paris: Picard, 1970.

St. John's College, Cambridge, MS S 35.

Salu, M. B., trans. *Ancrene Riwle.* London: Burns and Oates, 1955.

Salverda de Grave, J. J., ed. *Enéas.* 2 vols. Paris: Librairie Ancienne Edouard Champion, 1929.

Schweigel, Max, ed. *Esclarmonde, Clarisse et Florent, Yde et Olive: Drei Fortsetzungen der Chanson von Huon de Bordeaux, nach der einzigen Turiner Handschrift zum erstenmal veröffenlicht.* Ausgaben und Abhandlungen aus dem Gebiete der romanischen Philologie 83. Marburg: Elwert'sche Verlagsbuchhandlung, 1889.

Simmons, Thomas Frederick, and Henry Edward Nolloth, eds. *Lay Folks' Catechism*. London: Kegan Paul, Trench, Trübner and Co., 1901.

Sinclair, Keith V., ed. *Tristan de Nanteuil*. Assen: Van Gorcum, 1971.

Smith, Thomas. *Catalogue of the Manuscripts in the Cottonian Library 1696 (Catalogus librorum manuscriptorum bibliothecae Cottonianae)*. Edited by C. G. C. Tite. Cambridge: D. S. Brewer, 1984.

Spector, Stephen, ed. *The N-Town Play: Cotton MS Vespasian D.8.* 2 vols. EETS, s.s. 11 and 12. Oxford: Oxford University Press, 1991.

Statutes of the Realm. 12 vols. 1810–28. Reprint, London: Dawsons, 1963.

Stevens, Martin, and A. C. Cawley, eds. *The Towneley Plays*. 2 vols. EETS, s.s. 13 and 14. Oxford: Oxford University Press, 1994.

Stevenson, Joseph, ed. *The Church Historians of England*. Vol. 4. London: Seeleys, 1854.

Stubbs, William, ed. *Chronicles and Memorials of the Reign of Richard I.* 2 vols. London: Longman, Green, Longman, Roberts, and Green, 1864. Reprint, Kraus, 1964.

Summer, H. Oskar, ed. *Lestoire de Merlin, The Vulgate Version of the Arthurian Romances*. Vol. 2. Washington, DC: Carnegie Institution, 1908.

Tanner, Norman P., ed. *Decrees of the Ecumenical Councils*. 2 vols. London: Sheed and Ward, 1990.

Taschereau, Jules-Antoine, et al. *Catalogue des manuscrits français*. 5 vols. Paris: Firmin Didot, 1868.

Taylor, John, Wendy R. Childs, and Leslie Watkiss, eds. and trans. *The St. Alban's Chronicle: The* Chronica maiora *of Thomas Walsingham, 1376–1394*. Oxford: Clarendon Press, 2003.

Tertullian. "The Apparel of Women." In *Disciplinary, Moral and Ascetical Works*. Translated by Rudolph Arbesmann, Sister Emily Joseph Daly, and Edwin A. Quain. New York: Fathers of the Church, 1959.

Thomas of Kent. *Le Roman d'Alexandre ou le roman de toute chevalerie*. Edited by Brian Foster and Ian Short. Paris: Honoré Champion, 2003.

Trésor de la langue française informatisé. Analyse et traitement informatique de la langue française—Centre National de la Recherche Scientifique, Nancy Université.

Venette, Jean de. *The Chronicle of Jean de Venette*. Edited by Richard A. Newhall. Translated by Jean Birdsall. New York: Columbia University Press, 1953.

Virgil. *Aeneid*. Translated by H. Rushton Fairclough. Loeb Classical Library 63. Cambridge, MA: Harvard University Press, 1999.

Weatherly, Edward H., ed. *Speculum Sacerdotale*. EETS, o.s. 200. London: Oxford University Press, 1936.

Wenzel, Siegfried, ed. and trans. *Fasciculus Morum: A Fourteenth-Century Preacher's Handbook.* University Park: Pennsylvania State University Press, 1989.

———. *Preaching in the Age of Chaucer: Selected Sermons in Translation.* Washington, DC: Catholic University of America Press, 2008.

William of Malmesbury. *Gesta regum Anglorum.* Edited and translated by R. A. B. Mynors, R. M. Thomson, and M. Winterbottom. Oxford: Clarendon Press, 1998.

William of Newburgh. *Historia rerum Anglicarum.* Edited by Hans Claude Hamilton. London: Sumptibus Societatis, 1856.

Winny, James, ed. and trans. *Sir Gawain and the Green Knight.* Toronto: Broadview, 2001.

Wright, Thomas, and James Orchard Halliwell, eds. *Reliquae Antiquae: Scraps from Ancient Manuscripts Illustrating Chiefly Early English Literature and the English Language.* Vol. 1. London: William Pickering, 1841.

Yunck, John A., ed. and trans. *Enéas.* New York: Columbia University Press, 1974.

Secondary Sources

Adams, Tracy. "'Arte regendus amor': Suffering and Sexuality in Marie de France's *Lai de Guigemar.*" *Exemplaria* 17, no. 2 (2005): 285–315.

———. "'Pur vostre cor su jo em paine': The Augustinian Subtext of Thomas's Tristan." *Medium Ævum* 68, no. 2 (1999): 278–91.

Aers, David. "Christianity for Courtly Subjects: Reflections on the *Gawain*-Poet." In *A Companion to the* Gawain-*Poet,* edited by Derek Brewer and Jonathan Gibson, 91–101. Cambridge: D. S. Brewer, 1997.

———. *Community, Gender, and Individual Identity: English Writing, 1360–1430.* London: Routledge, 1988.

———. *Faith, Ethics, and Church: Writing in England, 1360–1409.* Cambridge: D. S. Brewer, 2000.

———. *Salvation and Sin: Augustine, Langland and the Fourteenth Century.* Notre Dame, IN: University of Notre Dame Press, 2009.

Akbari, Suzanne Conklin. *Seeing through the Veil: Optical Theory and Medieval Allegory.* Toronto: University of Toronto Press, 2004.

Allen, Peter L. "The Ambiguity of Silence: Gender, Writing, and *Le Roman de Silence.*" In *Sign, Sentence, Discourse: Language in Medieval Thought and Literature,* edited by Julian N. Wasserman and Lois Roney, 98–112. Syracuse: Syracuse University Press, 1989.

Amodio, Mark C. "Tradition, Modernity, and the Emergence of the Self in *Sir Gawain and the Green Knight*." *Assays* 8 (1995): 47–68.

Anciaux, Paul. *La Théologie du sacrament de pénitence au XIIe siècle*. Louvain: E. Nauwelaerts, 1949.

Appadurai, Arjun, ed. *The Social Life of Things: Commodities in Cultural Perspective*. Cambridge: Cambridge University Press, 1986.

Astell, Ann. "*Sir Gawain and the Green Knight*: A Study in the Rhetoric of Romance." *Journal of English and Germanic Philology* 84 (1985): 188–202.

Auerbach, Erich. *Mimesis: The Representation of Reality in Western Literature*. Translated by Willard R. Trask. Princeton: Princeton University Press, 1953.

Baildon, W. Paley. "A Wardrobe Account of 16–17 Richard II, 1393–4." *Archaeologia* 62 (1911): 497–514.

Baldwin, Frances. *Sumptuary Legislation and Personal Regulation in England*. Baltimore: Johns Hopkins University Press, 1926.

Baldwin, John W. *Aristocratic Life in Medieval France: The Romances of Jean Renart and Gerbert de Montreuil, 1190–1230*. Baltimore: Johns Hopkins University Press, 2000.

———. "The Image of the Jongleur in Northern France around 1200." *Speculum* 72, no. 3 (1997): 635–63.

———. *Masters, Princes, and Merchants: The Social Views of Peter the Chanter and His Circle*. 2 vols. Princeton: Princeton University Press, 1970.

Barr, Helen. "Pearl—or 'The Jeweller's Tale.'" *Medium Aevum* 69, no. 1 (2000): 59–70.

Barron, W. R. J. *English Medieval Romance*. London: Longman, 1987.

———. *Trawthe and Treason: The Sin of Gawain Reconsidered*. Manchester: Manchester University Press, 1980.

Barthes, Roland. *The Pleasure of the Text*. Translated by Richard Miller. New York: Hill and Wang, 1975.

Baswell, Christopher. *Virgil in Medieval England: Figuring the Aeneid from the Twelfth Century to Chaucer*. Cambridge: Cambridge University Press, 1995.

Baudrillard, Jean. *The Ecstasy of Communication*. Brooklyn: Autonomedia, 1988.

Beal, William. "Letter from the Rev. Wm. Beal, Vicar of Brooke, Norfolk, addressed to Dawson Turner, Esq., V.P., Descriptive of Certain Mural Paintings Lately Discovered in his Church." In *Norfolk Archaeology: Miscellaneous Tracts Relating to the Antiquities of the County of Norfolk, Published by the Norfolk and Norwich Archæological Society*, vol. 3, 62–70. Norwich: Charles Muskett, Old Haymarket, 1852.

Beaulieu, Michèle. "Le Costume français: Miroir de la sensibilité (1350–1500)." In *Le Vêtement: Histoire, archéologie, et symbolique vestimentaires au*

Moyen Age, edited by Michel Pastoureau, 255–77. Paris: Léopard d'Or, 1989.

Beaurepaire, Charles de. "Complainte de la bataille de Poitiers." *Bibliothèque de l'Ecole de Chartres* 12 (1851): 257–63.

Bennett, Michael J. "The Court of Richard II and the Promotion of Literature." In *Chaucer's England,* edited by Barbara Hanawalt, 3–20. Minneapolis: University of Minnesota Press, 1992.

Benson, Larry D. *Art and Tradition in* Sir Gawain and the Green Knight. New Brunswick, NJ: Rutgers University Press, 1965.

Besserman, Lawrence. "Gawain's Green Girdle." *Annuale Mediævale* 22 (1982): 84–101.

Bestul, Thomas H. "Chaucer's *Parson's Tale* and the Late-Medieval Tradition of Religious Meditation." *Speculum* 64, no. 3 (1989): 600–619.

Biggins, D. "*Canterbury Tales* X (I) 424: 'The Hyndre Part of a She-Ape in the Fulle of the Moone.'" *Medium Aevum* 33, no. 3 (1964): 200–203.

Biller, Peter, and A. J. Minnis, eds. *Handling Sin: Confession in the Middle Ages.* Woodbridge: York Medieval Press, 1998.

Birkett, Helen. "The Pastoral Application of the Lateran IV Reforms in the Northern Province, 1215–1348." *Northern History* 43, no. 2 (2006): 199–219.

Blanc, Odile. "From Battlefield to Court: The Invention of Fashion in the Fourteenth Century." In *Encountering Medieval Textiles and Dress: Objects, Texts, Images,* edited by Désirée G. Koslin and Janet E. Snyder, 157–72. New York: Palgrave, 2002.

———. "Historiographie du vêtement: Un bilan." In *Le Vêtement: Histoire, archéologie, et symbolique vestimentaires au Moyen Age,* edited by Michel Pastoureau, 7–33. Paris: Léopard d'Or, 1989.

———. "Vêtement féminin, vêtement masculin à la fin du Moyen Age: Le Point de vue des moralistes." In *Le Vêtement: Histoire, archéologie, et symbolique vestimentaires au Moyen Age,* edited by Michel Pastoureau, 243–51. Paris: Léopard d'Or, 1989.

Blanton, Virginia. "Chaste Marriage, Sexual Desire, and Christian Martyrdom in *La vie seinte Audrée.*" *Journal of the History of Sexuality* 19, no. 1 (2010): 94–114.

Bloch, R. Howard. *The Anonymous Marie de France.* Chicago: University of Chicago Press, 2003.

———. "The Medieval Text—'Guigemar'—as a Provocation to the Discipline of Medieval Studies." *Romanic Review* 79 (1988): 63–73.

———. *The Scandal of the Fabliaux.* Chicago: University of Chicago Press, 1986.

————. "Silence and Holes: The *Roman de Silence* and the Art of the Trouvère." *Yale French Studies* 70 (1986): 81–99.

Bloomfield, Morton. *Seven Deadly Sins*. East Lansing: Michigan State College Press, 1952.

Blumreich, Kathleen M. "Lesbian Desire in the Old French *Roman de Silence*." *Arthuriana* 7, no. 2 (1997): 47–62.

Boucher, François. *Histoire du costume en Occident de l'antiquité à nos jours*. Paris: Flammarion, 1965.

Boyle, Leonard E. "The Date of the *Summa Praedicatium* of John Bromyard." *Speculum* 48, no. 3 (1973): 533–37.

————. "The Fourth Lateran Council and Manuals of Popular Theology." In *The Popular Literature of Medieval England*, edited by Thomas Heffernan, 30–43. Knoxville: University of Tennessee Press, 1985.

————. "The Inter-Conciliar Period, 1179–1215, and the Beginnings of Pastoral Manuals." In *Miscellanea Rolando Bandinelli Papa Alessandro III*, edited by F. Liotta, 45–56. Siena: Accademia Senesi degli Intronati, 1986.

————. *Pastoral Care, Clerical Education, and Canon Law, 1200–1400*. London: Variorum Imprints, 1981.

————. "Summa Confessorum." In *Les Genres littéraires dans les sources théologiques et philosophiques médiévales: Définition, critique, et exploitation*, 227–37. Louvain-la-Neuve: Université Catholique de Louvain, 1982.

Bradfield, Nancy. *Historical Costumes of England*. 3rd ed. New York: Barnes and Noble, 1971.

Brahney, Kathleen J. "When Silence Was Golden: Female Personae in the *Roman de Silence*." In *The Spirit of the Court: Selected Proceedings of the Fourth Congress of the International Courtly Literature Society*, 52–61. Dover, NH: Brewer, 1985.

Braswell, Mary. *The Medieval Sinner: Characterization and Confession in the Literature of the English Middle Ages*. Rutherford, NJ: Fairleigh Dickinson University Press, 1983.

Brewer, Charlotte, and Alastair Minnis, eds. *Crux and Controversy in Middle English Textual Criticism*. Cambridge: D. S. Brewer, 1992.

Brewer, Derek. "The Arming of the Warrior in European Literature and Chaucer." In *Chaucerian Problems and Perspectives: Essays Presented to Paul E. Beichner*, edited by Edward Vasta and Zacharias P. Thundy, 221–43. Notre Dame, IN: University of Notre Dame Press, 1979.

————. "The Popular English Metrical Romances." In *A Companion to Romance: From Classical to Contemporary*, edited by Corinne Saunders, 45–64. Malden, MA: Blackwell, 2004.

Brewer, Derek, and Jonathan Gibson, eds. *A Companion to the* Gawain-*Poet.* Cambridge: D. S. Brewer, 1997.

Brown, Peter R. L. *The Cult of the Saints: Its Rise and Function in Latin Christianity.* Chicago: University of Chicago Press, 1982.

Bruckner, Matilda Tomaryn. *Shaping Romance: Interpretation, Truth, and Closure in Twelfth-Century French Fictions.* Philadelphia: University of Pennsylvania Press, 1993.

Brumlik, Joan. "The Lyric Malmariée: Marie's Subtext in *Guigemar.*" *Romance Quarterly* 43, no. 2 (1996): 67–71.

Bullough, Vern L. "Transvestites in the Middle Ages." *The American Journal of Sociology* 79, no. 6 (1974): 1381–94.

Bullough, Vern L., and Bonnie Bullough. *Cross Dressing, Sex, and Gender.* Philadelphia: University of Pennsylvania Press, 1993.

Burger, Glenn. *Chaucer's Queer Nation.* Minneapolis: University of Minnesota Press, 2003.

———. "Kissing the Pardoner." *PMLA* 107 (1992): 1143–56.

Burgess, Glyn S. *The* Lais *of Marie de France: Text and Context.* Athens: University of Georgia Press, 1987.

Burns, E. Jane. *Bodytalk: When Women Speak in Old French Literature.* Philadelphia: University of Pennsylvania Press, 1993.

———. *Courtly Love Undressed.* Philadelphia: University of Pennsylvania Press, 2002.

———, ed. *Medieval Fabrications: Dress, Textiles, Cloth Work, and Other Cultural Imaginings.* New York: Palgrave, 2004.

———. "Why Textiles Make a Difference." In *Medieval Fabrications: Dress, Textiles, Cloth Work, and Other Cultural Imaginings,* edited by E. Jane Burns, 1–18. New York: Palgrave, 2004.

Burrow, John A. *A Reading of* Sir Gawain and the Green Knight. London: Routledge and Kegan Paul, 1965.

———. "The Two Confession Scenes in *Sir Gawain and the Green Knight.*" *Modern Philology* 57, no. 2 (1959): 73–79.

Busby, Keith. *Codex and Context: Reading Old French Verse Narrative in Manuscript.* Amsterdam: Rodopi, 2002.

Caiger-Smith, A. *English Medieval Mural Paintings.* Oxford: Clarendon Press, 1963.

Camille, Michael. "The Pose of the Queer: Dante's Gaze, Brunetto Latini's Body." In *Queering the Middle Ages,* edited by Glenn Burger and Steven F. Kruger, 57–86. Minneapolis: University of Minnesota Press, 2001.

Carlson, David R. *Chaucer's Jobs.* New York: Palgrave Macmillan, 2004.

Carruthers, Leo. "The Duke of Clarence and the Earls of March: Garter Knights and *Sir Gawain and the Green Knight." Medium Ævum* 70, no. 1 (2001): 66–79.

Cartlidge, Neil. "Introduction." In *Boundaries in Medieval Romance,* edited by Neil Cartlidge, 1–11. Woodbridge: D. S. Brewer, 2008.

Cautley, H. Munro. *Suffolk Churches and their Treasures.* 5th ed. Woodbridge: Boydell, 1982.

Chapman, Coolidge O. "The Parson's Tale: A Medieval Sermon." *Modern Language Notes* 43 (1928): 229–34.

Clark, Robert L. A. "A Heroine's Sexual Itinerary: Incest, Transvestism, and Same-Sex Marriage in *Yde et Olive."* In *Gender Transgressions: Crossing the Normative Barrier in Old French Literature,* edited by Karen J. Taylor, 89–105. New York: Garland, 1998.

————. "Queering Gender and Naturalizing Class in the *Roman de Silence."* *Arthuriana* 12, no. 1 (2002): 50–63.

Classen, Albrecht. *The Medieval Chastity Belt: A Myth-Making Process.* New York: Palgrave, 2007.

Clein, Wendy. *Concepts of Chivalry in* Sir Gawain and the Green Knight. Norman, OK: Pilgrim Books, 1987.

Colby, Alice M. *The Portrait in Twelfth-Century French Literature.* Geneva: Librairie Droz, 1965.

Cooper, Helen. *The English Romance in Time: Transforming Motifs from Geoffrey of Monmouth to the Death of Shakespeare.* Oxford: Oxford University Press, 2004.

————. "The Supernatural." In *A Companion to the* Gawain-*Poet,* edited by Derek Brewer and Jonathan Gibson, 277–91. Woodbridge: D. S. Brewer, 1997.

————. "When Romance Comes True." In *Boundaries in Medieval Romance,* edited by Neil Cartlidge, 13–27. Woodbridge: D. S. Brewer, 2008.

Cooper, Kate Mason. "Elle and L: Sexualized Textuality in *Le Roman de Silence."* *Romance Notes* 25, no. 3 (1985): 341–60.

Cowell, Andrew. "Deadly Letters: 'Deus Amanz,' Marie's Prologue to the Lais and the Dangerous Nature of the Gloss." *Romanic Review* 88, no. 3 (1997): 337–56.

Crane, Susan. "Anglo-Norman Cultures in England, 1066–1460." In *The Cambridge History of Medieval English Literature,* edited by David Wallace, 35–60. Cambridge: Cambridge University Press, 1999.

————. *Insular Romance: Politics, Faith, and Culture in Anglo-Norman and Middle English Literature.* Berkeley: University of California Press, 1986.

————. *The Performance of Self: Ritual, Clothing, and Identity during the Hundred Years War.* Philadelphia: University of Pennsylvania Press, 2002.

Crowfoot, Elisabeth, Frances Pritchard, and Kay Staniland. *Textiles and Clothing, c. 1150–c. 1450.* Woodbridge: Boydell, 2001.

Davenport, Millia. *The Book of Costume.* Vol. 1. New York: Crown, 1948.

Davenport, Tony. "'Lusty fresche galaunts.'" In *Aspects of Early English Drama*, edited by Paula Neuss, 111–25. Cambridge: D. S. Brewer, 1983.

Davis, Fred. *Fashion, Culture, and Identity.* Chicago: University of Chicago Press, 1992.

De Jong, Mayke. "Transformations of Penance." In *Rituals of Power from Late Antiquity to the Early Middle Ages*, edited by Frans Theuws and Janet L. Nelson, 185–224. Leiden: Brill, 2000.

Denery, Dallas G., II. *Seeing and Being Seen in the Later Medieval World: Optics, Theology and Religious Life.* Cambridge: Cambridge University Press, 2005.

Dillon, Viscount, and W. H. St. John Hope. "Inventory of the Goods and Chattels Belonging to Thomas, Duke of Gloucester, and Seized in his Castle at Pleshy, Co. Essex, 21 Richard II (1397)." *Archaeological Review* 54 (1897): 275–308.

Dinshaw, Carolyn. *Chaucer's Sexual Poetics.* Madison: University of Wisconsin Press, 1989.

Dronke, Peter. "Peter of Blois and Poetry at the Court of Henry II." *Mediaeval Studies* 38 (1976): 185–235.

Dubost, Francis. "Les motifs merveilleux dans les lais de Marie de France." In *Amour et merveille: Les Lais de Marie de France*, edited by Jean Dufournet, 41–80. Paris: Honoré Champion, 1995.

Duby, Georges. *Guerriers et paysans, VIIe–XIIe siècle: Premier essor de l'économie européenne.* Paris: Gallimard, 1973.

Duffy, Eamon. *The Stripping of the Altars.* New Haven: Yale University Press, 1992.

Dupreel, Ernest. "Le problème sociologique du rire." *Revue philosophique de la France et de l'étranger* 106 (1928): 213–60.

Dupront, Alphonse. "Pèlerinages et lieux sacrés." In *Mélanges en l'honneur de F. Braudel*, 2:189–206. Toulouse: Privat, 1973.

Durling, Nancy Vine, ed. *Jean Renart and the Art of Romance: Essays on Guillaume de Dole.* Gainesville: University Press of Florida, 1997.

———. "The Knot, the Belt, and the Making of *Guigemar*." In *Assays: Critical Approaches to Medieval and Renaissance Texts* 6, edited by Peggy Knapp, 29–54. Pittsburgh: Carnegie Mellon University Press, 1991.

Edwards, A. S. G. "The Manuscript: British Library MS Cotton Nero A.x." In *A Companion to the* Gawain-*Poet*, edited by Derek Brewer and Jonathan Gibson, 197–220. Cambridge: D. S. Brewer, 1997.

Erler, Mary C. "Fifteenth-Century Owners of Chaucer's Work: Cambridge, Magdalene College MS Pepys 2006." *The Chaucer Review* 38, no. 4 (2004): 401–14.

Evans, Joan. *Dress in Mediaeval France*. Oxford: Clarendon Press, 1952.

Everett, Walter. "*The Clensynge of Mannes Soule:* An Introductory Study." *Southern Quarterly* 13, no. 4 (1975): 265–79.

Faral, Edmond. *Les Jongleurs en France au Moyen Age*. Paris: Librairie Honoré Champion, 1910.

Finlayson, John. "The Satiric Mode and the *Parson's Tale.*" *The Chaucer Review* 6 (1971): 94–116.

Firey, Abigail, ed. *A New History of Penance*. Boston: Brill, 2008.

Flugel, J. C. *The Psychology of Clothes*. London: Hogarth Press, 1930. Reprint, New York: International Universities Press, 1969.

Foley, Michael. "Gawain's Two Confessions Reconsidered." *The Chaucer Review* 9, no. 1 (1974): 73–79.

Frantzen, Allen J. "The Disclosure of Sodomy in the Middle English *Cleanness.*" *PMLA* 111, no. 3 (1996): 451–64.

Frazer, J. G. *Taboo and the Perils of the Soul*. London: Macmillan, 1914.

Freeman, Michelle A. "Marie de France's Poetics of Silence: The Implications for a Feminine 'Translatio.'" *PMLA* 99, no. 5 (1984): 860–83.

Garber, Marjorie. *Vested Interests: Cross-Dressing and Cultural Anxiety*. New York: Routledge, 1997.

Gaunt, Simon. "From Epic to Romance: Gender and Sexuality in the *Roman d'Enéas.*" *Romanic Review* 83, no.1 (1992): 1–27.

———. *Gender and Genre in Medieval French Literature*. Cambridge: Cambridge University Press, 1995.

———. "The Significance of Silence." *Paragraph* 13 (1990): 202–16.

Gertz, Sun Hee Kim. "Echoes and Reflections of Enigmatic Beauty in Ovid and Marie de France." *Speculum* 73, no. 2 (1998): 372–96.

———. *Echoes and Reflections: Memory and Memorials in Ovid and Marie de France*. Amsterdam: Rodopi, 2003.

Gibbs, Marion, and Jane Lang. *Bishops and Reform, 1215–1272*. Oxford: Oxford University Press, 1934. Reprint, London: Cass, 1962.

Gill, Miriam. *Seven Deadly Sins and Seven Corporeal Works of Mercy*. Database of British wall paintings. University of Leicester, 2001. http://www.le.ac.uk/ha/seedcorn/contents.html. Last accessed 28 June 2011.

Gillespie, Vincent. "Vernacular Books of Religion." In *Book Production and Publishing in Britain, 1375–1475*, edited by Jeremy Griffiths and Derek Pearsall, 317–44. Cambridge: Cambridge University Press, 1989.

Gilmore, Gloria Thomas. "Marie de France's *Bisclavret:* What the Werewolf Will and Will Not Wear." In *Encountering Medieval Textiles,* edited by Désirée G. Koslin and Janet E. Snyder, 67–84. New York: Palgrave, 2002.

Giraudias, Etienne. *Etude historique sur les lois somptuaires.* Poitiers: Société Française d'Imprimerie et de Librairie, 1910.

Goddard, Eunice Rathbone. *Women's Costume in French Texts of the Eleventh and Twelfth Centuries.* Baltimore: Johns Hopkins University Press, 1927.

Goering, Joseph. "The Internal Forum and the Literature of Penance and Confession." In *The History of Medieval Canon Law in the Classical Period, 1140–1234,* edited by Wilfried Hartmann and Kenneth Pennington, 379–428. Washington, DC: Catholic University of America Press, 2008.

———. "The Scholastic Turn (1100–1500): Penitential Theology and Law in the Schools." In *A New History of Penance,* edited by Abigail Firey, 219–37. Boston: Brill, 2008.

———. *William de Montibus (c. 1140–1213): The Schools and the Literature of Pastoral Care.* Toronto: Pontifical Institute of Medieval Studies, 1992.

Goggin, Cheryl Gohdes. "Copying Manuscript Illuminations: The Trees of Vices and Virtues." *Visual Resources* 20, no. 2 (2004): 179–98.

Golding, Brian. "Gerald of Wales, the *Gemma Ecclesiastica* and Pastoral Care." In *Texts and Traditions of Medieval Pastoral Care: Essays in Honour of Bella Millett,* edited by Cate Gunn and Catherine Innes-Parker, 47–61. Woodbridge: York Medieval Press, 2009.

Gransden, Antonia. *Historical Writing in England.* Vol. 1. London: Routledge, 1974.

Green, Richard Firth. "'Allas, Allas! That evere love was synne!': John Bromyard v. Alice of Bath." *The Chaucer Review* 42, no. 3 (2008): 298–311.

———. "Sir Gawain and the *Sacra Cintola.*" *English Studies in Canada* 11, no. 1 (March 1985): 1–11.

Gross, Gregory W. "Secret Rules: Sex, Confession, and Truth in *Sir Gawain and the Green Knight.*" *Arthuriana* 4, no. 2 (1994): 146–74.

Gunn, Cate, and Catherine Innes-Parker, eds. *Texts and Traditions of Medieval Pastoral Care: Essays in Honour of Bella Millett.* Woodbridge: York Medieval Press, 2009.

Haldon, John. "Humor and the Everyday in Byzantium." In *Humour, History and Politics in Late Antiquity and the Early Middle Ages,* edited by Guy Halsall, 48–71. Cambridge: Cambridge University Press, 2002.

Hamilton, Sarah. "The Unique Flavor of Penance: The Church and the People, c. 800–c. 1100." In *The Medieval World,* edited by Peter Linehan and Janet L. Nelson, 229–45. London: Routledge, 2001.

Hammond, Eleanor Prescott. *Chaucer: A Bibliographic Manual.* New York: Macmillan, 1908.

Hanna, Ralph. "Producing Manuscripts and Editions." In *Textual Editing and Criticism: An Introduction,* edited by Erick Kelemen, 333–62. New York: W. W. Norton, 2009.

———. *Pursuing History: Middle English Manuscripts and Their Texts.* Stanford: Stanford University Press, 1996.

Hanning, Robert W. "The Talking Wounded: Desire, Truth Telling, and Pain in the *Lais* of Marie de France." In *Desiring Discourse: The Literature of Love, Ovid through Chaucer,* edited by James J. Paxson and Cynthia A. Gravlee, 140–61. Selinsgrove: Susquehanna University Press, 1998.

Hardman, Phillipa. "Gawain's Practice of Piety in *Sir Gawain and the Green Knight.*" *Medium Aevum* 68, no. 2 (1999): 247–68.

Haren, Michael. "Confession, Social Ethics, and Social Discipline in the *Memoriale Presbiterorum.*" In *Handling Sin: Confession in the Middle Ages,* edited by Peter Biller and A. J. Minnis, 109–22. Woodbridge: York Medieval Press, 1998.

Harris, Jennifer. "'Estroit vestu et menu cosu': Evidence for the Construction of Twelfth-Century Dress." In *Medieval Art: Recent Perspectives,* edited by Gale Owen-Crocker and Timothy Graham, 89–103. Manchester: Manchester University Press, 1998.

Harte, N. B. "State Control of Dress and Social Change in Pre-Industrial England." In *Trade, Government, and Economy in Pre-Industrial England,* edited by F. J. Fisher, D. C. Coleman, and Arthur H. John, 132–65. London: Weidenfeld and Nicolson, 1976.

Hartung, Albert E. "'The Parson's Tale' and Chaucer's Penance." In *Literature and Religion in the Later Middle Ages,* edited by Richard Newhauser and John A. Alford, 61–80. Binghamton: Medieval and Renaissance Texts and Studies, 1995.

Hauerwas, Stanley, and David Matzko. "The Sources of Charles Taylor." *Religious Studies Review* 18 (1992): 286–89.

Heller, Sarah-Grace. *Fashion in Medieval France.* Woodbridge: D. S. Brewer, 2007.

———. "Limiting Yardage and Changes of Clothes: Sumptuary Legislation in Thirteenth-Century France, Languedoc, and Italy." In *Medieval Fabrications: Dress, Textiles, Cloth Work, and Other Cultural Imaginings,* edited by E. Jane Burns, 121–36. New York: Palgrave, 2004.

Hendrickson, Hildi, ed. *Clothing and Difference: Embodied Identities in Colonial and Post-Colonial Africa.* Durham, NC: Duke University Press, 1996.

Heng, Geraldine. "Feminine Knots and the Other *Sir Gawain and the Green Knight*." *PMLA* 106 (1991): 500–514.

Hentschell, Roze. "Moralizing Apparel in Early Modern London: Popular Literature, Sermons, and Sartorial Display." *Journal of Medieval and Early Modern Studies* 39, no. 3 (2009): 571–95.

Hess, Erika E. *Literary Hybrids: Cross-dressing, Shapeshifting, and Indeterminacy in Medieval and Modern French Narrative.* New York: Routledge, 2004.

Hodges, Laura F. *Chaucer and Clothing: Clerical and Academic Costume in the General Prologue to the* Canterbury Tales. Woodbridge: D. S. Brewer, 2005.

———. *Chaucer and Costume: The Secular Pilgrims in the General Prologue.* Woodbridge: D. S. Brewer, 2000.

Hœpffner, Ernest. "Marie de France et *l'Enéas*." *Studi Medievali*, n.s. 5 (1932): 272–308.

———. "Pour la chronologie des *Lais* de Marie de France." *Romania* 60 (1934): 36–66.

Hollander, Anne. *Sex and Suits*. New York: Alfred A. Knopf, 1994.

Hooper, Vincent Foster. "Greyon and the Knotted Cord." *Modern Language Notes* 51, no. 7 (November 1936): 445–49.

Hotchkiss, Valerie R. *Clothes Make the Man: Female Cross Dressing in Medieval Europe.* New York: Garland, 1996.

Huchet, Jean-Charles. *Le Roman médiéval.* Paris: Presses Universitaires de France, 1984.

Hughes, Jonathan. "The Administration of Confession in the Diocese of York in the Fourteenth Century." In *Studies in Clergy and Ministry in Medieval England,* edited by David M. Smith, 87–163. York: University of York, Borthwick Institute of Historical Research, 1991.

Hunt, Alan. *Governance of the Consuming Passions: A History of Sumptuary Law.* New York: St. Martin's Press, 1996.

Hunt, Tony. "Glossing Marie de France." *Romanische Forschungen* 86 (1974): 396–418.

Ingledew, Francis. Sir Gawain and the Green Knight *and the Order of the Garter.* Notre Dame, IN: University of Notre Dame Press, 2006.

Izbicki, Thomas. "Forbidden Colors in the Regulation of Clerical Dress from the Fourth Lateran Council (1215) to the Time of Nicholas of Cusa (d. 1464)." In *Medieval Clothing and Textiles*, vol. 1, edited by Robin Netherton and Gale Owen-Crocker, 105–14. Woodbridge: Boydell, 2005.

Jacobs, Nicholas. "Notes and News: Gawain's False Confession." *English Studies* 51, no. 5 (1970): 433–35.

Jaeger, C. Stephen. *The Envy of Angels*. Philadelphia: University of Pennsylvania Press, 1994.

————. *The Origins of Courtliness: Civilizing Trends and the Formation of Courtly Ideals, 939–1210*. Philadelphia: University of Pennsylvania Press, 1985.

James, M. R. "The Wall Paintings in Brooke Church." In *A Supplement to Blomefield's Norfolk*, edited by Clement Rolfe Ingleby, 15–26. London: Clement Ingleby, 1929.

Jauss, Hans Robert. *Toward an Aesthetic of Reception*. Minneapolis: University of Minnesota Press, 1982.

Johnson, Lynn Staley. *The Voice of the* Gawain-*Poet*. Madison: University of Wisconsin Press, 1984.

Jolliffe, P. S. *A Checklist of Middle English Prose Writings of Spiritual Guidance*. Toronto: Pontifical Institute of Medieval Studies, 1974.

Jonin, Pierre. "Merveilleux celtique et symbolisme universel dans 'Guigemar' de Marie de France." In *Mélanges de philologie et de littératures romanes offerts à Jeanne Wathelet-Willem*, edited by Jacques DeCaluwé, 239–55. Liège: Marche Romane, 1978.

Jurney, Florence Ramond. "Secret Identities: (Un)masking Gender in the *Roman de Silence* by Heldris de Cornouaille and *L'enfant de sable* by Tahar Ben Jelloun." *Dalhousie French Studies* 55 (2001): 3–10.

Karras, Ruth Mazo. "Misogyny and the Medieval Exemplum: Gendered Sin in John of Bromyard's *Summa Praedicantium*." *Traditio* 47 (1992): 233–57.

Kaske, Carol V. "Getting around the Parson's Tale: An Alternative to Allegory and Irony." In *Chaucer at Albany*, edited by Rossell Hope Robbins, 147–77. New York: Burt Franklin, 1973.

Kelly, Douglas. *Medieval Imagination: Rhetoric and Poetry of Courtly Love*. Madison: University of Wisconsin Press, 1978.

Kelly, Francis M., and Randolph Schwabe. *A Short History of Costume and Armour, 1066–1485*. 2 vols. 1931. Reprint, New York: Arco, 1972.

Kieckhefer, Richard. "Erotic Magic in Medieval Europe." In *Sex in the Middle Ages*, edited by Joyce E. Salisbury, 30–55. New York: Garland, 1991.

Kindrick, Robert L. "Gawain's Ethics: Shame and Guilt in *Sir Gawain and the Green Knight*." *Annuale Mediaevale* 20 (1981): 5–32.

Klerks, Suzanne. "The Pain of Reading Female Bodies in Marie de France's *Guigemar*." *Dalhousie French Studies* 33 (1995): 1–14.

Knapton, Antoinette. *Mythe et psychologie chez Marie de France dans* Guigemar. Chapel Hill: North Carolina Studies in the Romance Languages and Literatures, 1975.

Koda, Harold. *Extreme Beauty: The Body Transformed.* New York: Metropolitan Museum of Art, 2001.

Koslin, Désirée G., and Janet E. Snyder, eds. *Encountering Medieval Textiles and Dress: Objects, Texts, Images.* New York: Palgrave, 2002.

Krause, Kathy M. "'Li Mireor du Monde': Specularity in the *Roman de Silence.*" *Arthuriana* 12, no. 1 (2002): 85–91.

Krueger, Roberta L. "Beyond Debate: Gender in Play in Old French Courtly Fiction." In *Gender in Debate from the Early Middle Ages to the Renaissance*, edited by Thelma S. Fenster and Clare A. Lees, 79–95. New York: Palgrave, 2002.

————. "Marie de France." In *The Cambridge Companion to Medieval Women's Writing*, edited by Carolyn Dinshaw and David Wallace, 172–83. Cambridge: Cambridge University Press, 2003.

————. *Women Readers and the Ideology of Gender in the Old French Verse Romance.* Cambridge: Cambridge University Press, 1993.

Kurath, Hans, ed. *Middle English Dictionary.* Ann Arbor: University of Michigan Press, 1954. http://quod.lib.umich.edu/m/med.

Lachaud, Frédérique. "Liveries of Robes in England, c. 1200–c. 1330." *The English Historical Review* 111, no. 441 (1996): 279–98.

Laskaya, Anne. *Chaucer's Approach to Gender in the Canterbury Tales.* Cambridge: D. S. Brewer, 1995.

Lawton, David. "Chaucer's Two Ways: The Pilgrimage Frame of the Canterbury Tales." *Studies in the Age of Chaucer* 9 (1987): 3–40.

Lea, Henry. *History of Auricular Confession and Indulgences in the Latin Church.* 2 vols. Philadelphia: Lea Brothers, 1896.

Lecoy de la Marche, Albert. *La Chaire française au Moyen Age.* Paris: Didier et Cie. Librairies, 1868.

————. *Le Rire du prédicateur.* 1888. Reprint, with introduction and notes by Jacques Berlioz, Paris: Brepols, 1999.

Le Goff, Jacques. "Laughter in the Middle Ages." In *A Cultural History of Humor from Antiquity to the Present*, edited by Jan Bremmer and Herman Roodenburg, 40–53. Cambridge: Polity Press, 1997.

Leupin, Alexandre. "The Impossible Task of Manifesting 'Literature': On Marie de France's Obscurity." *Exemplaria* 3, no. 1 (1991): 221–42.

Liddell, Mark H. "A New Source of the Parson's Tale." In *An English Miscellany*, 255–77. Oxford: Clarendon Press, 1901.

————. "The Source of Chaucer's 'Person's Tale'" *The Academy* 1259 (June 20, 1896): 509.

Lindberg, David C. *Theories of Vision from Al-Kindi to Kepler.* Chicago: University of Chicago Press, 1976.

Little, Katherine. "Chaucer's Parson and the Specter of Wycliffism." *Studies in the Age of Chaucer* 23 (2001): 225–53.

Little, Lester K. "Pride Goes before Avarice: Social Change and the Vices in Latin Christendom." *The American Historical Review* 76, no. 1 (1971): 16–49.

———. *Religious Poverty and Profit Economy in Medieval Europe*. Ithaca: Cornell University Press, 1978.

Lochrie, Karma. *Covert Operations: The Medieval Uses of Secrecy*. Philadelphia: University of Pennsylvania Press, 1999.

Low, Anthony. *Aspects of Subjectivity: Society and Individuality from the Middle Ages to Shakespeare and Milton*. Pittsburgh: Duquesne University Press, 2003.

———. "Privacy, Community, and Society: Confession as a Cultural Indicator in *Sir Gawain and the Green Knight*." *Religion and Literature* 30, no. 2 (1998): 1–20.

MacIntyre, Alasdair. *After Virtue: A Study in Moral Theory*. 2nd ed. Notre Dame, IN: University of Notre Dame Press, 1984.

Madou, Mireille. *Le Costume civil*. Turnhout: Brepols, 1986.

Manly, John M., and Edith Rickert. *The Text of the Canterbury Tales: Studied on the Basis of All Known Manuscripts*. 8 vols. Chicago: University of Chicago Press, 1940.

Mann, Jill. "Courtly Aesthetics and Courtly Ethics in *Sir Gawain and the Green Knight*." *Studies in the Age of Chaucer* 31 (2009): 231–65.

———. "Sir Gawain and the Romance Hero." In *Heroes and Heroines in Medieval English Literature*, edited by Leo Carruthers, 105–17. Cambridge: D. S. Brewer, 1994.

Mansfield, Mary C. *The Humiliation of Sinners: Public Penance in Thirteenth-Century France*. Ithaca: Cornell University Press, 1995.

Marshall, Anne. *Medieval Wall Painting in the English Parish Church: A Developing Catalogue*. 2000, 2008. http://www.paintedchurch.org.

McCash, June Hall. "*La vie seinte Audree*: A Fourth Text by Marie de France?" *Speculum* 77, no. 3 (2002): 744–77.

McCracken, Peggy. "'The Boy Who Was a Girl': Reading Gender in the *Roman de Silence*." *Romance Review* 85, no. 4 (1994): 517–36.

McLaughlin, R. Emmet. "Truth, Tradition and History: The Historiography of High/Late Medieval and Early Modern Penance." In *A New History of Penance*, edited by Abigail Firey, 19–71. Boston: Brill, 2008.

Mead, George H. *Mind, Self, and Society*. Chicago: University of Chicago Press, 1934.

Mehl, Dieter. *The Middle English Romances of the Thirteenth and Fourteenth Centuries*. New York: Barnes and Noble, 1969.

Ménard, Philippe. *Le rire et le sourire dans le roman courtois en France au Moyen Age, 1150–1250.* Geneva: Librairie Droz, 1969.

———. *Les Lais de Marie de France: Contes d'amour et d'aventure du Moyen Age.* Paris: Presses Universitaires de France, 1979.

Mitchell, R. J. "English Students at Padua, 1460–75." *Transactions of the Royal Historical Society,* 4th ser., 19, no. 1 (1936): 101–17.

Monson, Don A. "Andreas Capellanus and the Problem of Irony." *Speculum* 63, no. 3 (1988): 539–72.

Mulvey, Laura. "Visual Pleasure and Narrative Cinema." *Screen* 16, no. 3 (1975): 6–18.

Murphy, James J. *Rhetoric in the Middle Ages: A History of Rhetorical Theory from Saint Augustine to the Renaissance.* Berkeley: University of California Press, 1974.

Murray, Alexander. *Reason and Society in the Middle Ages.* Oxford: Clarendon Press, 1978.

Myers, W. David. *"Poor, Sinning Folk": Confession and Conscience in Counter-Reformation Germany.* Ithaca: Cornell University Press, 1996.

Newhauser, Richard. "Avarice and Apocalypse." In *The Apocalyptic Year 1000: Religious Expectation and Social Change, 950–1050,* edited by Richard Allen Landes, Andrew Colin Gow, and David C. Van Meter, 109–19. Oxford: Oxford University Press, 2003.

———. *The Early History of Greed: The Sin of Avarice in Early Medieval Thought and Literature.* Cambridge: Cambridge University Press, 2000.

———. "The Meaning of Gawain's Greed." *Studies in Philology* 87, no. 4 (1990): 410–26.

———. "The Parson's Tale." In vol. 1 of *Sources and Analogues of the Canterbury Tales,* edited by Robert M. Correale and Mary Hamel, 529–614. Cambridge: D. S. Brewer, 2002.

———. "Peter of Limoges, Optics, and the Science of the Sense." *Senses & Society* 5, no. 1 (2010): 28–44.

———. "The Sin of Curiosity and the Cistercians." In *Erudition at God's Service,* edited by John R. Sommerfeldt, 71–95. Kalamazoo, MI: Cistercian Publications, 1987.

———. *The Treatise on Vices and Virtues in Latin and the Vernacular.* Turnhout: Brepols, 1993.

Newman, Barbara. *From Virile Woman to Woman Christ.* Philadelphia: University of Pennsylvania Press, 1995.

Newton, Stella Mary. *Fashion in the Age of the Black Prince.* Woodbridge: Boydell Press, 1980.

Nichols, Stephen G. "Deflections of the Body in the Old French Lay." *Stanford French Review* 14 (1990): 27–50.

Owen, Charles A. *The Manuscripts of the Canterbury Tales.* Cambridge: D. S. Brewer, 1991.

Owst, G. R. *Literature and Pulpit in Medieval England.* Oxford: Blackwell, 1961.

Pairet, Ana. "Magie et pureté dans *Tristan, Cligès,* et *Raoul de Cambrai.*" In *Souillure et pureté: Le corps et son environnement culturel,* edited by Jean-Jacques Vincensini, 258–66. Paris: Maisonneuve et Larose, 2003.

Pantin, W. A. *The English Church in the Fourteenth Century.* Cambridge: Cambridge University Press, 1955.

Partner, Nancy F. *Serious Entertainments: The Writing of History in Twelfth-Century England.* Chicago: University of Chicago Press, 1977.

Patterson, Lee. "Chaucer." Accessed on 9 February 2011. http://www.yale.edu /engl125/text-only/lectures/lecture-1.html.

———. "The 'Parson's Tale' and the Quitting of the 'Canterbury Tales.'" *Traditio* 34 (1978): 331–80.

Payen, Jean-Charles. "La Pénitence dans le contexte culturel des XIIe et XIIIe siècles." *Revue des sciences philosophiques et théologiques* 61 (1977): 399–428.

Payer, Pierre. "The Humanism of the Penitentials and the Continuity of the Penitential Tradition." *Mediaeval Studies* 46 (1984): 340–54.

Pearsall, Derek. *The Canterbury Tales.* London: George Allen, 1985.

———. "Courtesy and Chivalry in *Sir Gawain and the Green Knight:* The Order of Shame and the Invention of Embarrassment." In *A Companion to the Gawain-Poet,* edited by Derek Brewer and Jonathan Gibson, 351–62. Cambridge: D. S. Brewer, 1997.

———. "Rhetorical 'Descriptio' in 'Sir Gawain and the Green Knight.'" *Modern Language Review* 50 (1955): 129–34.

Pelikan, Jaroslav. *The Growth of Medieval Theology (600–1300).* Vol. 3 of *The Christian Tradition: A History of the Development of Doctrine.* Chicago: University of Chicago Press, 1978.

Perret, Michèle. "Travesties et transsexuelles: Yde, Silence, Grisandole, Blanchandine." *Romance Notes* 25, no. 3 (1985): 328–40.

Perry, G. G., ed. *Religious Pieces in Prose and Verse.* EETS, o.s. 26. London: N. Trübner and Co., 1867; rev. 1914; reprint 1973.

Petersen, Kate Oelzner. *The Sources of the Parson's Tale.* Boston: Athenaeum Press, 1901.

Peterson, Ingrid J. *William of Nassington.* New York: Peter Lang, 1986.

Pfander, Homer G. "Some Medieval Manuals of Religious Instruction in England and Observations on Chaucer's Parson's Tale." *Journal of English and Germanic Philology* 35 (1936): 243–58.

Pinckaers, Servais. *The Sources of Christian Ethics*. Translated by Sr. Mary Thomas Noble. Washington, DC: Catholic University of America Press, 1995.

Piponnier, Françoise. "Une révolution dans le costume masculin au XIVe siècle." In *Le Vêtement: Histoire, archéologie, et symbolique vestimentaires au Moyen Age*, edited by Michel Pastoureau, 225–42. Paris: Léopard d'Or, 1989.

Piponnier, Françoise, and Perrine Mane. *Dress in the Middle Ages*. Translated by Caroline Beamish. New Haven: Yale University Press, 1997.

Pitard, Derrick G. "Sowing Difficulty: *The Parson's Tale*, Vernacular Commentary, and the Nature of Chaucerian Dissent." *Studies in the Age of Chaucer* 26 (2004): 299–330.

Plummer, John. "'Beth Fructuous and that in Litel Space': The Engendering of Harry Bailly." In *New Readings of Chaucer's Poetry*, edited by Robert G. Benson and Susan J. Ridyard, 107–18. Cambridge: D. S. Brewer, 2003.

Poschmann, Bernhard. *Penance and the Anointing of the Sick*. Translated by Francis Courtney. London: Burns and Oates, 1964.

Post, Paul. "La Naissance du costume masculin moderne au XIVe siècle." In *Actes du premier Congrès international d'histoire du costume, Venise, 31 août–7 septembre 1952*, 28–41. Venice: Centro Internazionale delle Arti et del Costume, 1955.

Putter, Ad. "Transvestite Knights in Medieval Life and Literature." In *Becoming Male in the Middle Ages*, edited by Jeffrey Jerome Cohen and Bonnie Wheeler, 279–302. New York: Routledge, 1999.

Raybin, David. "'Manye been the weyes': The Flower, Its Roots, and the Ending of *The Canterbury Tales*." In *Closure in the* Canterbury Tales: *The Role of the Parson's Tale*, edited by David Raybin and Linda Tarte Holley, 11–43. Kalamazoo, MI: Medieval Institute Publications, 2000.

Raymo, Robert R. "Works of Religious and Philosophical Instruction." In vol. 7 of *A Manual of the Writings in Middle English, 1050–1500*, edited by Albert E. Hartung, 2255–2378, 2467–2582. New Haven: Connecticut Academy of Arts and Sciences, 1986.

Reed, Thomas L., Jr. "Marie de France's *Guigemar* as Art of Interpretation (and Ambiguity)." In *Speaking Images: Essays in Honor of V. A. Kolve*, edited by Robert F. Yeager, Charlotte Morse, and V. A. Kolve, 1–26. Asheville, NC: Pegasus Press, 2001.

Reid, Thomas Bertram Wallace, William Rothwell, and Louise W. Stone. *Anglo-Norman Dictionary*. Publications of the Modern Humanities Research Association 8. London: Modern Humanities Research Association, 1977. http://www.anglo-norman.net/gate. Last accessed 26 February 2010.

Reinhard, John R. *The Old French Romance of Amadas and Ydoine.* Durham, NC: Duke University Press, 1927.

Richards, Earl Jeffrey. "Les Rapports entre le *Lai de Guigemar* et le *Roman d'Enéas:* Considérations génériques." In *Le Récit bref au Moyen Age,* edited by Danielle Buschinger, 45–56. Paris: Librairie Honoré Champion, 1980.

Riddy, Felicity. "Jewels in *Pearl.*" In *A Companion to the* Gawain-*Poet,* edited by Derek Brewer and Jonathan Gibson, 143–55. Cambridge: D. S. Brewer, 1997.

Riggins, Stephen Harold, ed. *The Socialness of Things: Essays on the Socio-semiotics of Objects.* Berlin: Mouton de Gruyter, 1994.

Ringer, Loren. "Exchange, Identity, and Transvestism in *Le Roman de Silence.*" *Dalhousie French Studies* 28 (1994): 3–13.

Robertson, D. W. "Marie de France, Lais, Prologue, 13–16." *Modern Language Notes* 64, no. 5 (1949): 336–38.

Roche-Mahdi, Sarah. "A Reappraisal of the Role of Merlin in the *Roman de Silence.*" *Arthuriana* 12, no. 1 (2002): 6–21.

Rosenthal, Margaret F., ed. "Cultures of Clothing in Later Medieval and Early Modern Europe." Special issue. *The Journal of Medieval and Early Modern Studies* 39, no. 3 (2009).

Rosewell, Roger. *Medieval Wall Paintings in English and Welsh Churches.* Woodbridge: Boydell, 2008.

Rothwell, W. "The 'faus français d'Angleterre': Later Anglo-Norman." In *Anglo-Norman Anniversary Essays,* edited by Ian Short, 309–26. London: Anglo-Norman Text Society, 1993.

Rouse, E. Clive. *Medieval Wall Paintings.* 4th ed. Oxford: Shire Publications, 1991.

Rowland, Beryl. "Chaucer's She-Ape (*The Parson's Tale,* 424)." *The Chaucer Review* 2 (1968): 159–65.

Saul, Nigel. *Richard II.* New Haven: Yale University Press, 1997.

Scanlon, Larry. "Introduction." In *The Cambridge Companion to Medieval English Literature, 1100–1500,* edited by Larry Scanlon, 1–8. Cambridge: Cambridge University Press, 2009.

———. *Narrative, Authority, and Power: The Medieval Exemplum and the Chaucerian Tradition.* Cambridge: Cambridge University Press, 1994.

Scattergood, V. J. "Literary Culture at the Court of Richard II." In *English Court Culture in the Later Middle Ages,* edited by V. J. Scattergood and J. W. Sherborne, 29–43. London: Duckworth, 1983.

———. "'Sir Gawain and the Green Knight' and the Sins of the Flesh." *Traditio* 37 (1981): 347–71.

Schwam-Baird, Shira. "Would a Gentleman Belt a Lady? Chastity Belts (and Knots) in Marie de France's *Guigemar*." *Mediaevalia* 22, no. 2 (1999): 323–42.

Scott, Margaret. *Medieval Dress and Fashion*. London: British Library, 2007.

Sedgwick, Eve Kosofsky. "Queer Performativity: Henry James's *The Art of the Novel*." *GLQ* 1 (1993): 1–16.

Short, Ian. "Denis Piramus and the Truth of Marie's Lais." *Cultura Neolatina* 67, nos. 3–4 (2007): 319–40.

Simpson, J. A., and E. S. C. Weiner. *The Oxford English Dictionary*. 20 vols. Oxford: Clarendon Press, 1989. http://www.oed.com.

Sleeth, Charles R. "Gawain's Judgment Day." *Arthuriana* 4, no. 2 (1994): 175–83.

Smith, Nicole D. "The Parson's Predilection for Pleasure." *Studies in the Age of Chaucer* 28 (2006): 117–40.

Soucy, A. Francis. "Gawain's Fault: 'Angardez Pryde.'" *The Chaucer Review* 13, no. 2 (1978): 166–76.

Southern, R. W. *The Making of the Middle Ages*. New Haven: Yale University Press, 1959.

Spearing, A. C. *The Gawain-Poet*. Cambridge: Cambridge University Press, 1970.

Spence, Sarah. "Double Vision: Love and Envy in the *Lais*." In *In Quest of Marie de France: A Twelfth-Century Poet*, edited by Chantal A. Maréchal, 262–79. Lewiston, Queenstown, Lampeter: Edwin Mellon Press, 1992.

Spencer, H. L. *English Preaching in the Late Middle Ages*. Oxford: Clarendon Press, 1993.

Spitzer, Leo. "The Prologue to the 'Lais' of Marie de France and Medieval Poets." *Modern Philology* 41, no. 2 (1943): 96–102.

Sponsler, Claire. *Drama and Resistance: Bodies, Goods, and Theatricality in Late Medieval England*. Minneapolis: University of Minnesota Press, 1997.

———. "Narrating the Social Order: Medieval Clothing Laws." *CLIO: A Journal of Literature, History, and the Philosophy of History* 21, no. 3 (1992): 265–83.

Staniland, Kay. "Court Style, Painters, and the Great Wardrobe." In *England in the Fourteenth Century: Proceedings of the 1985 Harlaxton Symposium*, edited by W. M. Ormrod, 236–46. Woodbridge: Boydell, 1986.

———. "Extravagance or Regal Necessity? The Clothing of Richard II." In *The Regal Image of Richard II and the Wilton Diptych*, edited by Dillian Gordon, Lisa Monnas, and Caroline Elam, 85–93. London: Harvey Miller, 1997.

———. "Medieval Courtly Splendour." *Costume* 14 (1980): 7–23.

Steele, Valerie. *Fetish: Fashion, Sex, and Power*. New York: Oxford University Press, 1996.

Stein, Robert M. "Desire, Social Reproduction, and Marie's *Guigemar*." In *In Quest of Marie de France*, edited by Chantal A. Maréchal, 283–86. Lewiston, Queenstown, Lampeter: Edwin Mellon Press, 1992.

Stock, Lorraine Kochanske. "'Arms and the (Wo)man' in Medieval Romance: The Gendered Arming of Female Warriors in the *Roman d'Enéas* and Heldris's *Roman de Silence*." *Arthuriana* 5, no. 4 (1995): 56–83.

———. "The Importance of Being Gender 'Stable': Masculinity and Feminine Empowerment in *Le Roman de Silence*." *Arthuriana* 7, no. 2 (1997): 7–34.

Strohm, Paul. "The Origin and Meaning of Middle English *Romaunce*." *Genre* 10, no. 1 (1977): 1–28.

Sturges, Robert S. "The Cross-Dresser and the *Juventus*: Category Crisis in *Silence*." *Arthuriana* 12, no. 1 (2002): 37–49.

Suthrell, Charlotte. *Unzipping Gender: Sex, Cross-Dressing, and Culture*. Oxford: Berg, 2004.

Tachau, Katherine H. *Vision and Certitude in the Age of Ockham: Optics, Epistemology, and the Foundations of Semantics, 1250–1345*. Leiden: E. J. Brill, 1988.

Tanner, Norman. "Pastoral Care: The Fourth Lateran Council of 1215." In *A History of Pastoral Care*, edited by G. R. Evans, 112–25. London: Cassel, 2000.

Taylor, Andrew. *Textual Situations: Three Medieval Manuscripts and Their Readers*. Philadelphia: University of Pennsylvania Press, 2002.

Taylor, Charles. *Sources of the Self: The Making of Modern Identity*. Cambridge, MA: Harvard University Press, 1989.

Teetaert, Amédée. *La Confession aux laïques dans l'Église latine depuis le 8e jusqu'au 14e siècle*. Wetteren: J. de Meester et fils, 1926.

Tentler, Thomas N. *Sin and Confession on the Eve of the Reformation*. Princeton: Princeton University Press, 1977.

Thorpe, Lewis. "Introduction." In *Le Roman de Silence*, edited by Lewis Thorpe, 1–62. Cambridge: W. Heffer and Sons, 1972.

———. "Raoul de Houdenc: A Possible New Poem." *Modern Language Review* 47 (1952): 512–15.

Tickle, Phyllis A. *Greed: The Seven Deadly Sins*. New York: Oxford University Press, 2004.

Trigg, Stephanie. "The Romance of Exchange: Sir Gawain and the Green Knight." *Viator* 22 (1991): 251–66.

Tristram, E. W. *English Wall Painting of the Fourteenth Century.* London: Routledge, 1955.

Trudel, Guy. "The Middle English Book of Penance and the Readers of the Cursor Mundi." *Medium Ævum* 74, no. 1 (2005): 10–33.

Vale, Malcolm. *The Princely Court: Medieval Courts and Culture in North-West Europe, 1270–1380.* Oxford: Oxford University Press, 2001.

Van Buren, Anne H. *Illuminating Fashion: Dress in the Art of Medieval France and the Netherlands, 1325–1515.* New York: The Morgan Library and Museum, 2011.

Vance, Eugene. "Chaucer's Pardoner: Relics, Discourse, and Frames of Propriety." *New Literary History* 20 (1989): 723–45.

Van Vleck, Amelia E. "Textiles as Testimony in Marie de France and *Philomena.*" *Medievalia et Humanistica* 22 (1995): 31–60.

Vogel, Cyrille. *En rémission des péchés: Recherches sur les systèmes pénitentiels dans l'Eglise latine.* Edited by Alexandre Faivre. Aldershot: Variorum, 1994.

Wallace, David. *The Cambridge History of Medieval English Literature.* Cambridge: Cambridge University Press, 1999.

Waters, Elizabeth A. "The Third Path: Alternative Sex, Alternative Gender in *Le Roman de Silence.*" *Arthuriana* 7, no. 2 (1997): 35–46.

Watson, Nicholas. "The *Gawain*-Poet as a Vernacular Theologian." In *A Companion to the* Gawain-*Poet,* edited by Derek Brewer and Jonathan Gibson, 293–313. Cambridge: D. S. Brewer, 1997.

Watt, Diane. "Behaving Like a Man? Incest, Lesbian Desire, and Gender Play in *Yde et Olive* and Its Adaptations." *Comparative Literature* 50, no. 4 (1998): 265–85.

Watt, J. A. "The Papacy." In *The New Cambridge Medieval History,* Vol. 5, *c. 1198–c. 1300,* edited by David Abulafia, 107–63. Cambridge: Cambridge University Press, 1999.

Waugh, Christina Frieder. "'Well-Cut Through the Body': Fitted Clothing in Twelfth-Century Europe." *Dress* 26 (1999): 3–16.

Wenzel, Siegfried. "Notes on the *Parson's Tale.*" *The Chaucer Review* 16, no. 3 (1982): 237–56.

———. "The Source for Chaucer's Seven Deadly Sins." *Traditio* 30 (1974): 351–78.

———. "The Source for the 'Remedia' of the Parson's Tale." *Traditio* 27 (1971): 433–53.

Wogan-Browne, Jocelyn. "General Introduction: What's in a Name: The 'French' of 'England.'" In *Language and Culture in Medieval Britain: The French of*

England, c. 1100–c. 1500, 1–13. Edited by Jocelyn Wogan-Browne. Woodbridge: York Medieval Press, 2009.

Wright, Monica L. "Chemise and Ceinture: Marie de France's *Guigemar* and the Use of Textiles." In *Courtly Arts and the Arts of Courtliness*, 771–77. Edited by Keith Busby and Christopher Kleinhenz. Cambridge: D. S. Brewer, 2006.

———. *Weaving Narrative: Clothing in Twelfth-Century French Romance*. University Park: Pennsylvania State University Press, 2009.

Yarwood, Doreen. *English Costume from the Second Century B.C. to 1967*. 3rd ed. London: B. T. Batsford, 1967.

Zeikowitz, Richard E. *Homoeroticism and Chivalry: Discourses of Male Same-Sex Desire in the Fourteenth Century*. New York: Palgrave Macmillan, 2003.

Zink, Michel. *La Prédication en langue romane avant 1300*. Paris: Editions Honoré Champion, 1976.

Index

Nicole D. Smith

is assistant professor of English at the University of North Texas.